Battle
of the
Bay

Battle
of the
Bay

Bashing A's, Thrilling Giants, and the Earthquake World Series

Gary Peterson

TRIUMPH
BOOKS

Library of Congress Cataloging-in-Publication Data
Peterson, Gary, 1956-
  Battle of the Bay : bashing A's, thrilling Giants, and the earthquake World Series / Gary Peterson ; [foreword by] Tony La Russa.
    pages cm
    ISBN 978-1-60078-933-5 (pbk.)
  1. San Francisco Giants (Baseball team)—History. 2. Oakland Athletics (Baseball team)—History. 3. World Series (Baseball) (1989) I. Title.
  GV875.S34P5 2014
  796.357'6409794609048—dc23   2013045048

This book is available in quantity at special discounts for your group or organization. For further information, contact:
    Triumph Books LLC
    814 North Franklin Street
    Chicago, Illinois 60610
    (312) 337-0747
    www.triumphbooks.com

Printed in U.S.A.

ISBN: 978-1-60078-933-5

Design by Sue Knopf

Photos courtesy of AP Images unless otherwise indicated

*To my mom, for impressing upon me
the value of making things fun,
and to my dad, for showing me the importance
of doing things right.*

Contents

Foreword

The 1989 World Series will always be remembered for Mother Nature upstaging a rare and potentially classic competition between neighboring teams. The Loma Prieta earthquake on October 17, 1989, with a magnitude of 6.9, severely shook the San Francisco Bay Area just minutes before Game 3's first pitch. It became the dominant storyline of the '89 World Series and rightfully so.

The timing of the earthquake and its tragic and destructive effects overwhelmed every other aspect of the A's-Giants matchup. The stories relating to the earthquake—describing tragedy, heroism, and rebuilding—made for compelling reading. Whether the A's could win two more games before the Giants could win four was a minor win/lose question versus the life-and-death issues suddenly thrust upon the region.

That said, the World Series story that was pushed aside by the earthquake deserves to be told and had its own fascinations. Two teams from the same geographic area were playing to determine the world baseball champion. That hadn't happened since 1956, two years before the Dodgers and Giants moved west. Before their migration it happened more often in the New York City area.

The A's versus Giants had that historical significance. In addition a healthy competition had developed between the organizations during the years preceding 1989. The A's were seeking their fourth title since moving from Kansas City in

1968. The Giants were making their second World Series appearance since leaving New York. Their first, in 1962, was a tough loss in seven games to the Yankees.

On paper the so-called Bay Bridge World Series figured to be an outstanding competition that could be decided in either direction. Both teams featured offenses that were among the very best in the major leagues. Both had solid pitching staffs at the beginning and end of games. Both had won their divisions and League Championship Series in convincing fashion. The Cubs and Blue Jays were very good teams that were beaten in five games. The ALCS ended on Sunday, and the NLCS ended on Monday.

Games 1 and 2 of the '89 World Series were played in Oakland starting on Saturday, October 14. Our wins in both games were remarkably similar and were highlighted by a cruel irony as far as the Giants were concerned. A's starting pitchers Dave Stewart and Mike Moore both turned in dominating performances. Along with their fastballs and sliders, they had excellent splitters. The irony was that Dave Duncan, the A's outstanding pitching coach, had perfected his coaching of that pitch in part thanks to Giants manager Roger Craig.

Craig was a baseball treasure. He had a storied career as a major league pitcher and became one of the game's best pitching coaches. As a pitching coach on Sparky Anderson's Tigers, he was one of the pioneers in developing the split-fingered fastball or forkball. Imagine his discomfort watching Stewart and Moore handcuff his Giants hitters with his signature pitch.

Craig had an outgoing personality, which was on display before and after games. He was a hard-nosed competitor. An example of his competitiveness, which provided a perfect lead into the pre-Game 3 earthquake, was his postgame comments after Game 2. He was his usual positive and competitive self. His statements were that the A's and their fans had their fun for the first two games. But once the Giants, and especially their fans, returned to Candlestick Park, they would have a loud and uncomfortable reception ready for the A's and their fans.

I was so certain that Craig had inspired Giants players and fans that our staff had made it a point to warn our team to expect their "energy" and to be prepared to bring our "bunker mentality" to the contests.

In fact, Craig's combination of warning us and challenging their fans became my answer to the most frequently asked World Series earthquake question: where were you when the Loma Prieta earthquake struck? I was sitting in the third-base dugout, awaiting team introductions. There were some players near the left-field foul line getting legs and arms loose. At 5:04 PM there was a definite noise and movement experience. My first impression was that the "noise" that close to the introductions was Giants fans responding to Roger's challenge. My first thought was that our "bunker mentality" would have to start much earlier than the first pitch.

My first indication that something bigger was afoot was the violent swaying of the outfield light standards. Once that realization hit home, the environment at Candlestick Park became very surreal, fueled by such things as fans reporting what they were learning about the devastating consequences throughout both sides of the Bay Area, the uncertainty of damage at the stadium, and the specter of potential aftershocks.

Commissioner Fay Vincent quickly decided to cancel Game 3 and suspend action until further notice. The immediate A's response was to collect our teammates and families on buses and return to the Oakland Coliseum. We had to detour south to and around San Jose and then north to Oakland. A 30-to 45-minute trip became a four-and-a-half-hour nightmare crawl. The atmosphere on the buses was a very tense combination of concern, confusion, and uncertainty.

The interruption of World Series play lasted 10 days. The unprecedented stoppage placed both teams in uncharted situations. We both attempted to maintain our physical and mental conditioning. The latter was especially tough because our winning and losing concerns paled in comparison to the difficulties everyone in the Bay Area was experiencing.

An important issue to confront was whether play *should* be resumed. Some were calling for the Series to be canceled without any resumption of play. Some critics went as far as to accuse our players of being selfish for ignoring the suffering and pursuing the championship prize. In my mind that issue quickly became moot when other sports and entertainment quickly resumed their usual schedules.

The Athletics' primary focus was keeping our mental edge. A perfect example of the lengths our organization would go to maintain our edge was the two-day trip to our Phoenix spring training complex when the Game 3 reschedule date was announced. Our ownership and front office supported the move, and once we were in uniform there, practicing before thousands of excited fans, the therapeutic benefits were obvious.

The A's won Games 3 and 4 with the same starting pitchers, Stewart and Moore, who had shackled the Giants in Games 1 and 2. Our sweep of the Giants did not reflect how good the National League champions were. It was much more a set of advantages that added up to the four straight wins. The Giants' pitching at the end was ailing and poor in spots. Ours was very talented and healthy. Our frame of mind was virtually perfect. We remembered the heartbreaking loss to the Dodgers in the 1988 World Series after dominating the regular season and ALCS and how we had made it a rallying cry in 1989—from the first day of spring training through the fourth game of the World Series.

The A's were on a mission to get back to the World Series and not be denied. It helped us deal with tough competition from manager Doug Rader's Angels and John Wathan's Royals. It also helped sustain us through several key injuries in the first half of the season. Most importantly, it kept everyone focused on the finish line.

I think the bigger advantage was the great team assembled by the A's ownership and the Sandy Alderson-led front office. The A's had it all—great starting pitching and relievers complemented by great position players in terms of talent, toughness, and knowledge of the game.

My lasting memories of the '89 World Series include the earthquake, but also that great team which, through no fault of its own, was not able to be recognized for its place in history. I'm proud of that team, but I'm also proud of the way the A's demonstrated their awareness and respect for all who suffered because of Loma Prieta. There was a muted clubhouse celebration and rally instead of champagne baths. But none of that—not even the understated civic celebration at Jack London Square—could dim our satisfaction at the realization of lifelong dreams.

—Tony La Russa

Founded in 1991, Tony La Russa's Animal Relief Foundation (ARF) saves dogs and cats who have run out of time at public shelters and brings them together with people to enrich each others' lives. For more information, visit www.arf.net or www.facebook.com\tlrarf.

Prologue

I t began as a subtle vibration—not unlike those caused by commercial airliners as they would pass over Candlestick Park on their ascent from nearby San Francisco International Airport. And briefly—for less time than it takes to articulate that thought—that's what I figured it was: an airplane. My second thought was one I'd had on many occasions over the years: *This would be a really crummy time for an earthquake.*

It wasn't an idle thought. My senior project for U.S. history, my final assignment as a high school student, was a term paper on earthquakes. I learned about P waves and S waves. I learned about the Richter scale, on which every point represents a magnitude order of 10. In other words a 2.0 earthquake isn't twice as powerful as a 1.0 earthquake; it's 10 times as strong. I learned that the next devastating earthquake to ravage the Bay Area was a question of when—not if. And most frighteningly, I learned that no matter what the building code or what we had learned about engineering over the years, there was nothing man could construct that a sufficiently powerful earthquake couldn't wreck.

My fondest dream was realized when after high school and four years of college, I was hired as a sportswriter by the *Valley Times* of Pleasanton, California, a part of the *Contra Costa Times* group. Soon, much sooner than I deserved, I was given a column that gave me an entrée to the full menu of Bay Area sports—the Giants,

A's, 49ers, Raiders, Warriors, Cal, Stanford. I spent a lot of time crossing the Bay Bridge, where traffic sometimes would come to a grinding halt and I would think to myself, *This would be a really crummy time for an earthquake.*

The same thought occasionally crossed my mind as I sat in a sold-out stadium or traveled an elevated freeway. Now, just minutes before the scheduled start of Game 3 of the 1989 World Series between the A's and Giants, as the subtle vibration began to morph into a gentle bouncing motion, I realized my greatest fear was coming true. There was no plane passing overhead. And even if there was, it wouldn't cause the arrhythmic jostling that was beginning to pitch me back and forth, side to side. This was an earthquake, alright. I had experienced earthquakes before. But this one seemed more insistent and more intense. I was seated in the dreaded auxiliary press box, where they put overflow media at big sporting events (in this case Section 1 in the upper deck at Candlestick Park). I began to bounce up and down.

No, seriously: This would be a really crummy time for an earthquake.

The bouncing intensified. We were beginning to rock and roll. I looked at the football press box, tucked under the canopy of the upper deck on the third-base side of the stadium. I had watched dozens of 49ers games from inside those Spartan quarters. Now its plate glass windows flexed in and out, reflecting funhouse mirror images as they moved. Beginning to panic just a little, I looked out at the second deck beyond center field. We were bouncing to such an extent that it seemed inconceivable that Candlestick Park, the most maligned stadium in sports, could stand the strain. Which part of the inelegant cement bowl would fail first? The light towers swayed like tall stalks of corn. Something had to give. But what? And when? The shaking and jolting went on for what seemed like minutes. And then it stopped.

A half beat later, the crowd let loose with a hearty cheer. Candlestick Park had taken Mother Nature's kick to the gut and was still standing. But I was consumed with dread. With earthquakes you can never be sure. Was what you felt a relatively small quake that seemed bigger than it was because it was epicentered just below your feet? Or was it a powerful event that traveled miles to reach you? I wasn't sure. But I was unsettled.

Within minutes, power was out at the stadium. I was armed with a Sony Watchman, a hand-held TV with a screen about half the size of today's smart phones. I had fresh batteries. I turned it on. It took what seemed like forever to locate a signal from one of the local TV stations. When I finally found one, the magnitude of the devastation was beyond what I had imagined. There were no cars in the water beneath the Bay Bridge as had been rumored almost instantly after the shaking stopped. But the bridge was impassable.

It would be long, slow minutes before we found out about the fires in San Francisco's Marina District and the collapse of the Cypress Structure Freeway in Oakland. But even before the official announcement, I was certain of one thing: there would be no baseball that day. It didn't take a genius to figure that out. There was no power at the stadium and a collapsed double-deck freeway just a few miles from where a World Series game was supposed to have been contested. Death. Destruction. The need for police and firefighting resources elsewhere around San Francisco. Clearly, the stadium would need to be inspected.

I began packing my briefcase.

"What are you doing?" asked a colleague.

"They aren't going to play this game," I told him. I made for the nearest ramp to the lower deck. I needed to get out of the stadium and circle around to the players' parking lot where my press credential would allow me access. I knew I would be expected to file a story—game or no game. The line leading out of the stadium moved slowly. As we shuffled down the ramps, some opportunists were already offering to buy ticket stubs for souvenirs. Occasionally you could feel the slight jostle of another quake.

This would be a really crummy time for a serious aftershock.

I finally made my way to the players' parking lot and began conducting interviews. I'd be lying if I said my heart was in it. The sun was beginning to set. The parking lot looked like an oil painting with thousands of cars sitting motionless with their taillights glowing.

I hooked up with two other colleagues. We needed a place to write. But where? We weren't keen on reentering the stadium and climbing back up to a blacked-out Section 1. We would learn later that some out-of-town reporters wrote their stories in the parking lot by the light of a rental car's headlights—a semicircle of scribes in a race to finish their stories before the car battery went dead.

I had a better idea. For years Major League Baseball has provided media and assorted VIPs a pregame brunch and postgame buffet at playoff games. They're nicely done. But the postgame buffets don't account for the hour or two newspaper reporters need to finish and file their stories. This was the third consecutive year I had covered the postseason. I had become accustomed to arriving at the postgame buffet just in time to see the last food table being wheeled out of the room. I didn't even bother bringing my postgame buffet tickets to Candlestick Park for Game 3 of the World Series. I surely would never use them, and my briefcase was cluttered enough as it was.

There would be no Game 3. But the huge tent erected in the Candlestick Park parking lot to host the brunch and buffet might be open, with its generator, tables, and chairs, maybe even food and drink. I suggested to my two colleagues that we head in that direction. I was right. The tent blazed, an oasis of light. Peering inside, we saw plenty of available tables and chairs. We approached the entrance. "Can I see your tickets?" a security guard asked us. My colleagues produced theirs. I informed the guard that I didn't have my ticket.

"Then you can't come in," he said. I was dumbfounded. "We're not here for a party," I said, not altogether pleasantly. "We're here to work."

"Sorry," he said.

At that moment, one of my colleagues recognized Connie Lurie, wife of Giants owner Bob Lurie, inside the tent. He called to her. She came over, and we explained our situation. "You let these gentlemen inside," she told the security guy. He did. Mrs. Lurie showed us to a table as if seating us at one of San Francisco's finest restaurants. She brought us something to drink. She brought us food and apologized because it was cold. "We have no way to warm it," she said. "We were planning a postgame party, but now we'll have a post-earthquake party." I knew there were horrific scenes playing out all over the Bay Area. At that moment I felt comforted by her simple act of kindness.

We wrote our stories and then had to solve another problem. The tent had no telephones. This was before air cards and wireless Internet access. The Internet itself was in its embryonic stage. We had Radio Shack TRS-80 word processors— covered wagons compared to the powerful laptops we use today. We needed an actual phone to transmit. And we knew there was only one place to find one: inside Candlestick Park.

It was dark by then. We left the safety of the tent and walked halfway around the outside of the stadium and up an incline so treacherously steep that it was known as Heartbreak Hill in memory of the Candlestick Park patrons who had succumbed to cardiac arrest trying to climb it. Finally, we reached the same open gate I had exited a few hours earlier. There was no one to stop us, so we reluctantly crept back into the murky darkness.

The pay phone banks in that part of the lower-deck concourse—essentially behind where home plate would be—were inside big cutouts in the stadium's cement wall. It was pitch black inside those alcoves. This wasn't going to be easy. Here's what transmitting a story entailed: I had to dial a prefix, then the 10-digit number of the computer at our Walnut Creek office. At the tone I had to dial a 16-digit calling card number to pay for the long-distance call. When I heard the familiar squealing tone, I had to place the phone's handpieces into my word processor's acoustical couplers (they looked like rubber suction cups), making sure the earpiece went into the coupler specific to the earpiece and the mouthpiece into the coupler specific to the mouthpiece.

The TRS-80 (we called them "Trash 80s") had a row of function buttons below the display screen. I had to find and push F4, then F3. Then I had to type the name of the document I wished to transmit and hit enter. It didn't transmit at the speed of light. Not being able to see the screen, I had no idea when the transmission was complete. I gave it plenty of time just to be on the safe side. Then I had to call the office—prefix, 10-digit number, tone, 16-digit number—to make sure the story had arrived intact. I don't recall how many tries it took me to successfully transmit and verify. More than one would be a safe guess. I do recall that every second inside that black hole was agony.

Eventually, we all filed our stories. Then there was the small matter of how to get home. With the Bay Bridge closed, the quickest way was over the San Mateo Bridge to the south of Candlestick Park. Before reaching the bridge, we heard a radio report that it had been inspected and cleared for traffic. To get on the bridge required driving on a long flyover, a high, elevated connector. I almost couldn't bring myself to do it.

It's difficult to explain to anyone who hasn't been through an earthquake. For a time afterward, sometimes days, you simply don't trust the ground. You can't be sure if it's done shaking or if the worst is over. You just don't know. It seemed as if we were on the flyover for hours. It was a relief to get on the bridge and an even bigger relief to get to the other side. Not long after getting off the bridge, we heard a radio report that it had been closed again for further inspection. Eventually, we made it back to the office. There wasn't much visible damage in the East Bay. I found a few items toppled over at my house when I got home. That was comforting. But anxiety continued to plague me. I simply couldn't settle down. I turned on the news and watched as much of the nonstop earthquake coverage as I could stand.

The images conveyed a sense of hell on Earth. It seemed as if things would never be the same again.

I tried to sleep but couldn't. I got up and turned on the TV again for as long as I could stand it. I tried to sleep, again unsuccessfully. The next day on very little sleep, I went into the office. I knew I would be expected to write a column. And I knew just what to write: "As far as I'm concerned, the World Series is over."

Chapter 1

The Offseason

Tony Phillips settled into his crouch in the left-handed batter's box. His team trailed by three runs with two out in the bottom of the ninth inning. The count was full. A runner was on third base. If Phillips could reach base, the tying run would come to the plate. And at that point, who knew what might happen?

It was the kind of win-or-go-home moment that the 1988 Oakland Athletics embraced with relish en route to winning 104 regular-season games—second most in the 88-year history of a franchise that boasted a colorful, checkered resume of sublime highs (three clusters of American League pennants that resulted in eight World Series championships) and slapstick lows (extended periods of benign neglect under owners Connie Mack and Charles O. Finley).

As recently as 1979, the A's had lost 108 games while drawing 306,763 fans. But in August 1980, Finley sold the team to Levi Strauss chairman Walter Haas. In midseason of 1986, Haas hired onetime A's bonus baby Tony La Russa to manage the club. And in 1988, La Russa guided the A's to their first World Series in 14 years. It was an eminently winnable World Series at that, against a Los Angeles Dodgers team that captured the National League West with 94 wins and rode the right arm of Orel Hershiser to a National League Championship Series upset of the New York Mets but entered the Fall Classic an uninspiring collection of wounded warriors and role players.

That collection stunned the A's with Kirk Gibson's epic Game 1 home run and Hershiser's Game 2 three-hit shutout. The teams split Games 3 and 4 in Oakland. Now in the ninth inning of Game 5, it was up to Phillips, Oakland's eight-place hitter, to keep the A's breakout season in play. With Carney Lansford on third base and eventual Rookie of the Year Walt Weiss on deck, Phillips looked out at the Oakland Coliseum's pitching mound and saw Hershiser, about to apply the capstone to perhaps the greatest six-week run of pitching in baseball history, staring back.

Hershiser stood straight as a tin soldier, tugged at the long sleeve on his right arm, hitched at his belt, got the sign from catcher Rick Dempsey, and then swung into his windup. He elevated his left knee as he tucked his left shoulder. Then he exploded in a riot of body parts toward home plate. Phillips swung through Hershiser's high fastball. Hershiser walked a couple steps off the mound, spoke a few words while looking at the sky, and then was hoisted off his feet by the onrushing Dempsey.

The Dodgers had won. The A's had been ushered into a disquieting offseason, a fate they could not have imagined when they convened for spring training as a team of dreams coming off an 81–81 season. In the short span of seven months, they had established themselves as a sexy, swaggering, star-laden potential dynasty. Jose Canseco had chartered the 40–40 club, becoming the first player in major league history to hit 40 home runs and steal 40 bases in the same season. Mark McGwire had encored his record-setting 49-homer effort as a rookie with 32 round-trippers and 99 RBIs. Dave Stewart, released by the Phillies in 1986, had turned in his second consecutive 20-win season. Bob Welch, acquired from the Dodgers during the offseason, had transitioned successfully to the American League with a 17–9 record. La Russa had begun construction of the modern bullpen with set-up men and a one-inning closer, making a star of Dennis Eckersley. The A's ripped off a 14-game win streak in late April and early May, establishing an eight-game lead in the AL West. They won the division in a romp.

They were more than good. They were intimidating by virtue of their ability and their physical stature. They quickly came up with a quirky, unique manner in which to express their size and strength to each other and—perhaps more importantly—to their opponents. It happened one day in spring training of 1988 when McGwire and Canseco banged arms while comparing their considerable muscles. The forearm bash was born.

Its architects could scarcely have been more different. Canseco was outgoing, flashy, demonstrative, and sassy. (He once referred to Giants first baseman Will Clark as "a three-toed sloth.") Canseco had every physical skill in the book. He also had a chip on his shoulder, having been the last pick in the 15th round of the 1982 draft. He had, he said, transformed himself into a superstar through hard work. He was proud of the transformation. McGwire was quiet, content to be just one guy on a 25-man roster. He had stupendous power. Although in time he would become a solid defensive first baseman and a .300 hitter in two different seasons, he was not the epitome of the five-tool player.

But they had one thing in common—they were big, strong, proud, power-lifting, power-hitting new generation A's. And now they had a signature move. Soon all A's players were celebrating home runs by raising one arm, clenching their fist, and clinking forearms with a similarly posed teammate. It was as an action as subtle as Paul Bunyan's blue ox. And it was a perfect fit. "We were looking to do something a little different," McGwire said. "We have a lot of guys who look like they'll hit home runs and we didn't want to just do high fives."

Size mattered to those A's. According to the official 1988 World Series media guide, the muscular McGwire stood 6'5" and weighed 220 pounds. Canseco was an equally muscular 6'3" and 210. Dave Parker was 6'5" and 230; Don Baylor was 6'1" and 210; Dave Henderson was 6'2" and 220; Terry Steinbach was 6'1" and 195; Ron Hassey was 6'2" and 195, and Carney Lansford was 6'1" and 195. The bash became an exclamation point after a home run into the 23rd row, the cherry on top of a bases-loaded double. No vanquished opponent could miss it. But perhaps its greatest value was giving the A's an identity they had lacked for a half-decade.

Until manager La Russa arrived, the A's were largely a faceless, featureless bunch. Canseco began to change the dynamic when he arrived at the end of the 1985 season. His Rookie of the Year season in 1986 was encored by McGwire's in 1987. Parker and Baylor were added to the roster during the 1987–88 offseason. When they began exchanging forearm shivers in 1988, it was as if they were kicking sand in the faces of their undersized opponents. Soon there was a video set to the tune of the 1962 Bobby "Boris" Pickett tune, "Monster Mash," and a Bash Brothers souvenir poster featuring McGwire and Canseco outfitted to resemble John Belushi and Dan Aykroyd in the film, *Blues Brothers.* "We had been looking for something that would be all ours," McGwire said. They succeeded *una-bash-edly.*

But their quest for a World Series title had been thwarted by a collection of superlative efforts and confounding, unexplainable turns of events. How confounding and unexplainable? Gibson's Game 1 homer, launched off two bad legs, made a loser of Eckersley, who led the majors with 45 saves during the regular season. Hershiser had as many hits as he allowed the A's in Game 2.

McGwire's walk-off homer in Game 3 gave the A's hope on an evening when the Dodgers lost starting pitcher John Tudor to an elbow injury in the second inning; lost right fielder Mike Marshall—their leading RBI man during the regular season—to a stiff back in the fourth; and had already gotten all they would get from Gibson.

NBC announcer Bob Costas set the stage for Game 4 by assessing the Dodgers starting lineup as "possibly one of the weakest to take the field in World Series history." And that was before catcher Mike Scioscia left with a bad knee in the bottom of the fourth. That weak lineup beat the A's and their ace, Stewart, 4–3.

Hershiser closed it out in Game 5, capping a phenomenal stretch in which he went 8–0 with one save in 12 appearances, struck out 66 in 97⅔ innings, allowed a miserly 55 hits, tossed seven shutouts, and compiled an ERA you needed a microscope to read: 0.46. Oakland's swaggering stars fell silent. Canseco was held to one hit, a roaring grand slam in Game 1, in 19 at-bats. McGwire had one hit, his Game 3 game-winner, in 17 at-bats. Lansford was 3-for-18; Weiss was 1-for-16. There was no disguising the A's disappointment. "My heart is broken," La Russa told *The New York Times.* "When you feel you're the best team and you don't win," Oakland designated hitter Dave Parker told reporters, "that bothers you. This will haunt us all winter."

The frustration was already bubbling over for Eckersley, one of the team's straightest shooters, both on and off the field. Eck shook his head over what he considered Hershiser's overly dramatic mannerisms, specifically the way he would reach in his back pocket for a card containing scouting reports on Oakland hitters, study it for several pregnant moments, and then shove it back in his pocket before climbing atop the mound. "His style, the way he plays to the crowd, really pisses me off," Eckersley told reporters as the Dodgers were still celebrating their conquest. "But you have to give him credit. He's the best in the business."

◆ ◆ ◆ ◆

The Giants' offseason of discontent was already 18 days old when Phillips took the A's final, futile swing of the year. The two Bay Area teams had this much in common—both had at one time or another entertained visions of a World Series parade in 1988. If the A's had reported to spring training in February of '88 with cautious optimism, the Giants had convened with unbridled ambition. General manager Al Rosen threw out the ceremonial first boast at a pre-spring training luncheon by predicting his team, coming off its first division title in 16 years, would win the World Series.

His optimism was understandable. Rosen had been hired during a disastrous 1985 season in which the Giants had lost 100 games for the first time in franchise history. He hired Roger Craig as his manager and with several shrewd personnel moves remade a roster that hadn't won a postseason game since Willie Mays was the team's center fielder. Rosen inherited Clark, selected with the second pick in the 1985 summer draft. Clark was at the fore of an influx of young talent that made the 1986 club and inspired an upbeat marketing campaign: "You gotta like these kids."

Clark made a fabulous series of first impressions, homering in his first spring training at-bat in 1986, homering off Nolan Ryan in his first major league at-bat, and homering in his home debut at Candlestick Park. Clark pulsed with confidence and intensity. Incredibly, the team, which finished 33 games out of first place in 1985, led the National League West at the All-Star break the following year. The Giants eventually faded to third. (An elbow injury cost Clark most of June and July.) There was no fading in 1987.

Buoyed by Rosen's midseason deals—he acquired slugger Kevin Mitchell and pitchers Dave Dravecky and Craig Lefferts in early July and then secured Pirates pitchers Rick Reuschel and Don Robinson in separate transactions—the Giants assumed sole possession of first place for good on Aug. 21.

They met the St. Louis Cardinals in the NLCS, taking a 3–2 lead after five games. Needing just one win in the final two contests (played in St. Louis) to reach the World Series, the Giants failed to score a run. Right fielder Candy Maldonado's attempt at a sliding catch on a blooper hit by Cards catcher Tony Pena (Maldonado would later contend he lost the ball in the stadium lights) resulted in a triple that led to the only run in Game 6. Starting pitcher Atlee Hammaker was rocked in Game 7. A three-run homer by Jose Oquendo, just his third home run in more than 900 major league at-bats, was the coup de gras in the Giants' series and season-ending 6–0 loss.

The dispirited Giants repaired to their downtown hotel where they were treated to the sound of joyous Cardinals fans honking their car horns for hours after the game. Those horns echoed into the spring of '88. "I stayed up all night," pitcher Mike Krukow said. "Those horns were more motivation than anything Al Rosen and Roger Craig could have provided."

The addition of center fielder Brett Butler, the classic leadoff hitter the team had lacked in 1987, fueled the Giants' optimism for 1988. On August 11 they were just two and a half games off the lead. But a relentless onslaught of injuries to the pitching staff doomed their chances. Dravecky went down first with a bum shoulder. His final appearance was on May 28. He had surgery on June 12. In September doctors biopsied a lump in his upper left arm and found it to be cancerous. During a nine-hour operation on October 7, Dravecky's 10th wedding anniversary, surgeons removed the tumor and much of Dravecky's deltoid muscle. Dr. George Muschler informed Dravecky that, barring a miracle, he had "zero chance" of ever pitching again.

That was by far the worst of it, but it wasn't the end of it. Mike LaCoss, a 13-game winner in 1987, had season-ending surgery to remove a bone spur from his right elbow on July 21. Ten days later, rookie Terry Mulholland suffered a fractured left wrist when hit by a line drive; his season was over. Kelly Downs was shut down after his August 24 start with an inflamed right shoulder and a 13–9 record. Krukow had season-ending surgery on his right shoulder on September 13. Reliever Joe Price was disabled twice. The malaise even extended to Mike Remlinger, the Giants' first-round pick in the 1987 draft, who was limited to 13 innings at Double A by ligament damage in his pitching elbow.

Needless to say, the Giants generated fewer headlines at the 1989 pre-spring training luncheon. This time Rosen was more circumspect. "A lot of people are picking us fourth in the division," he told the assembled Bay Area media, "but I see where Las Vegas has us at 7–1 to win the pennant, second only to the Mets in our league." Said Craig at the same event: "I'm not going to make any predictions."

In the summer of 2013, Craig, the man who both invoked and answered to the baseball expression "Humm Baby," recalled feeling a cautious optimism about his team's chances. "There were probably some teams better than we were," he said. "But we had a solid infield with Will Clark and Robby Thompson and [Jose] Uribe and Matt [Williams], so we could catch the ball defensively in the infield and outfield. Our pitching was okay."

Humm Baby was an all-purpose phrase Craig used when he first joined the Giants. He was coy about its origins. (The consensus was that it was a take-off on a form of infield chatter.) The more he used it—as a noun, an adjective, an exhortation, a homily, an expression of approval—the more its meaning became a subject of debate in the Bay Area. Craig would refer to certain players at times as a Humm Baby. For example, Bob Brenly was called such on the day he made four errors at third base in one inning and then wound up winning the game with a walk-off home run. Over time, people started referring to Craig as the Humm Baby. During the 1987 NLCS, Craig described the expression as such: "Humm Baby means aggressive, hard-nosed baseball. It can mean a great double play, a well-executed hit-and-run, or a beautiful girl." That was its beauty: it could mean anything you wanted it to mean.

Also looking back nearly a quarter-century, Clark recalled having "high hopes" for 1989. If others in the Giants organization felt likewise, it was probably because they were pinning their hopes on him—and for good reason. Clark's first major league game came 26 days after his 22nd birthday; he finished fifth in the 1986 Rookie of the Year voting. In 1987 he hit 35 homers with a .308 average and finished fifth in the MVP balloting. In 1988 he made his first All-Star team and led the National League in RBIs. "You're talking about a kid," Dave Dravecky said in 2013. "The stuff he had done up to that point was amazing. You're talking about a guy with Hall of Fame talent and those kinds of characteristics. The organization had compiled a very good baseball club, Will being at the head of that. He really was the centerpiece."

A confident young man with a high-pitched cackle of a voice, Clark relished being the guy people looked to in important situations. "I really enjoyed being able to run out there every day," he said in 2013. "My teammates knew that, hey look, he's going to be there and he's going to give it the max effort. I want to be out there on the field with him." At least one of his managers felt likewise. "He was a great defensive player," Craig said in 2013. " He's a winner. You get a couple guys like him and you're going to win some ballgames. He leads by example."

♦ ♦ ♦ ♦

Canseco came up with what appeared to be the perfect antidote to postseason baseball heartache. Five days after the final game of the 1988 World Series, he married Esther Haddad in a civil ceremony in Miami. In doing so he pocketed

$10,000, winning a wager with teammate Stewart, who had bet Canseco that he wouldn't tie the knot before November 5.

If Canseco needed further balm to soothe his World Series wounds, he got it on November 8, when he was voted the Associated Press Player of the Year (in a landslide over Orel Hershiser) and again on November 16, when he was named American League Most Valuable Player. He was the first unanimous AL choice since another A's right fielder of note, Reggie Jackson, in 1973.

For the rest of the offseason Canseco displayed an astonishing gift for generating headlines but not always for the right reasons. He led the majors in no-shows, failing to appear for a parade in his honor in his hometown of Miami, for an appearance at a Bay Area Sports Hall of Fame function at which he was to receive an award, and for a baseball card show in New Jersey. On January 22, 1989, Canseco and his traveling companion, David Valdez, were detained at the Detroit airport when Valdez was found to be carrying a gun and a bag of pills. Two months later, tests would reveal the pills were steroids.

Back in Oakland, A's general manager Sandy Alderson and manager La Russa began clinically deconstructing the World Series and making plans for spring training 1989. That process figured to come naturally to Alderson, a Dartmouth graduate who joined the Marines (for whom he was, literally, a recruiting poster boy), served in Vietnam, and then earned a law degree from Harvard.

Outwardly, Alderson was stoic and contemplative. He seemed to have a cool, measured response to any crisis. He was to the prototypical baseball executive what white shoes were to wool uniforms. That he was in baseball at all was a freak of circumstance. He worked at the same San Francisco law firm as Roy Eisenhardt at the time Eisenhardt's father-in-law, Walter Haas, bought the A's. Eisenhardt left the law firm to become the A's president. He convinced Alderson to join him as the team's general counsel. In 1983, Alderson was named general manager. For a man of achievement, Alderson exuded no airs. He may have had a button-down education, but he favored a button-fly wardrobe. He was so low-key that for years, including 1989 and 1990, his biography was conspicuously absent from the A's annual media guide. Whatever disappointment he felt after the 1988 World Series failed to impair his critical thinking. "When you win 104 games and go to the World Series," he would tell reporters during the 1989 postseason, "you know you have a decent team. It's not like you have to tear things down and start over again.

It allows you to focus in on one or two changes you might make and try to make them with a little more confidence."

Alderson's first confident decision was to sign free-agent pitcher Mike Moore to a three-year contract worth a reported $3.95 million, which gave him a $1.31 million average yearly salary. Of the 1988 A's, only Carney Lansford had earned as much. A risk? Moore had posted a 66–96 record in his first seven big league seasons, all spent with the woeful Seattle Mariners. Although he had top-drawer physical skills, his personal winning percentage (.407) was even worse than that of the M's (.439) during his time in Seattle. But the A's saw enough to believe they needed to be the first team to welcome him to the open market. "I remember making the visit to Arizona with Sandy and Wally [Haas, son of the owner] to talk to Mike Moore," La Russa said. "And all of a sudden, you get this pitcher, and we sell him on us before he could get into this free-agent stuff. Now we've got Mike Moore to go along with [a proven starting rotation]."

Alderson's second decision was more or less made for him. The Cuban-born Canseco, for all his off-field missteps, was unlike any major league player before him. He was huge and sculpted with phenomenal bat speed, superior strength, and stunning foot speed for a man of 6'3" and 210 pounds. In his first three full major league seasons, Canseco averaged 35 home runs, 118 RBIs, and 23 stolen bases. He improved his average each year, from .240 to .257 to .307. He improved his defensive skills to the point that La Russa moved him from left field to right field for the 1988 season.

Canseco was eligible for arbitration and he held all the cards. On February 1 his agent, Dennis Gilbert, asked for $1.64 million for the 1989 season. Alderson countered with an offer of $1.3 million. But he sensed how things were going to play out. "To say I'm pessimistic would probably be too much of an understatement," he told the *San Jose Mercury News*. Two days later the A's avoided the contentious arbitration process by signing Canseco to a one-year deal worth every penny of the $1.64 million Gilbert had requested. It represented a $1.245 million bump from Canseco's 1988 salary, the biggest raise in major league history at the time. "It's a reflection of our feeling that the number he submitted [for arbitration] was a fairly reasonable one," Alderson told reporters.

One week later Canseco was pulled over by the Florida Highway Patrol for driving his $75,000 customized candy-apple-red Jaguar (license plate: Mr. 40–40) at 125 miles per hour in South Broward County. He was cited for reckless driving and allowed to drive away. Like it or not, the A's were all in on Canseco, and the risk-reward proposition he would embody for the balance of his first term with the team.

If Alderson was mired in practical concerns, La Russa was equally concerned with the psychology of the coming season. Unlike the measured Alderson, La Russa was a potent blend of fire and ice, at once supremely intense and utterly logical. What's more, he'd been down this path before. In 1983, as a 38-year-old already in his fifth year as a big league manager, La Russa guided the Chicago White Sox to a runaway title in the American League West. They finished 20 games ahead of the Kansas City Royals, clinching the division on September 17. It was the team's first pennant in 24 years and La Russa's first taste of success as a manager at the major league level. The White Sox squeaked out a 2–1 win against the Baltimore Orioles in Game 1 of the American League Championship Series behind 24-game-winner and eventual Cy Young Award recipient LaMarr Hoyt. Then they fell hard, losing the final three games of the best-of-five series by a combined score of 18–1.

La Russa reflected upon the spring of 1984 as a lost opportunity to set the proper tone for his defending division champs. Winners of 99 games in 1983, the Sox plummeted to 74 wins in 1984. They improved to 85 in 1985 but were in the throes of a 90-loss season when La Russa was fired on June 20, 1986.

A voracious reader, La Russa bought Lakers coach Pat Riley's book *Showtime* after the 1988 season, seeking insight into how to motivate players who have already performed at a high level. He made plans to bring Jackson, with whom he played in 1968–71 and whom he managed in 1987, to spring training to enlighten current A's players on how to encore success with more success. La Russa also performed his winter ritual of reviewing the just completed season in spare-no-feelings fashion. The first thing he admitted was that the 1988 A's, relentless from spring to fall, had let down in Game 1 of the World Series. "When Jose hit the grand slam, for the first time all year, this relentless [team], I think, we lost an edge," La Russa said in 2013.

When the team met for the first time in spring training, La Russa told his club what he had told selected veterans—he called them "co-signers"—in advance. "That first day of spring training, I just laid it out what our [veteran] guys had already agreed upon," he recalled. "I told the rest of the squad, 'We're going to be on a mission. This is what we did last year. It got away from us.' I said, 'But we've got to get there first…What I remember about that club starting out was saying that, and guys were just nodding [their heads in agreement]. They knew we'd missed the opportunity. They wanted it again."

◆ ◆ ◆ ◆

The Giants had more questions than answers in the offseason. Would Dravecky be able to come back? If not, who would replace him? How many of their legion of pitchers injured in 1988 would be good to go at the start of the 1989 season? Would Maldonado, who nose-dived in 1988, regain the form he displayed for the Giants in 1986–87, when he averaged 19 home runs and 85 RBIs?

While division rivals beefed up—the Dodgers acquired veteran All-Stars Willie Randolph (to replace departed free agent Steve Sax) and Eddie Murray, and the San Diego Padres traded for slugging first baseman Jack Clark and signed free agent pitcher Bruce Hurst—it seemed all the Giants did was lose during the offseason.

Catcher Bob Brenly, who joined the team in 1981 as a 27-year-old rookie and liked to joke that he left his best seasons on a bus during six long minor league campaigns, signed a free-agent contract with the Toronto Blue Jays. At 35, Brenly's best playing days were clearly behind him. But his wisecracking leadership and his yin-and-yang relationship with pitcher Mike Krukow, another quick-witted clubhouse presence, had provided glue that helped Craig's early Giants teams bond. They seemed like characters straight out of *Bull Durham*. They had developed a rapport that began during a 1984 game in San Diego. It was a story they loved to tell. "I gave up six runs in the first inning, the last on a three-run dinger by [No. 8 hitter] Garry Templeton," Krukow recalled after a 1986 game. "Bob waited until the umpire flipped him a new ball, then he walked out to me and said, 'Let's see if you can get the fucking pitcher out.' From that day forward, he's been in charge."

On the first trip of the season to Chicago, where he pitched six seasons for the Cubs, Krukow would dispatch Giants teammates on an after-hours mission to a lakefront park and a statue of General Philip Sheridan astride his horse Winchester. There, in a ritual that has been embraced by other teams and continues to this day, they would spray-paint the horse's testicles in the Giants' team colors.

Brenly was, as all good catchers are, a calming influence. On the Giants' final road trip in 1987, during which they clinched the division title, they woke up in Los Angeles at 7:42 AM to a 5.9 earthquake. The temblor rattled the downtown area and left the team hotel without power or hot water. The hotel was evacuated as a precaution. Players, team officials, and reporters in various states of dress and bed head rushed down the stairs and onto the sidewalk. Sitting on a retaining wall, Brenly set up shop and began issuing sartorial critiques of people stumbling out of the building. Soon it was like a Giants locker room with Brenly holding court surrounded by others reveling in his witty banter.

Now Brenly was gone, and Krukow was an unknown quantity coming off season-ending surgery, leaving the Giants without a veteran leader. While Rosen made a couple tweaks, swapping outfielders with the Montreal Expos (Mike Aldrete for Tracy Jones) and catchers with the Orioles (Bob Melvin for Terry Kennedy), he did nothing to address the Giants' biggest on-field concern coming into spring training in 1989—the lack of a bona fide closer. Craig, guru of the split-fingered fastball, had a plan. It wouldn't last long.

Chapter 2

A Burgeoning Rivalry

The A's hired two security guards for their initial 1989 spring training workouts at Scottsdale (Arizona) Community College in anticipation of larger than normal crowds drawn by their breakout 1988 season. One by one as players and team officials trickled into town, the subject of the team's World Series defeat was addressed through the soft lens of hindsight.

But in one sense, it was business as usual. Jose Canseco was late to camp for the third consecutive year. In 1987, he arrived late due to a contract dispute. In 1988, he was at a card show. He was never officially AWOL since the collective bargaining agreement (CBA) stipulated that players weren't required to report to their teams until March 1. But per the TLR (Tony La Russa) agreement, the A's first full-squad workout was scheduled for February 22, and the full squad was expected to be on hand. And for the third time in three years, Canseco wasn't there. Not that this came as any great surprise. "The good news," La Russa told the *San Jose Mercury News* the night before the first full-squad workout, "is he says he's going to be here. The bad news is he's driving to camp."

Canseco wasn't the only no-show. Outfielders Luis Polonia, Stan Javier, and Felix Jose—all residents of the Dominican Republic—were waiting for their visas to be cleared by the U.S. Embassy. But Canseco was well on his way to being judged on many levels by a different standard than your average ballplayer. It was a fact of his new life that he lamented when he finally arrived at camp on February 23. "The publicity I'm getting is kind of negative," he told the *Mercury News*. "But I don't think people see the other side." Canseco complained that he was hounded by fans even at his Miami home. Because of that and other unwanted attention that came his way, he occasionally carried a gun, for which he had a permit. Canseco wasn't the first surpassing athlete to transcend the game he played so well and then complain about the inevitable scrutiny that ensued. But he was at the head of that class in the late winter of 1989. If he bristled at the confines of his carefully constructed celebrity, so did the A's.

La Russa blamed the tardy arrival on Canseco's buddy, David Valdez. But when Canseco finally arrived on-site, La Russa endeavored to make light of the transgression the way members of teams often do—by razzing a player to let him know how much he was missed. So it happened that a Scottsdale Community College football coach showed up that day as well, playing the role of Valdez in a La Russa-orchestrated skit. La Russa gave the faux Valdez a playful pat-down. It was a jocular way of saying to Canseco, "Glad you're here." But it underscored the reality that Canseco was separating himself from the team—in ways both good and bad.

On the evening of March 1, Canseco was stopped by Phoenix police for running a red light. He was cited for three other violations: failure to carry a driver's license, failure to carry proof of insurance, and because his Jaguar bore plates that were issued to another vehicle. Canseco and his twin brother, Ozzie, a non-roster invitee to the A's spring training camp, were in his Jaguar. Jose's wife, Esther, followed in a Corvette, and Ozzie's wife was in a third car. Jose complained he had been treated like "a common criminal." He blamed the license plate mix-up on his father confusing the plates for his Jaguar with the plates for his Corvette. "I don't want special treatment," he told the *Mercury News*. "I just want to be treated like a human being." When the news hit camp, La Russa expressed little sympathy for his reigning MVP. "He says, 'Why am I different? I want to be like everybody else,'" La Russa told the paper. "Well, if you are in the public eye, you are not like everybody else."

But the incident was the subject of some in-house humor the following day. Canseco playfully swiped a reporter's notepad and pen and asked La Russa in the third person about his incorrigible right fielder. "I heard you wanted to be his lawyer," Canseco said.

"When I first heard Jose's version, yes," La Russa, a law school graduate who had passed the bar, told Canseco/reporter. "Since then, I've contacted the Phoenix Police Department and, hearing their version, I would rather prosecute him."

Canseco's envelope-pushing aside, the 1988 World Series was Topic A. Looking back 24 years, Eckersley recalled that the novelty of his new normal—newfound sobriety, a trade to the A's, and a career rebirth as a closer—helped him cope with the disappointment of the loss to the Dodgers. "Something like that is devastating," he said, "but I was okay. I think Tony was more concerned with my psyche. That's how he is. He wants to be on top of everything. I'd got a second chance. So when that happened to me, I wasn't like *poor me*. I was lucky I was doing what I was doing. I had resurrected my career. I was kind of digging the attention and success. And even though [the World Series loss] was a killer, I'd been around the block. If anybody could handle it, it would be someone like me."

The *Mercury News* devoted a lengthy story to the 3–2 backdoor slider Eckersley threw Gibson—the pitch Dodgers scout Mel Didier reportedly had advised the team's left-handed hitters to expect. "It's not the only pitch he could have hit," La Russa said, referring to the fact that Gibson had injuries to both legs. "But it's the only one he could have hit out of the ballpark." Catcher Ron Hassey disagreed. "To this day I will not believe what they said—that Eck throws a lot of 3–2 sliders," he said. "I had no hesitation at all [calling it]."

Twenty-four years later the '88 World Series still gnawed at Dave Stewart, who stood to be the winning pitcher in Game 1 before fate intervened. "Any time you underachieve, you're always going to feel some disappointment whenever the topic comes up," he said. "For me [the postseason] is a difficult time. You always have flashbacks and think of the ones that got away."

♦ ♦ ♦ ♦

For the 1989 Giants, Matt Williams, a slick-fielding, power-hitting shortstop from UNLV selected with the third pick of the 1986 draft, was their best chance for a marked improvement from 1988 based on the players currently under contract. Williams had the physical tools—quick feet and soft hands on defense, power to all fields as a hitter—that would have been the envy of any player. But the Giants rushed him to the big leagues, and he struggled. He made the team out of spring training in 1987 as a 21-year-old phenom. On July 3 he was demoted to Triple A with eight homers and a .192 average. He was recalled when the rosters expanded in September but finished at .188 with 68 strikeouts in 245 at-bats. Slow breaking balls were his catnip.

Williams began 1988 in the minors but was recalled in early June when shortstop Jose Uribe faced a family tragedy; his wife, Sara, died of heart failure shortly after delivering the couple's third child. In his second game, Williams bashed a grand slam off Nolan Ryan in an 8–2 San Francisco victory. Even after that triumphant moment he looked uncomfortable in the postgame locker room, eyes wide and unblinking as he was surrounded by reporters. He finished the season with a .205 average in 156 at-bats. He reported a week early to spring training in 1989, showing off a new body designed by fitness guru Mackie Shilstone, who had transformed Will Clark from a scrawny gap hitter into a power threat. "I hope he taught [Williams] how to hit the breaking ball, too," Craig cracked.

If the A's spring training question marks were decidedly pedestrian—Glenn Hubbard, Tony Phillips, and Mike Gallego were in a three-headed competition to start at second base; lefty Curt Young and right-hander Todd Burns were the leading candidates to be the fifth starter—the Giants were confronted with a doozy: who would be the closer?

Seven pitchers combined for 42 saves for the 1988 Giants, but there was no leader in the clubhouse at season's end. Craig anointed one in the offseason: Scott Garrelts, a tall, lean, whip-armed practitioner of the split-finger fastball. In parts of seven big league seasons, Garrelts had appeared in 283 games, 257 as a reliever. He led the Giants in saves in each of the previous four years, though never with more than 13. He was the Giants' only All-Star in their train wreck of a season in 1985, finishing with a 2.30 ERA. But his ERA rose to 3.11 in 1986 and to 3.22 in 1987. He converted just 22 of 38 save opportunities in the two seasons combined. He was a tantalizing enough talent in 1988, a year in which the Giants bullpen posted a record of 18–30, to earn, in Craig's estimation, first crack at the closer's job in 1989.

The logic may have been sound, but Craig's decision inspired some arched eyebrows outside the organization. Although Garrelts was dominating at his best, there were those who believed he wasn't at his best often enough. He was so enigmatic during the 1987 season that Craig began calling his pitches for him. Garrelts and teammates Atlee Hammaker and Kelly Downs were alike in the sense that they made scouts salivate with the movement on their pitches. Craig's oft-used line about Hammaker was that he couldn't throw the ball straight if he tried. But they seemed to be lacking an essential ingredient when it came to consistently achieving results commensurate with their ability. Confidence? Conviction? The ability to block out what other people might think or say? It wasn't clear. But this much was—Craig was committed to Garrelts as the closer to the point of calling the 27-year-old bespectacled right-hander his special project for spring training.

Meanwhile, the Giants had a situation on their hands. Had it involved Canseco, the world might have stood still. But because it involved a quiet slick-fielding, slap-hitting shortstop named Jose Uribe, it barely made a ripple. Uribe came to San Francisco in a multi-player trade after the 1984 season that sent Jack Clark, the closest thing the Giants had to a franchise player, to the St. Louis Cardinals. At the time, Uribe was known as Jose Gonzalez. After joining the Giants, he asked to be called Jose Uribe. Then-Giants third-base coach Rocky Bridges cracked, "Uribe literally is the player to be named later."

Uribe won his teammates' affection and the fans' hearts with his terrific defense. He was cast as a sympathetic figure when his wife died. So the news from the Dominican Republic on February 10 was unsettling. Uribe, who had signed a one-year contract for $687,500 in January, had been charged with threatening a woman with a gun and raping her. He was jailed for three days and was not allowed to leave the country before he was tried. His agent, Jim Bonner, was confident the matter would be resolved within 72 hours. Bonner was prophetic. Two days later, a judge ruled there was insufficient evidence to try Uribe, who was released on February 13. He reported to camp on February 26, claiming the entire episode had been an effort to extort money from him.

◆ ◆ ◆ ◆

From 1958–67 the Giants had the Bay Area to themselves. They were hailed as heroes when they arrived from New York before the '58 season. An estimated 200,000 fans turned out for what the Associated Press called a "riotous" parade through downtown streets the day before the team's first game on the West Coast. In that first decade, the Giants won more games (887) than any other National League team, and their average annual attendance of 1.499 million was second only to the Dodgers.

The A's arrived in Oakland in 1968. During their first decade of cohabitation, the A's and Giants averaged a combined 1.58 million in attendance per season—slightly more than the Giants had averaged on their own from 1958–67 but in twice the number of home dates. The fight for survival was on in a baseball town believed by many too small to accommodate two teams. Competitively speaking, the two franchises were on divergent paths in the late 1960s. In the midst of logging five consecutive second-place finishes, the Giants boasted a veteran core group of future Hall of Famers. But that group was aging. Before the 1968 season was over, Willie Mays would be 37. Juan Marichal, Willie McCovey, and Gaylord Perry would all be 30. They were being paid like stars. The Giants announced Mays' 1968 salary as $125,000, which would have made him the highest-paid player in baseball (though baseball-reference.com pegs it at $105,000, second to Frank Robinson's $120,000).

No four Athletics players combined could equal Mays' salary, and the team averaged 98 losses during its final four years in Kansas City. But it was loaded with young talent. Reggie Jackson, Rollie Fingers, and Joe Rudi were 21 on Opening Day 1968. Jim "Catfish" Hunter had just turned 22 (and would soon throw a perfect game). John "Blue Moon" Odom was 22. Sal Bando was 24. Bert Campaneris was 26.

There wasn't much to separate the teams during their first three years as regional bedfellows. From 1968–70 the Giants won five more games than the A's and outdrew Oakland by slightly less than 250 fans per home date. In 1971, Bay Area baseball fans entertained their first fantasies of a Bay Bridge World Series. With Mays apparently having located the fountain of youth, the keys to a time machine, or both, the Giants raced to a 12–2 start. Mays opened the season in style, belting his 629th career home run on his first swing on opening night. One longtime Mays observer believed it to be an omen. "If you will remember," Hall of Fame broadcaster Lon Simmons told his KSFO radio audience, "in 1962 when the Giants won the pennant, Willie Mays in his first time at-bat in the season hit a home run off Warren Spahn, and the Giants went on to win it."

Mays, one month shy of his 40th birthday, homered in the second game as well, and the third and the fourth. It was the first time in major league history that feat had been performed—and the only time until Mark McGwire reprised it at the dawn of his record-breaking 1998 season. By May 15, the Giants were 27–9 and led the National League West by nine games. On the final day of the month, Mays hit a game-tying home run in the eighth inning of a home game against the Mets and then scored the game-winner in the 11th. It gave the Giants two straight walk-off wins, a five-game win streak, a 37–14 record, and a 10½-game lead. Jerry Reed's catchy "When You're Hot, You're Hot" moved from 32 to 28 on the Billboard charts that week. It got plenty of play on KSFO.

The A's were almost as combustible. They lost their first three games, but by their 15th they had assumed the American League West lead for good. "Hot" didn't begin to describe Vida Blue. A 21-year-old fireballer from Mansfield, Lousiana, Blue made his major league debut in 1969 just a few hours before Neil Armstrong took man's first steps on the moon. During his second cup of coffee with the A's late in the 1970 season, he threw a one-hitter against the Kansas City Royals (allowing a single with two out in the eighth) and no-hit Minnesota. On the verge of clinching their second consecutive division crown, the Twins were gracious enough to send a few bottles of champagne to the Oakland clubhouse.

Named the 1971 Opening Day starter by Oakland manager Dick Williams, Blue lasted just one and two-thirds innings against the Washington Senators. But from that point until the Fourth of July, Blue blazed to a 17–2 record in 20 starts with six shutouts and 169 strikeouts in 171⅔ innings. He was a national sensation, featured on the cover of *Time* magazine. With a record 17 wins at the break, he was the natural choice to be the American League's starting pitcher in the All-Star Game in Detroit. Though he had faded along with his team during June, Mays was the sentimental choice to start in center field for the National League. Entrusted with an embarrassment of offensive firepower, NL manager Sparky Anderson decided to bat Mays in the leadoff spot.

So there they were to start the game. Blue vs. his boyhood idol Mays. Oakland vs. its civic big brother San Francisco. Promise vs. achievement. The sleeveless jerseys of the A's vs. the traditional shirts of the Giants. Blue got Mays to ground out to shortstop on the second pitch of the game. Two innings later Blue retired Mays on a high fly ball to right-center field. The game has become known for the six home runs hit by future Hall of Famers. One stood out, literally, above the rest—a colossal shot off the bat of Oakland's Jackson, pinch-hitting for his teammate Blue, that struck a transformer atop the roof at Tiger Stadium. The American League snapped an eight-year All-Star losing streak that night.

The A's charged through the second half, going 38–23 from the All-Star Game through their division-clinching victory on September 15. Blue finished the season 24–8 with a 1.82 ERA and 301 strikeouts. He would be voted the Cy Young Award winner and Most Valuable Player. The Giants, meanwhile, staggered down the stretch. Mays looked and felt his age. McCovey was tormented by his sore knees. Rookie slugger Dave Kingman gave the team a boost when he was called up from Triple A in July but was lost for six weeks after an appendectomy. Still the Giants held an eight-and-a-half-game lead over the Los Angeles Dodgers on September 4. Ten days later, the lead was one. It came down to the last night of the season with the Giants leading by a game and playing the Padres in San Diego. Marichal woke up the echoes with a snappy five-hitter. Mays broke a scoreless tie with an RBI double in the top of the fourth. Two batters later, Kingman, playing right field for an ailing Bobby Bonds, belted a two-run homer. As the Giants celebrated their 5–1 win in the clubhouse in traditional fashion, Mays sat in a corner, too weary to join in the revelry.

The Bay Area barely had time to experience the symptoms of baseball fever. Within the week the Giants had been run from the National League Championship Series in four games by the Pittsburgh Pirates. The A's had been swept in the American League Championship Series by the Baltimore Orioles. The anticipated Bay Bridge Series never reached the toll booth.

◆ ◆ ◆ ◆

Giants owner Horace Stoneham was a baseball man. He took over ownership of the team—then the New York Giants—from his father, Charles. He had no other business. The team was his life and livelihood. He already had experienced the economic squeeze of a multi-team market. For more than a half-century, the Giants shared New York with the American League Yankees and the National League Dodgers. But with the dawning of the 1950s came a demographic sea change in the United States. The well-to-do began migrating from city centers to new suburbs. Television began eating away at baseball ticket sales. Though the Giants and the rival Dodgers were going gangbusters on the field—one team or the other represented the National League in every World Series from 1951–56—attendance was falling off a cliff.

The Giants ranked second in the league in attendance during their miraculous pennant-winning season of 1951. They fell to third in 1952, fifth in 1953, jumped back to second while winning the World Series in 1954, then placed sixth in '55, eighth in '56, and eighth again in '57. The Dodgers fared somewhat better, but owner Walter O'Malley was frustrated by his inability to secure a new ballpark. With the Dodgers' move to Los Angeles a foregone, if unannounced, conclusion, Stoneham confirmed on August 19, 1957 that he was moving the Giants to San Francisco. Asked what he would tell the young fans of his team, Stoneham replied, "I feel bad about the kids, but I haven't seen many of their fathers at the ballpark lately."

It was happening again. Crowded by the A's and saddled by a payroll largely devoted to stars beginning to lose their sparkle, Stoneham saw no recourse. Less than one month into the strike-delayed 1972 season, Stoneham traded Mays to the New York Mets. A few weeks after the 1973 season, McCovey was dealt to the Padres. A couple months after that, Marichal was sold to the Boston Red Sox. On July 22, 1975, Stoneham was instructed by the team's board of directors, of which he was a member, to make "every effort" to sell the club. It was difficult to argue the logic. While the A's were reeling off a superlative run—three consecutive World Series Championshops nested within a string of five straight division titles from 1971–75—the Giants were suffering four consecutive seasons of diminished attendance. They lost $3 million in 1974–75. At the conclusion of the 1975 season, it was reported their $125,000 rent on Candlestick Park was nine months overdue.

After months of rumors and breathless speculation that had a) the Giants moving, b) Stoneham making a pitch to keep the team, and c) a recommendation by Major League Baseball's Franchise Committee that the Giants stay put while the A's relocate to Seattle, the Giants' board of directors agreed in principal to sell to an investor group that would move the team to Toronto. An injunction blocking the transfer of the team was within hours of expiring when on February 11, 1976, Bob Lurie, a member of the Giants board, and former Washington Senators owner Bob Short put forth an $8 million offer. The deal was imperiled when Short abruptly withdrew his half of the offer. But San Francisco mayor George Moscone helped rustle up a new partner—Bud Herseth, a Phoenix cattle and meat-packing baron. If the Giants continued to spin their wheels on the field, they at least had stable ownership. It was the fans of A's turn to be nervous.

With the advent of free agency in 1976, A's owner Charlie O. Finley became a baseball anachronism. He had no stomach for a free-market game and proved as much by trading some of his more marketable players rather than pay them what other teams thought they were worth. Some of his transactions worked out better than others. Just before Opening Day in 1976, Finley dealt Jackson, who would be a free agent at season's end, to the Orioles in a six-player deal. Charlie O. was just warming up.

On June 15, the non-waiver trade deadline in those days, Finley sold Blue to the Yankees for $1.5 million and peddled Fingers and Rudi to the Red Sox for $1 million apiece. As it happened the Red Sox were in Oakland at the time. Rudi and Fingers donned Boston uniforms and spent the game on the visitor's bench, though they did not play. Their Red Sox tenure didn't last long. Three days later, commissioner Bowie Kuhn struck down the deals, regarding them as contrary to the best interests of baseball. Finley responded by calling Kuhn "the village idiot" and ultimately by letting Fingers, Rudi, Bando, Campy Campaneris, Gene Tenace, and Don Baylor (acquired in the Reggie trade) leave as free agents at season's end. He kept Blue, reluctantly. Three months after Kuhn voided a December 1977 deal that would have sent Blue to the Cincinnati Reds for $1.3 million and a minor league player, Finley dealt him to the Giants.

At the same time he had been negotiating the Blue trade, Finley also was negotiating with Denver oilman Marvin Davis, who wished to bring Major League Baseball to Colorado. The talks seemed so promising that Lurie sought and received from San Francisco permission to play 40 home games in 1978 at the vacated Oakland Coliseum. "It's possible we could play our first game there as early as April 8," Lurie said at a press conference.

The problem was that discussions between Finley and Davis fell apart on March 27. Davis and Kuhn, anxious to be rid of his tart-tongued adversary, laid the blame at Finley's feet. Two weeks later, the A's staged their home opener before a sparse crowd and—until batting practice was cloaked in near-darkness—without artificial light. "I bet the lights are on in Denver!" a Seattle player hollered into the gathering gloom.

The A's drew 17,283 fans for opening night. They averaged 2,491 for the final five games of the homestand. But 1978 was just a warm-up act for the 1979 season, in which the A's lost 108 games and attracted an average of 3,787 fans per home date. Finley created some magic in 1980 when, in one final iconoclastic masterstroke, he hired Berkeley native Billy Martin as manager. Before that season was over, Finley sold the team to Walter Haas for $12.7 million—more than six times what he had paid for it in 1960.

A few years later, tag! The Giants were it. After eight years of calling Candlestick Park home, Lurie was ready for an upgrade. Even as his organization made plans to host the 1984 All-Star Game, he was openly stumping for a new stadium. In the final week of the 1985 season, Lurie announced a plan to buy out the final nine years of the Giants' Candlestick Park lease and play as many as four seasons in the Oakland Coliseum while a new stadium was built in San Francisco. "The San Francisco Giants will not under my ownership play at Candlestick Park beyond this season," he said.

Lurie had engaged in preliminary conversations with A's and Oakland Coliseum officials, which was enough to convince him that his plan had their blessing. But the announcement caught them off guard. The A's were noncommittal. Oakland mayor Lionel Wilson, who hoped to attract an NFL team—ideally the prodigal Los Angeles Raiders—to the Coliseum, vowed to inform the Coliseum board of his opposition to the idea.

Ultimately, the matter was settled with a letter sent from Haas to Lurie, owner to owner, in which Haas stated he was against the move because it would adversely affect A's attendance. Nothing came of a trip the Giants took to Denver to discuss temporarily locating there. Lurie wound up going back to Candlestick for the 1986 season. Three years later windy, arctic, inhospitable Candlestick Park remained a festering issue.

◆ ◆ ◆ ◆

By the spring of 1989, the Bay Area baseball market was positively robust. The Giants, buoyed by preseason ticket sales inspired by their 1987 division title, drew 1.785 million fans in 1988, the third-highest total in their San Francisco history. The A's were coming off a World Series appearance and a franchise-record attendance of 2.287 million fans. Both teams were appraised at $75 million, more than seven times what Lurie had paid for the Giants and six times what Haas had paid for the A's. Both teams were expected to sell 1.2 million tickets for the 1989 season before Opening Day.

Both teams had committed and decorated ownership and leadership. A's general manager Sandy Alderson had been named co-winner of UPI's Executive of the Year Award for 1988. Giants GM Al Rosen was *The Sporting News* Executive of the Year for 1987. La Russa was the Baseball Writers' of America Association AL Manager of the Year in 1983 (with the White Sox) and 1988. Roger Craig was the Associated Press NL Manager of the Year for 1987.

Not as visible were the teams' marketing directors. The A's Andy Dolich and the Giants' Pat Gallagher were sharp, savvy, good friends, and skilled pranksters. Dolich was the driving force behind the Athletics' BillyBall campaign that celebrated the aggressive, daring nature of manager Billy Martin. Gallagher was the genius behind the Croix de Candlestick, a cheap little button awarded only to fans who stayed until the final out of an extra-inning night game at Candlestick Park. Suddenly a wholly unappealing fate—braving Candlestick's oft-arctic climes into extra innings—became, literally, a badge of honor.

The two liked to rib each other. In 1987 the year the A's hosted the All-Star Game, Gallagher bought a billboard on the freeway near the Coliseum and posted the message: "Andy Dolich is celebrating his 40th birthday by giving away free All-Star tickets." Included on the billboard was Dolich's office telephone number. Dolich retaliated on Gallagher's next birthday, arranging for a 40-foot inflatable A's player and a 12-foot bobblehead to be placed in front of Gallagher's house.

The further up the organizational ladder, the higher the stakes and the less jocular the relationship between the clubs. Success mattered, but it couldn't come at any price. "Even today we have to be very flexible in how we approach the things we do," Alderson said in spring training 1989. "One of the real tough things is keeping track of how much paper you use and how many pencils you buy, [then] giving a guy a $500,000 contract, which is all the pencils in the world."

In the dugout it was highly contentious, especially where La Russa was concerned. One of the first things La Russa sensed upon taking the A's managerial job in 1986 was that the Giants seemed to get more attention for doing less. They had been in the area longer. They had the strongest radio station in the market with 50,000-watt KNBR having succeeded KSFO in 1979, while the A's always seemed to settle for a secondary station.

It nagged at the A's. There were times when the A's fell out of the race late in the season, and some Bay Area newspapers would pull their beat writers off Oakland road trips to save money. It wasn't unheard of for Alderson to drop in on various local sports editors to express concern over the lack of coverage. It seemed to nag La Russa most of all. After a late-season win in September 1987, reporters awaiting a postgame audience with the A's skipper received a surprise when he opened the door to his office to reveal wadded-up newspaper pages littering the floor. His not-so-subtle message: the A's are doing well and not getting any credit for it.

Now preparations for the 1989 season were under way. As the rivalry between two teams trying to carve out a living in the Bay Area—where the entertainment dollar can waft in any number of directions—heated up, and as the desire of both teams to upstage the other was at a fever pitch, the Bay Area baseball market never looked like such a cash cow. "And now," Gallagher said, "the question is where to put the third team, right?"

Chapter 3

A World Series Preview

T he Cactus League schedule-maker wasn't stupid. Spring training was evolving into big business. An estimated 600,000 fans attended Cactus League games in 1988. Fans enjoyed the relaxed pace of early workouts, the weather, and the intimacy of small ballparks where they had a chance to hear the pop of the glove, catch a foul ball, or snag an autograph. Another reason: immediacy. Phoenix Sky Harbor International Airport, of course, is a short, direct flight from the Bay Area. So it was only good business sense to schedule A's-Giants exhibition games in pairs, on the weekend if possible, to make it convenient for Bay Area tourists. The first two games between the teams in early 1989 came in a home-and-home set on Saturday and Sunday, March 11–12.

Schedule-makers and fans weren't the only ones who considered A's-Giants spring training games something special. The teams themselves conceded as much in 1982 when they decided to conclude spring training with what they termed the "Bay Bridge Series"—home-and-home exhibition games in the Bay Area. Based on a suggestion from the teams' marketing whizzes, Andy Dolich of the A's and Pat Gallagher of the Giants, the Bay Bridge Series was extended to three games in 1989. "We played the A's so many times in spring training that we got our own little rivalry going," Will Clark said in 2013. "It was good for the Bay Area. They got a chance to see the Giants taking steps in the right direction as well as the A's. It was a good time to be a baseball fan in the Bay Area. Those games were always packed. I guarantee you both organizations definitely did want to win."

Tony La Russa didn't get it at first. During his first spring training with the A's in 1987, he treated a date with the Giants as just another game on the schedule. He received an eye-opener after the Giants whipped the A's 19–8 in a game at Phoenix Stadium. "As soon as the game was over," La Russa said in 2013, "I see Roger [Craig] go over and I think it was to [Bob] Lurie and [Al] Rosen, and man, they're high-fiving and hugging. And I went, 'Wow.'"

When La Russa reached the Oakland clubhouse, he was greeted by a stone-faced quartet of team executives—owner Walter Haas, his son Wally, Roy Eisenhardt, and Sandy Alderson. They looked as if they had lost more than an exhibition game. "I went, 'I'm missing something here,'" La Russa said. "So Sandy and Wally explain it: well, there is a competition between the two franchises. I remember thinking it's a lot like the White Sox and the Cubs—the Cubs here [his left hand held high] and the White Sox here [right hand held low]. The White Sox had to go harder to get the same attention and so did the A's. So they became games we couldn't afford to lose. The Giants could lose them. We couldn't. We were second-class citizens."

The competition between ownerships trickled down to the dugout. La Russa said he never rooted against the Giants and in fact liked Roger Craig and his staff. "But I think you felt that the ownerships took great pride in their teams and I'm not sure they wanted the other team to be good," La Russa said. "They wanted to own the market. After my experience in '87, I made sure the club understood that maybe some guys are going to play when they didn't think they were going to play. And the Giants sure were going to play that way against us, so be ready."

The first of nine exhibition games the teams played in 1989 went to Oakland 6–2. Mark McGwire launched a pair of home runs over the center-field fence—410 feet away at Phoenix Municipal Stadium. Starting pitcher Bob Welch held the Giants to one run in five innings. The crowd of 8,663 represented the A's first home sellout of the Cactus League season.

The next day the teams met at the Giants' spring home at Scottsdale Stadium. The ramifications of that game would send ripples into the regular season. The A's jumped to a 3–1 lead after three and a half innings—thanks in part to another McGwire homer (his fifth of the spring). The Giants answered with five runs in the bottom of the fourth, three on a Matt Williams home run. The A's tied the game 6–6. San Francisco catcher Terry Kennedy untied it with a solo home run off A's lefty set-up man Rick Honeycutt.

The first eight innings were entertaining by any measure. But they were just an appetizer for the ninth. That was when Craig handed the ball to Scott Garrelts for his first save opportunity since being designated the team's closer during the offseason. "Just what I wanted," Craig told reporters after the game, "a one-run lead and him coming in there in the ninth inning." It could scarcely have gone worse.

The first batter, Luis Polonia, singled. So did the second batter, Stan Javier. Garrelts walked the third batter, Doug Jennings, to load the bases. Then he walked Felix Jose to force in the tying run. Billy Beane singled home the go-ahead run, and Ron Hassey followed with a two-run single. That was the end of Garrelts but not of the inning. Smelling blood in the water, the A's continued their assault against rookie reliever Doug Robertson. He allowed the last of the six runs charged to Garrelts to score and then was charged with five more of his own before Craig removed him after two-thirds of an inning. Rookie right-hander John Burkett got the final out, but by then the A's had scored 14 runs on nine hits and turned a 7–6 deficit into a 20–7 win—their sixth in a row. "It seemed unreal," Garrelts told reporters the following day. "Why did it have to be that game that was televised back to the Bay Area?"

The A's and Giants got a reprieve from one another for 10 days before their next home-and-home, tourist-friendly set. In the meantime, as spring training began to hit its stride, the teams set about assessing what they had. The Giants knew this much: Kevin Mitchell was hitting the snot and slobber out the baseball.

♦ ♦ ♦ ♦

Mitchell, a product of one of San Diego's roughest neighborhoods, went undrafted. He was signed as an amateur free agent by the New York Mets in 1980. He arrived in New York when the rosters expanded at the end of the 1984 season. He made the team out of spring training in 1986 as a stocky, strong, natural-born power hitter who played six different positions in 108 games for the eventual world champions. His biggest contribution in the 1986 postseason came in Game 6 of the World Series. With the Mets trailing 5–3, Gary Carter on first base, and down to their last out in the bottom of the 10th inning, Mitchell served an 0–1 pitch from Boston Red Sox reliever Calvin Schiraldi into center field for a single. He eventually scored the tying run on a wild pitch by Bob Stanley just moments before Mookie Wilson's squibber trickled through the legs of Bill Buckner. The Mets went on to win Game 7, giving Mitchell a World Series ring in his first full season.

Mitchell was still a young, wild, untamed talent with a troubling past. When, during the offseason, the Mets had a chance to include him in a deal to acquire slugging left fielder Kevin McReynolds from the Padres, they jumped. Mitchell was coming home to San Diego. You'd have been hard-pressed to find anyone who thought that was a good idea. Southeast San Diego, after all, had been the hardscrabble part of town where Mitchell's parents went their separate ways, leaving their son to be raised by his grandmother, Josie Whitfield. It's where he ran with gangs, where he was shot at, and where his 16-year-old stepbrother was fatally gunned down.

Mitchell didn't play terribly in front of his hometown fans, but the 1987 Padres were a wretched bunch. They lost 39 of their first 50 games, falling 17 games off the pace by May 30. Come July 4, the Padres were sellers in the trade market. Giants general manager Al Rosen took them to the cleaners. Rosen sent pitchers Keith Comstock, Mark Grant, and Mark Davis (a future Cy Young Award-winning reliever) and talented but enigmatic third baseman Chris Brown to the Padres for Mitchell, starting pitcher Dave Dravecky, and reliever Craig Lefferts. "That trade was the hardest," Mitchell told the *Los Angeles Times*. "I wanted to ask the Padres, 'Why did you trade for me and mess around with me?' I was happy. I could have stayed with the Mets."

Mitchell played for the Padres on July 4 in Montreal. He was in the starting lineup for the Giants July 5 in Chicago. He cranked a two-run home run his first time up for San Francisco. He later tagged a second two-run homer as the Giants rallied from a 5–2 deficit to win 7–5 against the Cubs. Mitchell had 15 home runs and 44 RBIs in half a season with San Francisco as the Giants romped to their first division title since 1971. And if manager Craig laid it on a little thick about Mitchell's heroic resolve to play in pain, it played well in San Francisco. Especially since the man he replaced in the hot corner, Brown, once pronounced himself unable to play because he had slept on his eye wrong. Mitchell belted 19 home runs and had 80 RBIs in 1988, during which he played mostly third base. Craig moved him to left field in spring training 1989, whereupon Mitchell began mauling the baseball. It wasn't so much the position switch that occasioned the turnaround as it was a couple of visits to the doctor.

One of the doctors was an ophthalmologist who fitted Mitchell with contact lenses. Suddenly, Mitchell could pick up the rotation on the baseball and quickly deduce whether the pitch was a breaking ball or a fastball. The other doctor performed arthroscopic surgery on Mitchell's right knee, his plant knee at the plate. Able to pick up the ball quicker and stay back longer, Mitchell began waging war on enemy pitchers.

◆ ◆ ◆ ◆

Jose Canseco was familiar with the zone Mitchell occupied, but he suddenly found himself reduced to a spectator. His left hand, in which he felt soreness during batting practice on March 9, was not getting much better. While teammate Eric Plunk allowed five ninth-inning runs in an 11–6 loss to the Chicago Cubs on March 18, Canseco took some swings on a practice field behind Municipal Stadium. The following day, La Russa told reporters that Canseco should be good to go for the Tuesday, March 21 game against the Giants.

Instead Canseco was limited to a simulated game that day. But there was bigger news breaking in Michigan, where David Valdez, Canseco's traveling companion when the two were detained in the Detroit airport in January, had been sentenced to a year's probation and a $250 fine. The 26 pills he was carrying that day had been tested. They were steroids.

It was the tip of an iceberg that many people in and outside the game wouldn't recognize (or wouldn't want to acknowledge) for years. The whispers about Canseco had begun in September 1988 when *The Washington Post* sports columnist Thomas Boswell told CBS that Canseco was "the most conspicuous example of a player who has made himself great with steroids." The comment drew national attention. In Game 1 of the 1988 American League Championship Series in Boston, Canseco broke a scoreless tie with a blast over the Green Monster off Bruce Hurst. As Canseco rounded the bases, Fenway Park echoed with the sing-song chant of "STER-roids! STER-roids!"

The chant greeted Canseco when he took his position in right field in the bottom of the inning. He looked into the stands and spread his arms as if to exclaim, *Who me?* Later in the game, a 2–1 A's win that presaged a series sweep, the chant sprung to life again. Canseco, clearly enjoying the interplay, struck a bodybuilder's pose. "Rumors are rumors," he said after the game. "Especially if you know yourself that it's just a rumor, why worry about it?"

It was just that easy to brush the story aside. Steroids? In track and field for sure. The previous month, sprinter Ben Johnson had his world-record victory in the 100-meter dash at the Summer Olympics stricken from the books when he tested positive for stanozolol. It seemed doping was part of the track and field culture. The NFL? Probably. Football players were getting suspiciously bigger, stronger, and faster every year. The very day Valdez was sentenced in Michigan, NFL commissioner Pete Rozelle took advantage of a window in the collective bargaining agreement to institute a steroid testing program. The tests, however, would not be random. And only a fool would test positive after being given advance notice.

For more than a century the conventional wisdom in baseball held that lifting weights was the worst thing a player—pitcher or batter—could do. All those muscles would bind you up. You would lose flexibility. The Giants took their first tentative step toward weight training in the early 1980s when they repurposed the players cafeteria at Candlestick Park into a weight room. A sign on the wall read: "The Room Where Champions Are Built."

Even given Canseco's comic book-superhero physique, the steroids accusation seemed fantastic. But it was being made for the second time in five months. Reporters wanted to know about the steroids Valdez had been carrying. He had claimed ownership, but whose were they really?

◆ ◆ ◆ ◆

A Scottsdale Stadium-record 5,770 fans turned out on March 21 to watch the Giants take a 7–2 lead over the A's after eight innings. Mike LaCoss, Craig's leading fallback choice as closer if Garrelts didn't work out, was dispatched to get the final three outs, even though it wasn't a save situation.

He didn't record an out. Just as Garrelts had done in the ninth inning in the previous meeting between the Giants and A's, LaCoss faced six batters, allowing four hits and walking two, before being yanked. The A's scored seven times with rookie outfield prospect Felix Jose delivering the knockout blow—a go-ahead three-run double. The A's won 9–7. A pattern was developing, one the A's were loving, and one Craig denied losing sleep over. "I didn't really emphasize winning and losing in spring training," he said in 2013. "One year right at the end, somebody said, 'You're not doing too well.' I asked him, 'Well, who won the Cactus League last year? Who won the Grapefruit League?' A lot of time in spring training you're playing a lot of players, you're giving guys a last look-see. You're giving somebody extended time because they're working on something. Playing Oakland, they had a hell of a ballclub and a great manager. We saw them and played them a lot. When you've got a great offense like they had, Canseco and McGwire, all those guys, if you play in Arizona where the ball jumps, they'd hit pop flies, and the ball would go over the fence. I didn't like it, but there's not much you can do. I know it matters to the fans, and the front office wants to win, so you draw more fans. But as a manager, you try to get through spring training without any injuries and get the guys ready."

The Giants' fans and front office enjoyed Wednesday's game in Phoenix. Outfielder Tracy Jones' two-run double in the 11th inning gave the Giants a 6–4 win. But Mitchell was the story—again. Before the game he bragged to his manager about how well he was swinging the bat. Then he went out and hit for the cycle. Mitchell's four hits included his fifth home run. They also boosted his average to .458 and his slugging percentage to .854.

A's catcher Terry Steinbach returned to the lineup two weeks after getting beaned and had two hits and an RBI. But it was a bad day for Canseco, who finally tested his sore left wrist under game conditions. After two swings in his first at-bat, he left the game with a 2–2 count. He hopped a plane back to the Bay Area, where he had the wrist examined at San Francisco Children's Hospital. The weirdest medical situation involved Giants pitcher Don Robinson, who went out to dinner after the game to celebrate the two-year contract extension worth $2.4 million he had signed the previous day. Robinson had an allergic reaction to shrimp and had to have an injection to reduce the swelling.

It was a freak occurrence. But that didn't stop Craig from wondering if the spring of '89 was an extension of the summer of '88, when his pitchers dropped like flies from various and sundry maladies. In four days the Giants had lost Robinson, Atlee Hammaker (back), Rick Reuschel (hamstring), Kelly Downs (back), and Terry Mulholland (chest). And Mike Krukow was still shaking off the rust from his September season-ending shoulder surgery. "Out of my five starters," Craig said, invoking dark humor, "six of them are down."

It was six days before the teams played again in back-to-back games in the Louisiana Superdome. The New Orleans Sports Foundation was showcasing the stadium in hopes of landing a major league team, and the games appealed to the Giants because Clark hailed from the New Orleans area. La Russa said he was working under the assumption that Canseco would not be available for Opening Day, let alone the side trip to the Big Easy. The A's skipper made that assessment even before doctors at San Francisco Children's Hospital projected that Mr. 40–40, who was late for his appointment, would be out three to five weeks with an inflamed ligament in his left wrist. Canseco's wrist was placed in a cast. Two days later that diagnosis was revised. A slight tear of the ligament had been detected on the outside of Canseco's wrist. The timetable for his return remained the same.

As for the Giants, Craig located an unlikely starter—would-be closer Garrelts. Against the Milwaukee Brewers in Chandler, Arizona, Garrelts, who had a 15.00 ERA in six relief appearances during spring training, threw three perfect innings. There was another development with Garrelts. He stopped granting interviews to the media. "I don't want to come off as being a jerk," he told the reporters after pitching in a B game on St. Patrick's Day. "I just feel it might be a distraction for me to talk to you guys. I'm through for the year."

Mitchell bombed another home run, his sixth of the spring, on March 24. He wasn't the only Giants outfielder having a strong spring. Candy Maldonado, a sensation in 1986 and '87 after being acquired in a rare Giants-Dodgers trade, had slumped badly after signing a new contract before the '88 season that raised his salary from $415,000 to $750,000. Rosen was among those who believed Maldonado had felt the pressure of his new deal. Maldonado didn't disagree.

After a big game in a win over the Seattle Mariners in Tempe, Arizona, Maldonado's spring average stood at .305 and his slugging percentage at .508. At the 1988 winter meetings, Rosen had offered Maldonado and Garrelts to Kansas City for slugging outfielder Danny Tartabull. Sometimes the best trades are the ones you never make. Was this one of them? The Giants were the subject of several trade rumors during the spring. Jose Uribe and a pitcher or two to the Phillies for closer (and 1987 Cy Young Award winner) Steve Bedrosian was one. Garrelts to Atlanta for shortstop Andres Thomas was another. Aside from acknowledging he had called the Phillies to inquire about Bedrosian, Rosen had no comment.

Just before the bulk of the team left for New Orleans, the Giants received a surprise visitor in Scottsdale. Dave Dravecky dropped in to say hello. On February 8, the Giants said that Dravecky, the guy who on October 7 had been told he had "zero" chance of ever pitching again after an operation to remove a cancerous tumor from his upper left arm, would miss most of spring training. He remained at his home in Boardman, Ohio, close to the Cleveland Clinic where he'd had his surgery.

On February 19 Dravecky told the *Mercury News* that he had been throwing a football for three weeks without pain. "From a purely medical standpoint," Dravecky said, "they honestly believe by midsummer we can make the attempt to get into a competitive mode." He expressed both optimism and realism and confessed he didn't know what would become of his attempted comeback. But he was committed to the cause. "I really wasn't all that concerned about playing baseball," Dravecky said of his mind-set 24 years later. "At the same time, there was something in me that said, *This doctor is saying that outside of a miracle, I'll never pitch again. I've got to try. I can't walk away now and always wonder if I could have come back or not.* I realized that if I put the right amount of effort into this, I might have a chance. I remember going to a doctor in Cleveland, and he said, 'As well as your rehab is going, maybe it's time to start trying to throw and see how it goes.' I realized there was something in front of me I could shoot for."

New Orleans provided a new venue, but it yielded familiar results. On Tuesday, March 28, Garrelts started and threw five shutout innings. The Giants took a 3–1 lead into the ninth, and LaCoss blew the save as the A's scored a 4–3 win to even their spring training mark at 13–13. The A's had scored 25 runs in the ninth inning in six spring training games against the Giants. They needed no dramatics the following day. McGwire belted his eighth home run of the spring as the A's beat the Giants again 4–2.

Craig recalled that two-game set 24 years later—not for the losses, but for the fellowship between he and La Russa. Yes, he understood the regional rivalry. "But I would have more so if they'd been in our league," Craig said. "I remember playing in New Orleans, and Tony saying, 'You're good at picking up signs. Can you watch me during the games and see if you can pick up a couple things?' I said, 'Tony, I have things to worry about on my own team.' As it turned out, I picked up something. I said, 'It's not much, but when you walk down the dugout with your right hand in your back pocket, you're giving your base runner the green light. I'm not sure he believed me," the Humm Baby said, chuckling.

◆ ◆ ◆ ◆

The teams returned to the Bay Area on Friday, March 31. It was a cold, windy evening at the Oakland Coliseum. Bob Welch stymied the Giants, holding them to one run on two hits over five innings as the A's romped 7–1. The Giants were without Mitchell, who was given permission to travel to San Diego to be with his mother, who had been injured in a car accident.

LaCoss, looking more and more like the default closer to open the season, coughed up two runs in two innings of work. Meanwhile, Rosen admitted he had contacted the agent for 37-year-old reliever "Goose" Gossage, who had been released by the Cubs three days earlier. At the same time, he acknowledged the obvious—Gossage wouldn't have been waived if he was the Goose of old. It was a tacit admission that the Giants, still in the market for a bona fide closer, were grasping at straws—and apparently for good reason.

On Saturday in Oakland, it happened again. The Giants took a 2–1 lead into the bottom of the eighth, and then Dave Henderson hit a go-ahead two-run home run off rookie reliever Jeff Brantley. Whether Brantley was rattled or the Giants had had enough—maybe both—the rookie grazed the uniform of the next batter, Carney Lansford. Both benches emptied. The unpleasantries didn't change the bottom line. The A's were 7–1 against the Giants during spring training, with four of the victories coming in Oakland's last at-bat. "As far as I know," Craig said after the game, "Al Rosen may be jumping off the Bay Bridge right now."

There was only one way spring training could end. On Sunday, April 2, the A's and Giants were tied 6–6 after eight innings at Candlestick Park. In the ninth, the Giants committed two errors that led to a pair of Oakland runs. It gave the A's an 8–1 spring training record against San Francisco with five of the wins coming in their final at-bat.

The A's won a team-record 19 games during spring training. Despite the brilliance of Mitchell—who returned from San Diego in time to go 4-for-4 and finish the spring with seven home runs, 21 RBIs, a .455 average, and a .774 slugging percentage—the Giants finished with their first losing spring record since 1983. "I've never had to give speeches on Opening Day," Craig told reporters. "But I think this team needs it. Tomorrow they're going to know how I feel. Tomorrow I'm gonna put some fire in 'em."

In the Oakland clubhouse, perhaps realizing there's nothing left to say after you've let your action on the field speak for you, La Russa already had turned the page. "I don't even want to talk about the Bay Bridge Series," he said. "Tomorrow's the real thing."

Chapter 4

Overcoming Adversity

In 1988, the outgoing message on Tony La Russa's home answering machine stated that the A's hoped to win 100 games. In 1989, according to the *Los Angeles Times*, La Russa's message went something like this: "Everyone asks if the A's can repeat. My answer is definitely yes. We want more wins, more fun, more championships. We're hungry for it and we're going for it." The A's launched their quest to be the first team since the 1978 Yankees to repeat as American League champions without reigning MVP Jose Canseco. Mr. 40–40 was in a wrist-to-elbow cast on his left arm. The show went on without him.

The pregame festivities on opening night at the Oakland Coliseum included Jeffrey Osborne singing the national anthem for the second consecutive year. There were fireworks and an elephant—the team's mascot since 1902, when New York Giants manager John McGraw referred to Connie Mack's Athletics as "white elephants"—throwing out the first pitch. Throwing might be a generous interpretation of what really happened. Akili the elephant, who had demonstrated a remarkable ability to fling a ball 40 feet with its trunk in practice sessions, apparently was unnerved by the sellout crowd. The pachyderm dropped the ball at its feet, leaving the team's marketing director to complete the toss to the catcher.

The A's got a soft touch on opening night. The Seattle Mariners were beginning their 13th season—the first 12 having resulted in losing records. There was some interesting symmetry involved. The M's new manager, Jim Lefebvre, had coached third base for the A's in 1988, and the A's current third-base coach, Rene Lachemann, had managed the Mariners for parts of three seasons in the early 1980s. The Mariners were still three seasons away from their first winning record, but the nucleus that would reverse that tradition of underachievement—rookies Ken Griffey Jr., Omar Vizquel, and Edgar Martinez—was on the field on opening night in 1989.

In his first major league at-bat, Griffey Jr. doubled off Dave Stewart in the first inning. But Stewart, who had declared after the Bay Bridge Series that "this is probably the best spring I've ever had," turned in a solid first outing, holding Seattle to two runs on four hits over five and one-third innings. Closer Dennis Eckersley notched a four-out save in the A's 3–2 victory. "Don't talk to me about last year, please," La Russa said afterward. "I had enough of '88 in the pregame ceremonies."

Giants manager Roger Craig had a closed-door meeting with his team before its opening game, a road contest against the San Diego Padres. It had no effect on Kevin Mitchell, who began the regular season the way he had ended spring training. He hit a two-run home run in the top of the first inning and added a two-run single in the seventh.

That had become a familiar sight. This was not: Mike LaCoss, the irascible redhead known to his teammates as "Buffy" for his resemblance to a character in the 1960s television series *Family Affair*, pitched two scoreless innings to save a 5–3 Giants win. It was LaCoss' seventh career save and first since June 4, 1985.

Following an off day, the A's polished off a sweep of the Mariners with victories of 11–1 (with Bob Welch throwing eight strong innings and Walt Weiss hitting two home runs) and 11–3. It was their first 3–0 start in five years.

◆ ◆ ◆ ◆

The Giants had an off day in Cincinnati on Thursday, April 6. But the Pete Rose stories, suggesting he bet on baseball, it seemed, never took a day off. That day a former housemate of Rose's, Thomas Gioiosa, was indicted in federal court for tax evasion and conspiracy to distribute cocaine. The indictment alleged Gioiosa falsely claimed and listed as income nearly $50,000 in gambling earnings. *Sports Illustrated* had previously reported that Gioiosa had placed bets for Rose with a bookmaker. "I'm guilty of one thing," Rose told reporters in response to Gioiosa's indictment. "I wasn't a very good picker of friends."

When the Giants and Reds took the field on Friday night, April 7—hours after Gioiosa had made bail—they comprised two-thirds of a three-way tie atop the National League West. Nearly five hours later, they were still playing. It was one of those games that provided ammunition for both sides of the debate on the seaworthiness of the San Francisco bullpen. The Giants took a 1–0 lead in the first on an RBI double by Candy Maldonado. The Reds answered in the second inning on Jeff Reed's two-run double off Scott Garrelts, making his first start since 1986. Terry Kennedy's clutch single off Nasty Boy reliever Rob Dibble drove in Clark in the top of the eighth to tie the game 2–2. There it stayed for the rest of Friday night and part of Saturday morning.

If you were a believer in the Giants relief corps—the eternally optimistic Roger Craig, for instance—you were heartened by the work of Craig Lefferts, LaCoss, and Atlee Hammaker, who combined for five shutout innings. You might not have been overly concerned about Jeff Brantley's two-and-two-thirds-inning stint in which he allowed one run on three hits.

If you were convinced the Giants bullpen was damp dynamite, you probably saw Brantley's effort in a different light. Robby Thompson had scampered home with the tie-breaking run on a wild pitch in the top of the 14th inning. Brantley needed three outs in the bottom of the frame to secure his second major league save. He got the first, getting Barry Larkin to fly out. But the next batter, Chris Sabo, doubled to right. Brantley wild-pitched Sabo to third and then got the dangerous Eric Davis on a comebacker. Craig called on left-hander Joe Price to face lefty Kal Daniels. Price's first pitch went to the backstop, and Brantley's runner scored to tie the game again at three.

The Reds played small ball on Price in the 16th. Herm Winningham bunted for a hit, stole second, and was bunted to third by Larkin. Craig had Price intentionally walk the next two batters—Sabo and Davis—to set up a force at any base. But Daniels hit the first pitch he saw in the air to left field, deep enough to score the fleet Winningham with the winning run and end the four-hour, 51-minute slog at 12:26 AM.

The Giants bullpen had displayed more heart than depth. Both teams were probably grateful for the storm clouds that rained out Saturday's game. But nothing could forestall the torrent of unsettling news where Rose was concerned. Two newspapers reported on Saturday that the Reds manager was being investigated by the IRS. Whatever the upshot of the various investigations targeting Rose, this much was becoming evident: he was unlikely to walk away unscathed. "The evidence is so large right now and aiming toward Pete in so many ways," Johnny Bench, a Reds broadcaster and a teammate of Rose's on the great Big Red Machine teams of the 1970s, said in an interview with a Cincinnati television station. "All of a sudden, we're trying to find ways for Pete to step down gracefully, and that is really sad."

By comparison the news from the Giants side was almost trivial. Craig announced that Garrelts would remain a starter. And general manager Al Rosen, a hard-hitting third baseman in his day and the 1953 American League MVP, took Matt Williams aside to give him a few batting tips. A desperate measure? Perhaps. But it was a desperate time. Williams, whom the Giants believed was on the brink of stardom, had begun the season 0-for-14 with six strikeouts.

Conditions weren't ideal Sunday—cloudy, 45 degrees, wet field—but they were good enough to play baseball. The first two San Francisco hitters, Brett Butler and Thompson, were retired on a combined five pitches by Reds starter Danny Jackson, coming off a 23-win season that would have earned him a Cy Young Award had it not been for a spectacular year by a fellow named Orel Hershiser. Jackson had given the Giants fits in 1988, winning three of four decisions while striking out 28 in 29⅔ innings. He already was 1–0 in 1989, having trumped the Dodgers on Opening Day. If his first five pitches were any indication, it was going to be a long day for the Giants followed by a long flight home.

Clark was the third hitter. He singled to right field. Mitchell followed with a deep but catchable ball to left-center field. Left fielder Daniels and center fielder Davis each pursued it, but both pulled up and looked at the other as the ball kangarooed off Riverfront Stadium's artificial surface and over the fence for a ground-rule double. Stunningly, the inning was still alive. Rose ordered Maldonado walked intentionally. Jackson, perhaps still shaken over the turn of events, then walked light-hitting catcher Kirt Manwaring to force in a run for a 1–0 Giants lead.

Williams, still 0-for-1989, was next. If you included spring training, which Williams ended on an 0-for-18 skid, the young third baseman was hitless in his previous 32 at-bats. He approached the batter's box with Rosen's advice in mind: stand closer to the plate. Williams did, and the count went to 1–1. Then Williams ripped a liner over the left-field fence for a grand slam. The Giants tacked on a run in the fourth and three in the sixth for a 9–1 win and a share of first place.

Buoyed by Williams' grand slam and three scoreless innings from their bullpen, they were flying high as they returned to the Bay Area for their home opener against the Dodgers.

◆ ◆ ◆ ◆

Oakland was out of first place for the first time since April 20, 1988. And the A's placed La Russa's right-handed set-up man, Gene Nelson, on the disabled list with a ribcage injury. Now two valuable players from the 1988 World Series roster— Nelson and Canseco—were on the disabled list. They would soon have company.

Stewart stopped the bleeding, striking out nine Chicago White Sox in eight and one-third innings in a 4–2 Oakland win. Some more good news arrived before Oakland's Monday, April 10, game against the California Angels. Trainer Barry Weinberg said Canseco would have his cast removed April 20 and would need 10 to 12 days of rehab after that before returning to the lineup. That meant Canseco could be back by May 1.

But there was also discouraging news in the third inning of the contest. Mark McGwire, who had just been named AL Player of the Week for his three home runs, nine RBIs, and .318 average in the season's first six games, experienced lower back pain after striking out. He was removed from the game, which the A's won 4–0 behind Welch's eight scoreless innings.

McGwire sat out Tuesday's game (as did center fielder Dave Henderson on a planned rest day). Bert Blyleven shut down the A's on four hits as the Angels eased to a 7–1 win. On Wednesday, as the A's were getting blanked 5–0, McGwire saw a back specialist. He was diagnosed with a herniated disk and placed on the 15-day DL. Now the '88 World Series team was down three players, including both Bash Brothers.

A strong effort by Mike Moore earned the A's a 5–0 win on Thursday and a split in the series. But Oakland played without shortstop Weiss, who had such a brutal case of the flu that he was tested for mono. (Results were negative.) This meant the 1988 pennant winners were down (if only temporarily) four men, including the past three American League Rookies of the Year. A few weeks later, Carney Lansford recalled a TV broadcaster saying that with Canseco and McGwire on the shelf, the A's were a "less than mediocre" team. Lansford also recalled thinking, *We'll see what he says the next time we're in Anaheim.*

◆ ◆ ◆

Hours before the first pitch of the Giants' April 10 home opener, the day's first triumph emerged. Dave Dravecky pitched off a mound for 10 minutes. He threw free and easy, nowhere near full throttle. Craig, a wily old pitcher, pitching coach, and guru of the split-finger fastball, described Dravecky's pitching motion as almost perfect.

A few hours later, Bill Walsh, slightly more than two months after leading the 49ers to a Super Bowl victory in his final game as an NFL head coach, took his turn on the mound, throwing out the ceremonial first pitch. Tower of Power played the national anthem. A Candlestick Park crowd of 53,015 showered the rival Los Angeles Dodgers with boos, saving their worst for L.A. manager Tommy Lasorda. The mood was festive, and the Giants obliged their fans over the first eight innings, eking out three runs against Hershiser—whose record consecutive-scoreless-innings streak carried over from 1988 was snapped at 56 innings in his previous start—shrugging off a home run by Kirk Gibson, and taking a 3–2 lead into the top of the ninth.

LaCoss was the team's new closer, but to start the ninth inning Craig summoned Hammaker for a lefty-vs.-lefty matchup with Mike Scioscia, who singled on a 2–1 pitch. When right-handed-hitting Mickey Hatcher was announced as a pinch-hitter for Hershiser, Craig called for Buffy. Hatcher squirted a single through the left side of the infield against LaCoss. Pinch-runner Mariano Duncan sped to third base. Leadoff hitter Willie Randolph then drew a walk. Dave Anderson, running for Hatcher, moved up to second. The bases were loaded with pinch-hitter Franklin Stubbs coming to the plate.

Say this about LaCoss: he wasn't afraid to challenge hitters. He had a mean streak on the mound and sometimes off it. He wasn't the type to think himself into a state of apoplexy or care what someone else might think or say. If he got beat, it wasn't because he shied away from the challenge. It was because the other guy was better. So he challenged Stubbs and got him to bounce into a fielder's choice with Duncan forced at home. He challenged Gibson, getting the reigning National League MVP to ground a ball to first base. Clark hadn't yet won a Gold Glove, but he soon would. He was decisive and reliable. Setting up to throw home for a force on Anderson, he dropped the ball. Everyone was safe. The game was tied 3–3.

Eddie Murray, the next hitter, had spent 12 years with the Baltimore Orioles, during which he hit 333 home runs and averaged 99 RBIs per season, won a World Series ring, was voted Rookie of the Year, selected to seven All-Star Games, and poured the foundation of a Hall of Fame career. It was his sixth game with the Dodgers. He came into it with no home runs, no RBIs, and an .095 average. But he remained an ominous sight in the batter's box, especially when the bases were full. His 14 career grand slams tied him with Gil Hodges for eighth all-time in major league history. On a 1–1 pitch, Murray broke that tie, hammering a long fly ball down the right-field line for his 15th career grand slam to give the Dodgers a 7–3 lead.

The Giants didn't fold. They loaded the bases with one out against L.A. closer Jay Howell. Lasorda lifted Howell in favor of Alejandro Pena, who got Thompson to fly out for the second out. That brought Clark to the plate as the tying run. Pena's balk, which scored Manwaring, didn't change that dynamic. Clark worked the count full with Mitchell on deck but struck out to end the game. The Giants rushed to LaCoss' defense afterward. "A lot of people will say my bullpen blew it, but [LaCoss] made the pitches," Craig told reporters. "We just didn't make the plays."

"I was going home with it," Clark said of Gibson's grounder. "I just booted it." LaCoss didn't sound like someone who had just experienced trauma that would leave emotional scars. "I did my best," he said. "I'll be out there tomorrow." All of which may have been true. But so was this: little more than 12 hours after Murray's grand slam, free-agent reliever "Goose" Gossage was throwing a three-inning simulated game at Candlestick Park under the watchful eyes of the Giants brass.

As they did countless times under Craig, whose positivity struck an authentic chord with players less than half his age, the Giants answered a difficult loss with a decisive victory. A few hours after Gossage's audition, Clark had two RBI doubles and a three-run homer in an 8–3 win. What's more, with the game tied 1–1 in the fifth and the Dodgers with runners on second and third, Craig ordered Kelly Downs to intentionally walk Gibson to load the bases for Murray. Downs held Murray to a long sacrifice fly.

Maybe there's some therapeutic value to having started the final game in Brooklyn Dodgers history, to having started the first game in New York Mets history (and lost 24 games in their first season), to having seen a perfect game in the World Series, to having been traded twice and released twice, to having been fired after two years as the Padres manager, to having been Sparky Anderson's pitching coach for the 1984 World Series champion Detroit Tigers, to having been hired as Giants manager at age 55, when he had reason to believe his baseball career was grinding to a halt. Whatever the source, Craig managed fearlessly. "What are the odds of [Murray] getting two grand slams in a row?" Craig asked reporters after the game. "I don't worry about things like that."

The Giants won the next game as well 3–1 with all their runs coming on Mitchell's prodigious three-run homer off Fernando Valenzuela in the first inning. They were off the next day, Thursday, April 13, but their general manager wasn't. Rosen was on the horn with Jerry Kapstein, Gossage's agent, trying to work out a deal. An announcement, the team said, was expected by Friday. Gossage, with 302 career saves, signed a one-year contract with the Giants for the major league minimum of $68,000. The Cubs picked up the balance of the $1.25 million owed Gossage for 1989.

The Giants didn't need the Goose on Friday—when Mitchell's two-run double and solo homer helped them to a 7–5 win against the Atlanta Braves and sole possession of first place—or on Saturday when Mitchell scored the game's only run after reaching second base when Dale Murphy misplayed his windblown fly ball into a two-base error. But Gossage got the call in Sunday's doubleheader. He made his Giants debut in a 7–2 loss in the first game, throwing two scoreless innings that extended the San Francisco bullpen's consecutive-scoreless-innings streak to 21⅓ since Murray's grand slam. A 13-inning no-hit streak by the San Francisco bullpen was broken in the nightcap and won by the Giants 6–1. Mitchell had a homer and five RBIs on the day.

The Padres then rolled into town. The Giants had taken two of three from them in the season-opening series. But San Diego paid them back. Garrelts opened the series in fine fashion Monday with his first shutout since 1983 and then ended his media boycott after the 9–0 win. "I just decided last Thursday that I would start talking again," he told reporters. "People have told me that I'm too nice a guy and that I listen to too many people. I don't know if that's true, but tonight I just tried not to think about anything."

◆ ◆ ◆ ◆

From Anaheim the A's flew to Chicago. Eckersley was late joining them. Eck had been called to Colorado Springs, Colorado, to testify in the trial of his brother Wallace, who was being tried for attempted murder, kidnapping, and sexual assault. Dennis Eckersley spent part of his time on the witness stand discussing his own history of alcohol abuse. A lot was made of the pitching transformation Eckersley experienced after he was traded by the Chicago Cubs to the A's in spring training

1987—from aging starter to the epitome of the modern-day closer. But that was a subplot to an even bigger transformation.

Eckersley, who grew up in Fremont, just a few miles south of the Oakland Coliseum, burst upon the major league scene at the age of 20. At 22 he threw a no-hitter and made the All-Star team in the last of his three seasons with the Cleveland Indians. At 23 he won 20 games for the ill-fated 1978 Boston Red Sox. In his first five seasons, Eckersley, a side-winding right-hander, was 77–50 with a 3.12 ERA, but over his next five seasons, he was 57–60 with a 4.24 ERA.

The Red Sox traded him to the Cubs in May 1984. Eck had a brief renaissance in Chicago, going 10–8 as the Cubs earned their first postseason berth since 1945. But by the spring of 1987, the Cubs were ready to be done with him and dealt him to Oakland for three players who would never spend a day in the majors. Suffice to say it was as big a shock to the pitcher as it was his new manager.

Before they were friends for life, La Russa and Eckersley were contentious adversaries. In the summer of 2013, La Russa recalled that when he was managing the White Sox and Eckersley was pitching for the Red Sox, his future closer had a knack for getting on his nerves. One thing La Russa especially disliked was Eckersley's habit of staring into the opposing dugout.

"What are you looking at?" La Russa yelled out at the mound.

"What are *you* looking at?" Eck hollered back.

La Russa also recalled berating Eckersley for what he believed to be bean balls deliberately thrown at his White Sox players. The two got a break from each other in 1984, when Eckersley was traded to the Cubs, who played and trained apart from the White Sox. They met again in 1987, at a spring training game in Mesa, Arizona. La Russa was in his first spring with the A's. Eckersley was the Cubs' starting pitcher that day.

The A's teed off on Eckersley. Canseco mashed a titanic home run in his first at-bat and ripped a double his second time up. Little of which unduly concerned Eckersley. Like a lot veterans in spring training, he was more focused on breaking a sweat than the final results.

La Russa, on the other hand, had his game face on.

"I get a little feisty sometimes," La Russa said. "So I gave Jose the sign to steal third." That's a bold strategy in a game that actually means something. In a game that means nothing, it's akin to a personal affront.

Canseco stole third.

"What are you doing?" Eckersley yelled at Canseco. "I'm just getting my work in!"

Canseco shrugged and pointed to the Oakland dugout.

Eckersley looked at La Russa.

"And I yell back, 'Yeah, I gave him the sign!'" La Russa recalled. "Four or five days later: [it's] 'Hey, Dennis. Welcome to the A's.' True story."

A lot of factors can contribute to a pitcher losing effectiveness over time—not the least of which is the unnatural physical act of throwing a baseball. From all appearances Eckersley's arm began dragging during the 1979 season. At the same time, Eck understood he was doing himself no favors with his hard partying lifestyle. His alcoholism became especially acute during his time with the Cubs, who played in Wrigley Field, the only major league ballpark without lights at the time. All those day games left him with too much time for nightlife.

In January 1987, on the verge of splitting up with his second wife, Eckersley entered rehab. The A's had no idea they were getting a new man when they traded for him three months later. Like another high-profile Bay Area athlete at the time, Golden State Warriors guard Chris Mullin, Eckersley had replaced one addiction (alcohol) with another (fitness).

As La Russa sorted out what he had during 1987, his first full season with the A's, he began to use Eckersley in relief. La Russa and pitching coach Dave Duncan liked what they saw. It took some selling on their part, but Eckersley eventually embraced his new assignment. He was driven by fear of failure. But when it came his way, he met it head on with unflinching honesty. He answered questions from reporters for nearly an hour after Gibson's home run in the 1988 World Series. Testifying at his brother's trial must have been another thing entirely.

As it turned out, the A's didn't need him on Friday, April 14. Stewart improved to 3–0 with six and one-third strong innings in a 7–4 victory against the White Sox in their home opener. It was the fast-starting Stewart's 12th consecutive winning decision in the month of April. Weiss, still in the throes of the flu, never left the hotel. Second baseman Glenn Hubbard exited in the sixth inning with a strained right hamstring. La Russa was then without five of the 24 men who had been on the 1988 World Series roster.

On Thursday, April 20, they played an exhibition against their Triple A Tacoma farm team. La Russa called on himself as a pinch-hitter. The career .199 hitter singled up the middle. The good feelings from that moment lasted barely longer than the team's off day on Thursday. Things on the Canseco front had been quiet. Too quiet. No speeding tickets. No steroids implications. But on Friday, April 21, during a visit to the UCSF medical center in San Francisco to have his injured wrist X-rayed, an employee noticed a 9mm handgun (later determined to be loaded) on the floor of Canseco's parked Jaguar. Police investigated and arrested Canseco when he returned to his car. He was taken to the Hall of Justice and booked on suspicion of possessing a firearm on university property (a felony) and possession of a loaded firearm in the passenger compartment of a vehicle (a misdemeanor). His wife, Esther, posted the $5,000 bond that allowed Canseco to be in uniform for that night's home game against the Angels.

This time there were no jokes when Canseco arrived at the Coliseum, no pretend interviews with La Russa. Canseco's story was that he carried the gun because of an incident that occurred during the offseason. Alderson told reporters he was "not unsympathetic" to Canseco and pledged to make sure he got the best legal support possible. But he added, "I'm embarrassed for the organization. My evaluation of Jose is that he's a fairly naïve young man who doesn't quite grasp the magnitude of interest in him or the consequences of not abiding by the same rules as you or I."

The pattern was unmistakable. La Russa had seen it before, would see it again, and was witnessing it now. "One of the realities of this time and of my 30-plus years [as a manager] was the ever present distractions of fame and fortune," La Russa said in 2013. "I can't tell you how serious those distractions could be. We had a real family among our players and our coaches. Jose was part of the family. What I remember is that Jose lost his way in '90. He was doing really well and signed a contract. As soon as he signed that contract, he had that classic quote he gave me. I said, 'Jose, you're not playing the game like you used to.' He said, 'Well, I'm more a performer than a player.' You could see him struggling. And if you watch athletes in all sports, young athletes that all of a sudden get fame and start to dream about fortune, not many guys handle it [well]."

Almost incidentally, the X-rays revealed a small stress fracture in Canseco's wrist. And the A's beat the Angels 10–6. The A's tore through the Angels that weekend, winning 4–3 Saturday and 2–0 Sunday as Moore threw seven and two-thirds shutout innings, and Eckersley picked up his sixth save. Oakland had a five-game win streak and was just one game back of the Texas Rangers.

The A's extended their streak to seven games with a two-game sweep of the Toronto Blue Jays on Monday and Tuesday and got healthy doing it. Tony Phillips' walk-off two-run double off Blue Jays All-Star closer Tom Henke won the first game. Nelson returned from the DL to get the win. Storm Davis (2–1), returning after missing a start with a bad back, won the second while tying a career high with nine strikeouts. Second baseman Hubbard played for the first time in 10 games, participating in two double plays.

That same day Canseco said he planned to start hitting off a tee on Friday. "If it's going to break," he said of the tiny bone in his left wrist, "we'd rather know early than two or three weeks from now."

◆ ◆ ◆ ◆

The Giants hit Los Angeles on Friday, April 21, and the Dodgers hit San Francisco starter Downs as if he were a piñata, knocking him out of the game in the third inning of an 8–2 L.A. win. It was the second consecutive rough outing for Downs, one of those Giants pitchers who seemed to need a little extra care and feeding. "He's pitching with no confidence at all," Craig said. "He's one of those pitchers going out there, looking for things to happen [to him]." Said Downs, who had records of 12–9 and 13–9 during the previous two seasons: "I feel like I've never pitched before."

The Giants won Saturday, but it wasn't pretty. Despite suffering from a stomach virus, Mitchell knocked in two runs, including the game-deciding run in the top of the ninth in a 5–4 win. Mitchell was so taxed by his busy night that he threw up in left field in the bottom of the ninth.

The rubber match featured another Giants bullpen malfunction. Trying to protect a 6–5 lead, LaCoss served up a tying RBI double to Hatcher in the bottom of the eighth. But he limited the damage. Facing Murray with the bases loaded for the second time in 12 days, LaCoss got the slugging first baseman on a swinging strike three. He then retired Scioscia on a liner to left. The contest spun into extra innings with the Giants leaving the bases loaded in the top of the 10th and Hammaker walking in the winning run in the bottom of the frame, leaving Craig gritting his teeth.

On the bright side, despite losing two of three to the Dodgers, the Giants still led the division by a half-game over the Reds. And Clark seemed to be warming up. He had his first career five-hit game Sunday and went 7-for-9 with six walks in the series. The next day it was announced he had succeeded teammate Mitchell as NL Player of the Week.

46

The Giants moved onto St. Louis and the resumption of unpleasantries with the Cardinals that dated back three years to when managers Craig and Whitey Herzog nearly came to blows during a bench-clearing melee at Busch Stadium. The hard feelings were cemented during the 1987 playoffs. Cardinals fans still recalled Jeffery Leonard's taunting home-run trot and Chili Davis' derisive description of St. Louis as a "cow town." That both antagonists had departed the Giants in the interim was immaterial. Many of the Giants who participated in the '87 National League Championship Series recalled the bitter disappointment of losing the final two games of the playoffs when one win would have sent them to the World Series. In the hours after Game 7, they had to listen to giddy, horn-honking Cardinals fans celebrate in the downtown area for most for the night.

The bad blood came to a full boil in St. Louis on July 24, 1988, when Clark slid hard into second baseman Jose Oquendo in an attempt to break up a double play. When Oquendo kicked at Clark, who was still on the ground, Clark came up swinging. Ozzie Smith threw a punch at Clark from behind, and soon the Giants' first baseman was swarmed by angry Redbirds. Maldonado, the batter on the play, came flying into the fracas and nailed Smith with a right hand, bloodying Ozzie's lip. After the Giants returned home from that road trip, someone got their hands on a tape of the brawl and popped it into a VCR before a game at Candlestick Park. Giants players gathered round to watch the fight over and over, roaring with laughter.

There were no sparks on April 25. San Francisco starter Don Robinson kept things nice and quiet. His seven shutout innings helped the Giants to a 4–0 win. Lefferts pitched the final two frames, recording his third save and boosting to 65⅓ the number of innings pitched by the team's bullpen—tops in the National League.

The following night the Giants fell 3–1 to the Cardinals, despite a bounce-back start from Downs, and out of first place in the NL West. But legions of YouTube fans will recall this game for one reason only. In the bottom of the first inning, Smith sliced a fly ball down the left-field line. Mitchell, nobody's idea of a Gold Glover, raced toward the corner. Realizing he had overrun the ball, he reached up with his bare right hand and caught it on the fly. It had nothing to do with Mitchell's torrid hitting, but it was one of those quirky plays that led you to believe he could do just about anything he wanted on a baseball field. When he returned to the dugout after the inning, his teammates playfully took his glove away. More than 1,700 miles away, the *San Francisco Examiner* had a photographer take a picture of a TV screen displaying Mitchell's amazing catch, and the photo ran on the front page of the sports section.

Clark was still shaking his head 24 years later. "Ozzie hits the ball down the left-field line in St. Louis, and Kevin's chasing it," Clark said. "He looked down to find the fence and when he did he recognized he had overrun the ball. He just stuck his big paw up there and made the barehand snag. I remember sitting in the dugout, and he's sitting next to me. And I'm laughing. And he's like, 'What are you laughing about?' I said, 'Do you not know that you will be on ESPN for the next 30 years because of that one catch?' He said, 'What are you talking about?' I said, 'Boogie, nobody barehands a ball in the middle of a game.' And about then he sort of caught on and he starting laughing."

◆ ◆ ◆ ◆

When did Canseco find time to sleep during the first four months of 1989? On Wednesday, April 26, he pled not guilty in San Francisco County Municipal Court to two weapons charges. He was represented by attorney Robert Shapiro, who five years later would gain fame—or perhaps notoriety—as part of O.J. Simpson's defense team. Later in the day, the California Egg Commission, which paid Canseco a reported $25,000 to appear in a commercial, dropped the ad after receiving complaints from farmers. Said commission president Robert Pierre, "Someone like that just doesn't portray the image we want to portray." Canseco had lost the farm vote.

Finally, Canseco had a wisdom tooth extracted, rendering him unable to lend his teammates moral support at that night's game against the Orioles. It was a good one to miss. Welch nursed a 1–0 lead through seven innings at the Coliseum but walked the first two batters in the eighth. The third batter, Billy Ripken, popped up a bunt with the runners in motion. Welch, catcher Ron Hassey, and first baseman McGwire—in his first game back from the DL—all pulled up short and let the ball land between them for a single. Orioles manager Frank Robinson later said he thought it was a certain triple play. Instead the O's scored twice in the inning and won 2–1. McGwire, who went 0-for-4 in his return, took a called third strike to end the game and the A's seven-game win streak.

He got his revenge the following afternoon, cracking a pair of home runs in a 9–4 victory. Oakland won again on Friday night, edging the Tigers 2–1. Eckersley pitched a scoreless ninth inning for his eighth save. Even the Canseco news of the day was promising. He took about 100 swings off a tee and soft tosses from hitting coach Merv Rettenmund and reported fatigue but no pain.

The A's won again on Saturday 3–2. It was their 10th win in 11 games and drew them to within percentage points of division-leading Texas. They lost on Sunday, but Canseco had another productive and uneventful hitting session. Two more of those and Canseco would head to Double A Huntsville on a rehab assignment. There he would meet up with his twin brother, Ozzie, who had just been cleared to play after having surgery to repair, eerily enough, a broken hamate bone in his hand.

On a lighter note, A's diminutive infielder Mike Gallego, a brilliant defensive player with a .223 career average coming into 1989, went 2-for-3 to increase his average to .442. At one point, he had appeared in the American League's top 10 hitters, above Wade Boggs. "I cut that [clipping] out. Are you kidding me?" said Gallego, an easy guy to root for. He was not only an agreeable sort, but he also had overcome testicular cancer that threatened to derail his career as a 22-year-old minor leaguer. By 1989 he had been cancer free for more than six years. Suddenly he was one of the American League's top hitters after one month of the season—or would have been, if he'd had enough at-bats to qualify. "That's okay," said Gallego, who was generously listed at 5'8" in the Athletics' media guide. "I've always been a little short."

◆ ◆ ◆ ◆

Even at the Giants' best under manager Roger Craig during the late 1980s, there were times when it seemed they were something of a house of cards—just one bad break or injury away from utter chaos. On Monday, May 1, they played their first home game after a 3–6 road trip that knocked them from first place to third. After their final game of the trip, an 11–1 loss in Pittsburgh, Craig expressed relief that the team was headed back to Candlestick Park, "because we play better there."

They did under Craig. Candlestick Park was windy. It was cold. The capricious breezes turned home runs into routine fly outs and simple fly balls into triples. In one of the two 1961 All-Star Games, a strong gust forced Giants reliever Stu Miller to shudder on the mound, thereby committing a wind-aided balk. When the concrete bowl opened in 1960, then-vice president Richard Nixon threw out the first pitch, proclaiming the facility "one of the most beautiful baseball parks of all time." But players seemed to be of two minds: some hated it; others despised it. Giants pitcher Bob Bolin said, "They ought to pull the cork out of this thing and sink it right out there in the bay." Outfielder Bobby Murcer stored his bats in the locker room sauna. Willie Montanez demanded to be traded because of the weather.

As part of his power-of-positive-thinking approach to managing when he took over the team late in the 1985 season, Craig forbid his players from complaining about the park. The bitching and moaning stopped. The winning started. In Craig's first three full seasons at the helm, the Giants won 137 home games (a .564 winning percentage), the third-best mark in the National League. "He was a great motivator," Will Clark said in 2013. "He reiterated the point all the time that, hey look, we're going to use Candlestick to our advantage. Needless to say, there's a lot of intricacies of Candlestick. We did a lot of stealing, a lot of bunting, a lot of squeezing, a lot of hitting and running because you never knew when the wind cranked up what would happen."

They were seeking comfort on their wind-whipped home turf. But after just three batters (all of whom reached base), Kelly Downs had to leave with tightness in his shoulder. Counted on to be one of the team's top starters in 1989, Downs had been up and down in his first five starts. Now he was out. Scott Garrelts took over with the bases loaded and no one out. He squirmed out of the jam, but not before allowing two runs. The Giants fell behind 3–0 after three innings against 1984 Cy Young Award winner Rick Sutcliffe. They rallied for two runs in the fourth, and tied the game in the eighth in a sequence more intriguing in hindsight than it was at the time.

Leadoff man Brett Butler grounded a single to right field and advanced to second on Tracy Jones' dribbler back to the mound. Cubs manager Don Zimmer then called for left-handed reliever Mitch Williams to pitch to Clark. The two had never faced each other in a major league game. Williams pitched with a corkscrewing fury, hurling the ball with such force that he would pivot wildly toward the third-base line in his follow-through. And he threw heat. His nickname of "Wild Thing" inspired by the 1989 movie *Major League* fit him like a glove.

His first pitch to Clark went whizzing to the backstop, allowing Butler to advance to third base. Clark blooped Williams' second pitch to short left field. Cubs left fielder Mitch Webster got his glove on it but couldn't hold on. Clark reached on what was ruled an error as Butler scored the tying run. The game spun into the 12th where Mike LaCoss, in his third inning of work, surrendered a home run to Chicago catcher Damon Berryhill. Matt Williams struck out to end the game, a 4–3 Giants loss. Minutes after the game, Williams, hitting .130 with 18 strikeouts in 54 at-bats, was sent down to Triple A. It was the ninth loss in 12 games for the Giants, who fell below .500 for the first time. Two young talents from whom they expected big seasons were out of the picture indefinitely, and their closer had as many losses (two) as saves.

But just that quickly, things turned around. The following night, Rick Reuschel threw seven and one-third shutout innings, "Goose" Gossage earned a save by getting out of a bases-loaded jam in the eighth and throwing a scoreless ninth, and Kevin Mitchell hit a two-run homer off Greg Maddux in a 4–0 win. And then they turned around again. The Pittsburgh Pirates came to town and beat the Giants for the third time in four meetings 5–3. Mitchell homered twice and hit two more balls to the warning track. The three bombs in two games gave him a major league-leading nine homers just 27 games into the season.

Mitchell homered again on Thursday against Pittsburgh. His two-run shot broke a 1–1 tie in the third inning and led to a 6–3 Giants win. Clark had three hits, raising his average to .369. Clark later posed with Mitchell for a Pacific Sock Exchange poster later in the 1989 season. He regarded Mitchell with awe. "I knew the potential was there," Clark said. "But we start off the season, and he is just on fire. And he was doing some weird stuff. Like I remember we were in Pittsburgh, and Kevin was swinging a 35-inch, 35-ounce bat and he only had a few of them left, and he broke his last one. He had nothing to fall back on. So he just basically took a broken bat and taped it up really good—and I'll never forget—first swing he hit one out to left-center. I was like, 'He just hit a home run with a *broken* bat.'"

Mike Krukow was the beneficiary of Mitchell's most recent power surge. He allowed two runs in five innings to earn his first win since his season-ending shoulder surgery in September 1988. Downs, on the other hand, had to shut down a throwing session with pitching coach Norm Sherry after just six pitches. He was placed on the disabled list the following day.

◆ ◆ ◆ ◆

As the second month of the season dawned, Jose Canseco was still trying to determine where he stood with his hand. On Monday, May 1, as his teammates flew to Toronto for a series against the Toronto Blue Jays, Canseco remained in Oakland, where he took four rounds of batting practice. He reported no pain and was told to report to Double A Huntsville, Alabama, the following Sunday for a rehab assignment.

The A's were reporting for their final series at Exhibition Stadium in Toronto, where the Blue Jays had played since their inception in 1977. The next time the A's passed through Toronto was immediately after the All-Star Game, and the Blue Jays were in their new $600 million (Canadian) playpen, a retractable-roof stadium called the SkyDome.

The series got off to a two-fisted start on Tuesday, May 2, beginning with a spritzing rain that delayed the first pitch and fell intermittently throughout the game. Oakland, trailing 4–1, rallied for three runs in the top of the seventh inning. Reliever Rick Honeycutt gave up the tie-breaking run in the bottom of the eighth. In the top of the ninth, Blue Jays reliever Tom Henke got to within one strike of nailing down the win—three times. A's left fielder Luis Polonia grounded a two-out, 2–2 pitch for a single to right field. The next batter, center fielder Dave Henderson, slapped a 1–2 pitch for a single to right. Designated hitter Dave Parker walked on a full-count pitch to load the bases for Mark McGwire. Big Mac, who had struck out in all six of his previous career meetings with Henke, didn't mess around, launching Henke's second pitch into the left-field stands for a grand slam that gave the A's an 8–5 lead.

The fun wasn't over. Honeycutt, starting his third inning of work, got two outs to open the bottom of the ninth. That brought up cleanup hitter George Bell, a right-hander. Though his team led by three runs with one out to go, manager Tony La Russa called on Gene Nelson to get a righty-righty matchup with Bell, the 1987 American League MVP. On the 1–2 pitch, Nelson hit Bell in the side. The excitable Bell, who was known to honor his first impulse to the exclusion of critical thinking, charged the mound. The benches emptied. The Associated Press reported that Bell and Henke threw most of the punches in the melee that ensued.

When order was restored, Alexis Infante was pinch-running for the ejected Bell, and Eric Plunk had been summoned to relieve Nelson. Plunk whiffed Tom Lawless on three pitches to end the game and put the A's in sole possession of first place for the first time since April 7. But it didn't end the conversation. Nelson later told reporters that Bell had pulled his hair at the bottom of the pile on the mound and "was saying he was going to kill me." La Russa said he could understand how Bell felt but swore "on my children" that Nelson wasn't trying to hit Bell. A chill rain. A scarcely believable comeback. A brawl. It was a game that had "To be continued" written all over it.

Things were a lot quieter the following night when Mike Flanagan hurled a four-hit shutout as the Blue Jays won 2–0. An off day followed, and Canseco departed for Huntsville.

Dave Stewart improved his record to 6–0 as Oakland won the first game of the Tigers series. Storm Davis was roughed up for six runs in a 6–3 loss on Saturday. On Sunday, McGwire singled, doubled, and hit his second homer of the series (and eighth of the year), and Eckersley logged his 10th save in a 5–4 win. The A's led the division, but they were scraping by offensively, having stranded 30 runners on base during the three-game series.

That, it turned out, was the good news. The bad news: Canseco injured his wrist in the second at-bat of his second rehab game in Huntsville. Athletics orthopedic surgeon Rick Bost said he expected the injury to require surgery.

♦ ♦ ♦ ♦

The Giants could give thanks that no team in the National League West was displaying much initiative. Despite falling to 14–14 after the Pirates series, they were still tied for second, two games behind the Cincinnati Reds. But the bullpen blues wouldn't go away. On Friday, May 5, in the opener of a three-game set with the St. Louis Cardinals, LaCoss inherited a 1–1 tie in the top of the eighth. He walked three of the five men he faced and committed a throwing error. The Giants lost 3–1 and fell a spot in the standings from a tie for second to a tie for third but lost no ground. They were still two games out. "We had a closer issue," Clark said in 2013. "But from an everyday player's standpoint, you're more worried about the starter because you want that lead going late into the game. If you don't have the lead going late into the game, the closer issue is a moot point. You wanted to go out there and do well against the [other team's] starter and get that lead and then hopefully the bullpen situation takes care of itself."

Craig had lost patience with Candy Maldonado, who was 3-for-33 and hadn't driven in a run since April 22. So he turned to Donell Nixon, who had batted .346 in a 59-game extended trial with the Giants in 1988. Nixon had no power to speak of, and whatever defensive skills he had were undermined by a below average throwing arm. But in the second game of the Cardinals series, a 9–0 San Francisco victory, he had three hits, scored twice, and drove in two runs. Reuschel won his fifth game with six shutout innings. (LaCoss, it should be noted, earned the save with three innings of scoreless relief.) In the series finale, Nixon went 2-for-4 in a 5–1 win.

But the true star of that Sunday win was Don Robinson dubbed Caveman by teammate Krukow for having endured and come back from six surgeries (five shoulder, one knee) during his career. Big, boisterous, friendly, and more than an able batsman, Robinson threw a complete game that day, adding a single and his ninth career home run. The Giants were in second place, one game behind Cincinnati.

On their off day on Monday, May 8, and propelled in part by the tailwind of the St. Louis series, the Giants took off for Chicago for a quick two-game series with the Cubs. Krukow won his second straight start on Tuesday, and Nixon had his fourth consecutive multi-hit game. It was a double loss for the Cubs, who learned that right fielder Andre Dawson required knee surgery and would be lost for about one month.

On Wednesday, the Giants rallied from a 3–0 deficit for a 4–3 win. Robby Thompson got the comeback started with a two-run double in the seventh inning. When Ed Jurak opened the eighth with a single, Zimmer hooked starter Mike Bielecki and called for Mitch Williams. Brett Butler, an excellent bunter, laid one down to the first-base side of the mound as Williams went whirling toward the third-base line. It was a base hit. Nixon tried to bunt the runners along but forced Jurak at third—which brought up Clark. This time Clark dropped a single down the right-field line, scoring Butler to tie the game and sending Nixon to third. With Mitchell batting, Williams balked Nixon home with the deciding run in a 4–3 Giants win.

That same day, the Giants, suddenly in need of third-base options with Williams trying to find himself in Phoenix, acquired veteran Ken Oberkfell from Pittsburgh. Craig Lefferts pitched an uneventful bottom of the ninth for his sixth save. The Giants were back in first place by a half-game.

Reuschel kept them there with a strong effort—one run allowed in eight and two-thirds innings—as the Giants won their fifth in a row 2–1 in the first of three games at Montreal. The win was the 200th for the famously reticent Reuschel, a big, round-faced, Charlie Brown of a man known to his teammates as Big Daddy. The milestone came four days before his 40th birthday. When reporters asked if he thought he would tell the story of his 200th win when he got older, Reuschel deadpanned: "I don't know. You'll have to ask me when I get older."

◆ ◆ ◆

On Tuesday, May 9, Canseco, on the eve of surgery to his left hand, was fined $500 by a Broward County, Florida, judge for his 125 miles per hour speeding ticket. Payment of the fine would expunge the associated reckless driving conviction from his record. Canseco's surgery went off on time. It lasted nearly two hours, after which Canseco's hand was placed in a cast. If all went well, the cast would come off after two to three weeks. Then he would wear a splint for two to three weeks. It was possible he could rejoin the A's immediately after the All-Star break.

Such was the competitive nature of the American League West race that the A's won three of four games against the Milwaukee Brewers in the subsequent wrap-around home series that extended through Monday but still saw their division lead halved from two games to one over the Kansas City Royals and California Angels. Emotions ran hot from the start of the first game. Henderson was hit by a pitch from Milwaukee starter Mike Birkbeck in the bottom of the first inning. One can only imagine how sweet it was for the man teammates called Hendu when, with the A's trailing 4–3 in the bottom of the ninth, he sent the crowd of 30,743 home happy with a game-winning two-run home run. "They made me angry," Henderson told reporters after the game. "And they made me a better hitter by making me angry."

At that point any late-game heroics only added to the legend Henderson launched during the 1986 postseason. With the Boston Red Sox down to their final strike in the ALCS, and with the opposing Angels at the top step of their dugout, awaiting the final pitch that would finally put manager Gene Mauch in the World Series, Henderson belted a go-ahead two-run home run off Angels closer Donnie Moore. After the Angels tied the game in the bottom of the ninth, Henderson hit a sacrifice fly off Moore, two innings later, to drive in the eventual winning run. The series shifted back to Boston, where the Red Sox won Games 6 and 7. Mauch, a fine manager whose legacy was burdened by the Phillies' collapse in the final days of the 1964 season and then the Angels' inability to close the deal in the 1986 playoffs, never made it to a World Series.

But Hendu did. What's more his tie-breaking home run off New York Mets reliever Rick Aguilera in the 10th inning of Game 6 put the Red Sox on the verge of their first world championship since 1918. That was the game that ended with Mookie Wilson's cue shot squirting between Bill Buckner's ankles of clay. It would take 18 more years before the Red Sox finally reversed their World Series curse, but Henderson's reputation as an uber-clutch performer was cast.

Henderson struggled during the regular season in 1987, losing his starting job to Red Sox rookie Ellis Burks. Batting just .234 with eight home runs at the end of August, he was shipped to the Giants for the bargain-basement price of a player to be named later. With his team closing in on its first division title in 16 years, Giants general manager Al Rosen was looking for insurance against the tender hamstring of slugging left fielder Jeffrey Leonard. But because he made the deal just after midnight on August 31, the deadline for adding players in time to be eligible for the playoffs, Henderson had no opportunity to reprise his postseason heroics in 1987. To say he was disappointed would be an understatement.

Hendu hit .238 with no home runs in limited action for the Giants that September. In slightly more than a calendar year, he had gone from being a decent if undecorated player for a poor Seattle Mariners team to a postseason sensation for the storied Boston franchise to an afterthought in San Francisco. He had been traded twice and was to be out of a contract at season's end. After the Giants clinched the '87 division title in San Diego, the team's players and coaches repaired to a celebration in a ballroom at the Marriott Marina Hotel. Reporters gathered at a more intimate hotel bar after filing their stories. They were surprised to see Henderson wander in, having eschewed the team function. "That's their celebration," Henderson said, almost sadly.

A free agent at year's end, he was scooped up by the A's with little fanfare four days before Christmas for the price of a one-year, $225,000 contract. His 24 homers, 94 RBIs, and .304 average in 1988 earned him a two-year deal for $1.7 million. He had found a home in Oakland.

Hendu encored his walk-off home run against the Brewers by singling home the decisive run in Oakland's 4–3 victory in the second game of the series. The Brewers fought back for a 2–1 win on Sunday, a game interrupted briefly in the fourth inning when benches cleared after Bryan Clutterbuck threw inside to A's outfielder Stan Javier. The A's ended the series with a bang, amassing season highs with 12 runs and 17 hits in a 12–2 triumph. Stewart cruised to his seventh win in eight decisions. You knew it was a laugher when La Russa dropped a postgame one-liner on the media. "Our basic strategy," he said, "is to get so far ahead I can't screw it up." There wasn't much La Russa could do about the onslaught of injuries. Second baseman Glenn Hubbard strained a hamstring in the final game against Milwaukee.

La Russa knew he couldn't expect his team to win every game. But he saw no reason why it couldn't win every series. The A's 6–2 win against the New York

Yankees on Thursday gave them their eighth win (with three splits) in their past 11 series. Designated hitter Dave Parker, off to a slow start, slugged a two-run home run off 45-year-old Tommy John in the penultimate start of his career. Weiss was placed on the DL with a sprained right knee. Mike Gallego shifted from second base to shortstop. Tony Phillips, out for 11 days with a sprained ankle, replaced Gallego at second.

The Red Sox followed the Bronx Zoo into Oakland for a three-game series to end the A's 10-game home stand. Henderson further embellished his reputation as a late-game miracle worker with a game-tying, two-run single in the bottom of the ninth inning of the Friday night game. But set-up men Nelson and Honeycutt loaded the bases with no one out in the 10th. Eckersley had no choice but to challenge former teammate Dwight Evans with a fastball. Evans hit it out for a grand slam. The 7–4 win was Boston's first in 10 games in Oakland, including the 1988 ALCS. "I threw him some high cheese, and he hits it out," Eck said after the game. "What are you going to do?" What the A's did was come back the next day to win 6–3. Eckersley preserved Stewart's major league-leading eighth win, escaping a bases-loaded jam in the eighth and pitching a scoreless ninth. So Eck was back? "I didn't know I was ever away," he said.

The A's beat Boston again on Sunday 5–4. It was another series win, achieved against Red Sox ace Roger Clemens, who pitched a complete game on three days' rest. Eckersley earned his 14th save, tops in the big leagues. And the A's, who at 29–14 led the division by one game over the Angels, drew their fourth consecutive home crowd of more than 40,000. It was an Oakland record.

◆ ◆ ◆ ◆

As a pitcher Craig lost 46 games during the expansion Mets' first two seasons. Perhaps that was why, as a mild-mannered manager, he wouldn't say horsefeathers if he had a mouthful. But he came close after the Giants game in Philadelphia on Monday, May 15. It was a scoreless tie after nine with San Francisco's Garrelts having limited the Phillies to three hits, and the Phillies' Don Carman having held the Giants to four hits. Both starters departed after regulation.

The Giants came close to breaking the scoreless deadlock in the 10th when Clark tried to score from second base on Maldonado's single. But Bob Dernier's throw cut down Clark at the plate. Clark took a more leisurely trip around the bases in the 12th after homering off Philadelphia closer Steve Bedrosian. Mitchell homered on the very next pitch for a 2–0 Giants lead. It had the look of a trademark Craig don't-get-your-dauber-down win as reliever Lefferts trotted out to the mound in the bottom of the frame for his third inning of work.

Lefferts allowed one-out singles to Dickie Thon and Steve Lake but retired Steve Jeltz on a pop fly for the second out. Up stepped Dernier, who pulled the 1–1 pitch into the left-field corner. It was a flip of the coin as to whether Lake, a catcher, could score from first with the tying run—until the ball skipped away from Mitchell. Dernier wound up circling the bases for a game-ending, three-run, inside-the-park homer. Craig closed the Giants clubhouse for a team meeting after the game. When he finally opened the door, he declared it the toughest loss he had ever experienced as a manager.

Once again, the Giants rebounded from bitter disappointment with a resounding victory—in this case with season highs in runs and hits in a 13–5 win. They concluded the series on Wednesday night with a 6–0 victory. One day after his 40th birthday, Reuschel retired the first 20 batters he faced. He lost the perfect game on Tommy Herr's single in the seventh. He left after eight scoreless innings. "It was getting past my bedtime," he cracked.

◆ ◆ ◆ ◆

On Tuesday, May 23, as the A's were starting a nine-game road trip in Milwaukee, Canseco was having stitches removed from his hand in the Bay Area. It was a small milestone—but a milestone nonetheless. The problem with his hand at last had been identified and surgically corrected. He was on his way back—and not a moment too soon. Competitively speaking, the A's had held the fort in his absence, going 29–14 through 43 games, good enough to lead the AL West by one game over the Angels. It was the same record they had achieved during the first 43 games of 1988 in a less demanding environment. That record had been good for a seven-game lead over the Texas Rangers. So Canseco's absence hadn't been ruinous. Stewart, speaking 24 years after the fact, thought the A's didn't miss him as much as people thought. "The team we had was pretty loaded," Stewart said, chuckling. "So when you ask, 'How much did it hurt?' Obviously he was one of the key pieces in our lineup, but we were a loaded baseball team. We missed him, but we didn't know we missed him."

Still the numbers told a stark story. After 43 games in 1988, Canseco had hit 11 homers, driven in 37 runs, scored 40 runs, stolen 15 bags in 20 tries, and compiled an on-base-plus-slugging percentage (OPS) of .911. Through 43 games in 1989, a consortium of five Oakland right fielders—Javier, Felix Jose, Billy Beane, Steinbach, and Lance Blankenship—had failed to homer in 155 at-bats while driving in 16 runs, scoring 15 runs, stealing three bases, and compiling an OPS of .581.

None of them changed the way an A's game was played in the manner Canseco did. Teams feared him. They tried to avoid him. They counted the batters until he was up next. At that point in his career, he could make a single play that would stand a game on its head. In the third game of the 1988 season, the A's hosted the Mariners. Steve Trout, a serviceable left-hander in his 11th year, started for the M's. Seattle scored a run in the top of the first inning, and Trout retired the first two A's batters in the bottom of the frame. Canseco was the third batter. Had he hit a ball so hard that it knocked a BART train off the tracks a half-mile beyond the center-field wall, it would merely have tied the game 1–1. Yet Trout nibbled, walking Canseco on four pitches. Then he walked Mark McGwire on five pitches. With Dave Parker, the No. 5 hitter, at the plate, Canseco took his lead off second base. He looked at third baseman Jim Presley, who was playing off the line for Parker, a pull-hitting left-hander. *I can get to third base before Presley can*, Canseco thought to himself. So with the pitcher Trout on the mound, holding the ball, Canseco took off running.

Trout stepped off the rubber and threw wildly to third base. Canseco scored with McGwire moving up to second. Seattle catcher Dave Valle later said that— Trout's intermittent spasms of wildness notwithstanding—he thought his pitcher had been rattled by Canseco's brash base-running gambit. Trout pitched like it, walking Parker. He walked Don Baylor. He threw consecutive wild pitches, allowing McGwire and then Parker to score. He walked Steinbach. Then he was gone. The A's scored four runs on one hit that inning. The fact that they coughed up the lead and lost that game 6–5 is almost immaterial. Canseco had made his point: relax around me at your own peril.

Would Canseco have made a difference in the A's game of Tuesday, May 23, at Milwaukee? Maybe not. The Brewers jumped Bob Welch for four runs in five and one-third innings in a 9–1 rout of Oakland. One of the few positives for the A's was the hot bat of third baseman Carney Lansford, who went 3-for-3 and was leading the American League with a .365 average.

The A's recorded a win and a loss Wednesday. Mike Moore pitched eight strong innings for his fifth win, a 6–2 triumph. The loss was Davis, who was placed on the 21-day disabled list with, well, you name it—right shoulder, right knee, hamstring.

Oakland fell flat 4–1 in Thursday's rubber game. Stewart took his first loss in 10 lifetime decisions against the Brewers. Lansford had three more hits—he was now on a 33-for-71 tear—to raise his average to .370. The news wasn't so good regarding Weiss, who was trying to work out the stiffness his right knee suffered on May 17. Weiss experienced fluid buildup on the knee following a Wednesday workout and had to take Thursday off.

The A's visit to Milwaukee resulted in their first series loss since mid-April. There was only one sure cure for that: a trip to New York to play the dysfunctional Yankees. A 4–0 win on Friday night, May 26, seemed almost too easy with Todd Burns, Honeycutt, and Plunk combining on a one-hitter. Rickey Henderson's infield single in the fourth was the Yankees' only hit. He was erased on a double play. New York sent the minimum of 27 men to the plate. The versatile Burns improved to 4–0 in his first start of the season. The A's shut out the Yankees again on Saturday 3–0, but the win had ominous overtones. Eckersley left with discomfort in his right shoulder after facing two batters in the bottom of the ninth inning. "I don't even want to think about it," Eck said after the game.

La Russa noted the difference between the pitching mounds in the visitors bullpen and on the playing field. The bullpen mound, he said, was much higher, inferring the difference could have contributed to Eckersley's injury. "I just addressed it to the general manager [Sandy Alderson]," La Russa told reporters. "I'm sure he'll address it to somebody."

Welch took the mound in Boston on Monday, May 29, knowing he had little, if any, relief support. La Russa had made nine pitching changes in the three-game sweep of the Yankees. Welch responded by pitching into the 10th inning for just the third time in his 12 major league seasons. He pitched well, too, allowing three runs on six hits. But it wasn't good enough to win. His 142nd pitch of the night was lined for a game-winning single by Boston's Marty Barrett. Off the field Eckersley was examined by Red Sox team physician Dr. Arthur Pappas. There was no apparent serious injury. A precautionary MRI was scheduled for Tuesday.

Sensing his players were dragging, La Russa canceled batting practice before Tuesday's game. It did wonders for Parker, who doubled, homered, and drove in three runs as the A's won 4–2. Stewart pitched seven sturdy innings to become the American League's first nine-game winner, and Honeycutt recorded his third save in four games.

The MRI results rolled in Wednesday. The image of Eckersley's right shoulder confirmed a strain. But the examination of Weiss' knee showed a tear in the cartilage that would require surgery and a six-week rehab. No one mentioned anything about the Curse of the Rookie of the Year, but they could have given Canseco's hamate bone surgery, McGwire's stint on the disabled list in April, and then Weiss' date with the orthopedic surgeon.

But once the game began, the A's battled hard, as they always seemed to do under La Russa, against Boston ace Roger Clemens. The Rocket was plenty good on that night, striking out 10 while holding Oakland to one run in eight innings. He was pulled by manager Joe Morgan after throwing 153 pitches and with the Sox ahead 2–1. But a throwing error by shortstop Jody Reed on what would have been the last out of the game allowed the A's to score the tying run in the top of the ninth. Parker led off the 10th with his eighth home run and fourth of the road trip.

Plunk, however, gave up the tying run in the bottom of the inning and departed with a man on third base and two out. The wheels began spinning. La Russa summoned southpaw Young for a between-starts relief appearance and instructed him to intentionally walk right-hander Nick Esasky to get to left-hander Rich Gedman. Red Sox manager Joe Morgan replaced Gedman with right-hander Rick Cerone, who lined a 1–1 pitch to center field for a 4–3 Boston victory. The A's posted a decent 5–4 record on the road trip, but the collateral damage was concerning.

♦ ♦ ♦ ♦

With three projected All-Stars performing at peak efficiency, the Giants looked like world beaters as they opened a homestand on Tuesday, May 23, with a 4–2 win against Montreal. Reuschel allowed two runs in seven and two-thirds innings against the Expos, improving his record to 8–2. His May totals were: 5–0, 0.48 ERA.

Mitchell drove in his major league-leading 43rd run in the top of the fifth inning to give the Giants a 2–0 lead. Clark doubled the lead with a two-run homer in the seventh, making him the majors' leader in hits (59) and average (.373). Reuschel and LaCoss, who earned his fifth save, took it from there. Craig gushed over his No. 3 and 4 hitters. "Will and Kevin lead by example," he told reporters. "It's not only their run production, but they were here at 2:00, ready to go." Expos starter Kevin Gross put the Giants offense to sleep Wednesday, striking out 11 (including Clark and Mitchell three times each) in a 1–0 Expos win. The San Francisco offense failed to show up again Thursday. With Mitchell out of the starting lineup with tendinitis in his left knee, the Giants fell 2–0.

The Giants still were in second place, two games behind the Reds. But they seemed to be treading water. Their competitive inertia was inspiring no end of rumors on the trade front. The speculation du jour on Friday, May 26, had the Giants sending Maldonado, pitcher Atlee Hammaker, and Williams to Toronto for closer Tom Henke and slugger George Bell. "No truth to it whatsoever," Rosen said. At 17–10 it was the Giants' first winning May since 1983. But since the team moved West in 1958, it was the June swoon that had proved its kryptonite.

Chapter 5

Swirling Trade Winds

After the first two months of the season, Kevin Mitchell led the majors with 15 home runs and 48 RBIs. Thirty-six of his 57 hits were for extra bases. His slugging percentage of .649 would have led the National League in each of the previous 17 years. No reasonable observer would have believed Mitchell could remain at that level of production. As it turned out, he didn't.

In June he got hotter.

After an off day June 1, the Giants opened a series in Atlanta with a 7–6 win. There was a lot to feel good about. Rick Reuschel, though he was hardly dominant, became the majors' first 10-game winner. The resurrection of "Goose" Gossage continued as he got the final two outs for his third save. Second baseman Robby Thompson connected for his third home run in seven days. But Mitchell was the story. He clobbered two home runs, one of them estimated at 440 feet, and drove in three runs. He made a diving catch. He threw out Atlanta Braves outfielder Dale Murphy trying to go from first to third on a single to left field.

Adding to the feel-good vibe, Reuschel and Will Clark were named the National League's Pitcher and Player of the Month for May. But there was a discouraging development. Starting pitcher Don Robinson had to leave the next day's game after three scoreless innings with a pulled muscle in his left buttock.

Robinson was a solid, rugged 6'4" and 225 pounds. His challenge was staying healthy. As a 22-year-old, he pitched through a sore shoulder to help the Pittsburgh Pirates win the 1979 World Series. It took two surgeries to find the nickel-sized bone fragment that was causing him pain. Built-up scar tissue at the end of the 1982 season led to related problems in 1983. Robinson had always hit like a position player. Considering the strength of his bat and the fallibility of his arm, the Pirates suggested after the '83 season that he play winter ball—as an outfielder.

He played just five innings of one game in left field for Pittsburgh in 1984. His arm held up well enough for him to pitch in 145 games from 1984–86. Shortly after the Giants traded for him in 1987 to help them nail down a division title, Robinson, however, estimated he'd had more than 200 cortisone shots during his career. He did help them win the division, pitching five brilliant innings of relief and hitting a home run in the clincher in San Diego. Robinson seemed at once indestructible and vulnerable, able to shake off the shots and the surgeries always seemingly one pitch away from another physical setback. Now the Caveman had been dinged again.

The Giants dropped the final game in Atlanta 6–3 despite Mitchell's 450-foot home run off a sign in the second deck. It was his 19th homer of the season, tying his 1988 total and putting him at least six homers up on every other major leaguer. It wasn't enough to overcome a rough outing by Mike Krukow, who was touched for five runs in four and two-thirds innings. His final pitch—the final pitch of his career it would turn out—was tagged for a three-run home run by former Giants teammate Darrell Evans. Krukow, 4–3 in eight starts with a 3.98 ERA in his comeback from shoulder surgery, was placed on the disabled list with right shoulder inflammation and sent back to San Francisco to be examined.

The Giants arrived in Cincinnati three percentage points behind the division-leading Reds. They leapfrogged into first place with an 11–8 win on Monday, June 5. Mitchell's two-run single in the fourth inning drove Cincinnati ace Jose Rijo from the game after allowing six runs in three and two-thirds innings. The teams played a doubleheader on Tuesday, which Mitchell kicked off with a three-run home run in the first inning of the first game. But those were the only runs the Giants scored. They lost 4–3 when closer Mike LaCoss walked Eric Davis with the bases loaded in the bottom of the ninth. No sweat. Mitchell homered twice more in the second game, including a solo shot off hard-throwing Rob Dibble for the eventual winning run in a 3–2 victory. "I threw him a good fastball in a decent spot," Dibble said, "and he just crushed it. The man's just not human right now."

"How many did he hit tonight? Three?" asked Giants manager Roger Craig. "I'm losing track." Mitchell had seven home runs and 13 RBIs on the first six games of the road trip. His streak defied description. But that didn't stop people from trying. "It's almost getting to the point where you don't wonder if he's going to hit one, but how far it's going to go when he does," Reuschel told reporters after winning the second game and becoming the quickest to win 11 games in San Francisco Giants history.

The Giants' stay in Cincinnati didn't end well. They lost 12–5 on Wednesday as Atlee Hammaker was torched and the defense made three errors. They fell 3–2 in the series finale as a result of yet another bullpen fiasco. Trying to preserve a 2–2 tie in the bottom of the eighth, LaCoss allowed singles to the first two batters and then went 2–0 on Dave Collins. Craig removed LaCoss for Craig Lefferts, who completed the walk and then threw a wild pitch to score Barry Larkin for the tie-breaking run. For all of Mitchell's heroics, the Giants merely split the eight games on the road trip, losing two games in the standings to the Reds. They were one game off the pace as they flew back to San Francisco on the team charter. Or was it on Mitchell's back?

◆ ◆ ◆ ◆

As the A's returned to Oakland, shortstop Walt Weiss bugged out for South Lake Tahoe. Surgery to repair a cartilage tear in his right knee was scheduled for Friday, June 2. It would be performed by Dr. Richard Steadman, chairman of medicine for the U.S. Olympic ski team. The timetable for Weiss' recovery wouldn't be known until Steadman was able to determine the extent of the damage. It might be as little as six weeks or as much as six months.

Before the Cleveland Indians game, Dennis Eckersley threw on the side. There were no setbacks, but he was not expected to pitch during the weekend. Things went downhill after the first pitch. Oakland starter Mike Moore lasted just four and one-third innings, long enough to walk five, throw two wild pitches, and allow four runs in a 5–3 A's loss. On top of that, Carney Lansford left the game with a sore left hamstring after grounding out in the fifth inning. In keeping with the unprecedented number and nature of injuries to hit the A's, Lansford wasn't sure how badly he was hurt. "I've never pulled a muscle before," he explained.

Lansford sat out Saturday's game, but he wasn't needed. Bob Welch improved to 7–4 with eight sharp innings as the A's blanked Cleveland 7–0. Oakland overwhelmed the Indians with a death-by-paper-cuts offensive attack of 14 hits—all singles.

In perhaps his sharpest outing of the season, Dave Stewart threw seven shutout innings, allowing just three hits, as the A's scored a 4–0 win on Sunday. Missing a solo shutout by six outs was the kind of thing that made Stew bristle. La Russa's groundbreaking and sometimes formulaic use of his bullpen late in a game may have been smart baseball, but it went against Stewart's fiercely competitive nature. But whatever misgivings Stewart may have felt being lifted a few steps short of the finish line, he never complained in public—notwithstanding the death stare he would unleash upon La Russa as he strode to the mound to ask for the ball.

On this occasion, however, Stewart took himself out of the game and was glad to do it. The trouble began in the bottom of the third inning with Lance Blankenship on second base in a scoreless game. Luis Polonia slapped a single to left field. Third-base coach Rene Lachemann waved Blankenship home, and his judgment was validated when Oddibe McDowell's throw to the plate was cut off. Blankenship scored to give the A's a 1–0 lead. But as he crossed the plate, Cleveland catcher Andy Allanson, aware the throw had been cut, threw an elbow at Blankenship.

Some managers give instructions to their pitches on when and how to retaliate against such transgressions of the baseball code. Stewart never needed to be told. On this occasion Stewart bade his time. Allanson came up in the fifth inning with the A's leading 4–0. Stewart pitched him straight up, getting him to line out to center field. But with two out and a man on second in the seventh, Stewart hit Allanson with his first pitch. The two jawed at each other after Allanson reached first base and had to be restrained as both benches emptied onto the field. Order was restored until Felix Fermin grounded out to end the inning. Stewart pointed at Allanson, Allanson charged Stewart, and the two brawled between the mound and second base. Both were ejected. "Just part of the game," Cleveland manager Doc Edwards said to reporters. "If you're going to be afraid, go get a dog."

The A's strong pitching continued against Minnesota the following day. Curt Young threw a complete game, allowing two runs. Unfortunately for him, the Twins combo of Francisco Oliveras and Jeff Reardon was better, combining on a six-hitter in a 2–1 win. In the day's most curious development, Major League Baseball released the first tabulation on balloting for the All-Star Game. Jose Canseco, who had yet to play a regular season game in 1989, ranked third among American League outfielders.

The A's had to take the final two games against the Twins to capture La Russa's cherished series win. Moore obliged on Tuesday, June 6, with a four-hit shutout on three days' rest. Oakland pitchers had thrown three shutouts in four games and allowed just two runs in the past 38 innings. But those pitchers didn't include Eckersley and wouldn't for at least two more weeks. Eck was placed on the 15-day DL with a right shoulder strain. Trainer Barry Weinberg said the muscles around the rotator cuff, which were "more weak than sore," were the problem.

That meant someone else would have to step up, and Todd Burns did on Wednesday. Called into the game in an Eck-like circumstance—the A's leading 3–2 with runners at the corners, two out, and a pinch-hitter at the plate—Burns fanned Greg Gagne on three pitches to end the game. It was Burns' third save, and it boosted the A's into sole possession of first place, one game ahead of the California Angels. Dominating it wasn't. But domination was a sometimes thing for the A's at that point with Canseco, Eckersley, Weiss, and Lansford all injured. To their credit the A's were winning the close ones. And it seemed they were all close ones. They were 13–6 in one-run games, and 20 of their 38 wins were by two runs or fewer.

◆ ◆ ◆ ◆

One of the few moves the Giants made during the 1988–89 offseason was trading outfielder-first baseman Mike Aldrete to the Montreal Expos for Tracy Jones, a fourth outfielder type who averaged .299 over his first three major league seasons. Jones broke in with Cincinnati where he was compared to a young Rose for his headfirst slides and intense manner. When he slumped to .229 in the first half of 1988, the Reds dealt him to Montreal. He perked up, hitting .333 for the Expos. The Giants acquired him as a backup outfielder, maybe even someone who could push the backsliding Candy Maldonado for the starting right-field job.

But Jones started painfully slow with San Francisco, batting .091 through 54 games—one-third of the season. San Francisco fans turned on Jones. It didn't help his cause that Aldrete was a homegrown product, having grown up in Carmel, California, and played college baseball at Stanford. Aldo had been a pleasant surprise on the Giants' 1987 division-winning team, batting .325 with 51 RBIs. Jones confessed that he was so upset by his slow start he had trouble sleeping. He lobbied Craig for at-bats. Craig played him seven times in the Giants' eight-game road trip through

Atlanta and Cincinnati, giving him four starts. The results were hardly revelatory: Jones hit .235 with two RBIs.

But it got Jones a start against the San Diego Padres in the first game of a 12-game homestand on Friday, June 9. His biggest contribution his first time up was shaking Mitchell's hand after Mitchell's 23rd home run of the year gave San Francisco a 1–0 lead in the second inning. In Jones' second time up, the Giants led 2–0 with the bases loaded and two out. He lined a single to left field off Bruce Hurst, driving in two runs.

He was back up again in the fifth, again with the bases loaded after an intentional walk to Mitchell. Jones grounded another single to left field, scoring two more runs. The Giants led 6–0; he had knocked in four of the six runs. One inning later he was up again with the bags loaded, this time facing reliever Greg Booker. He rolled a single up the middle, good for two more runs. Jones had come into the game with three RBIs all season. Suddenly he had six in six innings. In his final at-bat against reliever Dave Leiper, Jones dunked a single into center field to score Maldonado. Jones had driven in seven runs, one short of the Giants record. "It's been hell," he told the press. "But I knew I was due." Said Mitchell impishly: "Tracy Jones was a hero today instead of a zero."

Even before spring training, there had been an off-the-field baseball competition in the Bay Area. Two groups, one representing San Francisco and the other representing Santa Clara County in the South Bay, were endeavoring to put together a ballpark proposal that would be endorsed by Giants owner Bob Lurie and placed on the November ballot. In its June 9 edition, the *San Francisco Chronicle* ran a poll conducted by a Southern California company in which 34 percent of Bay Area respondents said the Giants should play at Candlestick Park, 23 percent said they should play in a park in downtown San Francisco, and 20 percent preferred a Santa Clara ballpark. Sunnyvale mayor Larry Stone, head of the Santa Clara County Stadium Task Force, thought it reeked of bias and called it the most ridiculous thing he'd ever heard.

Interestingly enough, the Giants Candlesticked—a windblown fly ball factored prominently—the Padres on Saturday. Scott Garrelts threw six shutout innings before leaving with a stiff elbow. He was nearly matched by Ed Whitson, a former Giant, who allowed just two hits in six innings. Gossage pitched one scoreless inning of relief, and Lefferts pitched two innings to secure his 11th save. It didn't prevent the rumor mill from suggesting that Giants general manager Al Rosen was trying to pry closer Lee Smith from the Red Sox.

There was nothing fluky about Sunday's win, which gave the Giants a sweep. It began as a snappy pitching duel between Reuschel and Dennis Rasmussen. The game was scoreless until the top of the eighth, when Tony Gwynn singled home a run for San Diego. Rasmussen took that 1–0 lead into the bottom of the ninth. Greg Litton, who had been called up when Matt Williams was sent down, hit Rasmussen's second pitch in the bottom of the inning for his first major league home run. Both Rasmussen and Reuschel went nine innings and allowed just one run. Neither would win. The game spun into the bottom of the 12th. With two out Thompson singled. Clark parked the first pitch from Padres closer Mark Davis over the right-center-field fence to win the game. Later he walked reporters through the final lefty-on-lefty matchup: "He has a good fastball, 92 or 93 miles per hour," Clark said, "and I was going to give him that until I got two strikes. I was sitting on the breaking ball and I got it."

After an off day during which the Santa Clara County Stadium Task Force added 45 acres to its ballpark proposal, the Giants were back at it against the Braves. Taking advantage of a horrendous third inning by Atlanta fielders, who committed four errors, the Giants scored a pair of runs that figured prominently in a 3–2 victory and a four-game win streak. And they did so without Mitchell, who sat out with a sore right knee.

On Wednesday, June 14, they made it five in a row, mauling the Braves 10–1 and taking over first place in the National League West. Jones, batting leadoff, had three hits to raise his average to .196. Thompson hit his seventh home run, matching his 1988 total. Robinson, apparently over his pulled buttocks muscle, allowed just one run in seven innings—a positive outing that took some of the sting out of the announcement that Downs was not expected back until after the All-Star break. Speaking of positive events, Williams was tearing up the Pacific Coast League, having hit 13 home runs since his May 1 demotion.

The Giants had no answer for Atlanta's John Smoltz, who was in his first full season, losing the series finale 2–1. Garrelts pitched well (two runs and three hits in seven innings). But nine San Francisco batters struck out against Smoltz, including Thompson, to end the game with two men on.

Jones' offensive resurgence, it turned out, did more than raise his average. It raised his profile. The Detroit Tigers were intrigued enough that on Friday, June

16, they pried him from the Giants in exchange for outfielder Pat Sheridan. Jones admitted that he had asked for a trade. Not only did the Giants announce that deal, but Rosen also admitted he had spoken with the Philadelphia Phillies about closer Steve Bedrosian. The upset would have been if he had not been actively trying to deal for a closer. At that point the combustible Giants bullpen was undeniably the team's Achilles' heel.

A crowd of 23,986 fans saw that for themselves that night. Getting a strong effort from Reuschel, the Giants took a 4–2 lead to the top of the ninth inning. Lefferts faced three batters, giving up a leadoff double to Todd Benzinger, getting Larkin on a foul pop, and allowing a run-scoring single to Paul O'Neill. That prompted Craig to call for Gossage. Davis launched the Goose's first pitch over the left-field fence to give the Reds a 5–4 lead that John Franco protected in the bottom of the inning. It was the Giants' 11th loss in the final inning. Their relievers led the National League with 21 saves, but they also had suffered 13 losses.

The trade market wasn't the only thing heating up. The ballpark issue was about to come to a head. Before Friday's game Lurie met with a small crowd in the South Bay. He said he expected to receive proposals from San Francisco and Santa Clara County in late July. The uncertainty seemed to be weighing on him. "I feel like we are part of the homeless from time to time," he told the group.

By Saturday, a Bedrosian trade seemed more a matter of when than if. The Phillies, with the National League's worst record, had little need for a closer, while it was becoming obvious that the Giants couldn't get where they wanted to go without one. "It's up to them," said Rosen, who was willing to take on a pitcher in the first year of a three-year, $4.25 million contract. Given Rosen's track record, Craig couldn't have been surprised. "Al Rosen did a terrific job when I was there," Craig said in 2013. "We became very close. When he hired me, I told him, 'Okay, but I want to take my wife on every road trip.' He said, 'I'll take mine, too. We can all go to dinner.' He was always asking, 'Who do you need? Do you like this guy?' He would pick up pitchers and would say, 'You can teach him the split-finger.'"

One of the young Giants pitchers rumored to be part of the deal, left-hander Dennis Cook, gave both prospective trading partners something to think about on Saturday, June 17, throwing a six-hitter as the Giants thumped the Reds 8–1. Mitchell ended a six-game homer drought. On Sunday the news broke. Rosen sent pitchers Cook and Terry Mulholland and minor league third baseman Charlie Hayes to the Phillies for Bedrosian, the NL's 1987 Cy Young Award winner. Incredibly, there were some boos from the crowd of 44,542 when the trade was announced on the stadium scoreboard during the game, a 2–1 Giants win. The game featured, coincidentally, two innings of scoreless relief from both LaCoss and Lefferts, who earned his 13th save—two better than his previous career high. Rose, whose team had battled the Giants and Houston Astros atop the division standings all season, tipped his cap to Rosen. "This makes them like us," Rose told reporters after the game. "They've got a good closer now."

"If there were any question marks out there, Al definitely went out and addressed them," Will Clark said, looking back 24 years. "That's the great part about Al Rosen. He wasn't one to sit back. He made things happen. If he saw a hole on the team, he addressed the need. We gave up two good prospects. We gave up Dennis Cook and Terry Mulholland to get Steve Bedrosian. And those guys later on wound up being Giants killers. For that run we needed somebody to step in and shut the door. Steve had been doing it over in Philly. He did it for us."

Bedrosian arrived in San Francisco in time for the Monday, June 19, game against the Astros. There was no booing to be heard. In fact Bedrosian, who had reported in the afternoon and shaved his beard to conform to team policy—Craig would soon relax that rule—got a standing ovation when he was called on in the ninth inning to protect a 3–2 lead. He allowed a leadoff single to Rafael Ramirez, who took second on a bunt and third on a ground out. But the man known as "Bedrock" got Billy Hatcher on a fly ball to center field for the final out. The Giants led the Astros by two games in the division, tying their biggest lead of the season.

With a new closer in hand and injuries to his starting pitchers, Craig made an obvious move, adding LaCoss to the rotation. And it was beginning to look like more help might be on the way. Dave Dravecky was scheduled to throw batting practice Wednesday. It would be his first time facing live hitters since his cancer surgery.

◆ ◆ ◆ ◆

The Texas Rangers were tired of being patsies, and you couldn't blame them. Born as the expansion Washington Senators in 1961—the year the original Washington Senators fled to Minnesota and became the Twins—they entered their 29th year a whopping 473 games under .500 and without ever having played a postseason game. They had tried bold moves; hiring Ted Williams and Billy Martin as managers; drafting high school phenom David Clyde and bringing him straight to the major leagues; hiring Eddie Stanky to manage the team in midseason 1977 (only to have him quit after one game); firing manager Don Zimmer in midseason 1982 (and asking him to manage three more games before naming his replacement).

Under the leadership of team president George W. Bush, son of the president, the Rangers were more aggressive than ever during the 1988–89 offseason, signing free agent Nolan Ryan and trading for slugging second baseman Julio Franco and promising first baseman Rafael Palmeiro. A little more than one-third of the way through the season, their plan seemed to be bearing fruit. The Rangers, who awaited the A's in Arlington for the start of a three-game series on Friday, June 9, had won five of their past seven games and were 32–25 (albeit in fourth place in the AL West).

They outslugged the A's 11–8 in the series opener. Stewart, in his first title defense since duking it out with Allanson, was knocked out in the fourth inning after allowing seven runs on nine hits. The A's fought back in a game that featured five lead changes. But the last lead belonged to Texas and was achieved on Pete Incaviglia's tie-breaking, two-run double in the bottom of the sixth. Mark McGwire's grand slam off Charlie Hough was rendered moot, and Lansford's return to the lineup (he went 0-for-4) was overshadowed.

But Oakland came back to win the next two games and, of course, the series. Eckersley threw 70 pitches in the outfield before the Saturday game and, though he felt better, pronounced himself "a ways away." Storm Davis returned from the DL to hold the Rangers to one run in five innings as the A's won 5–1. They won Sunday by the same score behind Moore, who gave up one run in six and one-third innings for his eighth win. Dave Parker and McGwire punctuated the victory with back-to-back home runs off live-armed Texas rookie Kevin Brown. The A's led the division by a season-high three games over the Angels.

The A's moved on to Kansas City and another three-game series. The first game on Monday, June 12, started poorly and ended worse. Welch left with a pulled right groin after three and two-thirds innings. The night ended in the bottom of the 12th inning when outfielder Jim Eisenreich singled to score Kevin Seitzer and give the Royals a 2–1 win. It was the A's fourth loss in four extra-inning games. And it was Exhibit A for anyone determined to make a case that the A's were not their explosive 1988 selves and that they were playing more games closer to the margin in 1989.

The following night's activities reinforced that presumption, starting with the A's decision to place Welch (and his 8–4 record and 2.81 ERA) on the 15-day DL, making him the ninth Oakland player to be disabled. The A's had so many walking wounded they had to play a shell game to officially render Welch hors de combat, which they did by moving Eckersley to the 21-day DL. The game was instantly forgettable. Young didn't last the fourth inning in a 5–3 Kansas City win. The onrushing Royals were now just one and a half games behind the division-leading A's.

Before the final game in Kansas City, Eckersley threw off a mound for the first time since straining his right rotator cuff. He was so excited that Weinberg had to tell him to dial it down. Oakland salvaged the series finale 2–1. Stewart held the Royals to one run in seven and two-thirds innings, making him the American League's first 11-game winner and running his record to 6–0 following A's losses. He was removed after 118 pitches despite what manager La Russa called one of his best death stares of the season. Parker lashed a tie-breaking double in the eighth, and Rick Honeycutt earned his fifth save. The A's left Kansas City two and a half games up in the AL West.

Then it was off to Baltimore and a Friday night doubleheader to make up for the rainout in early May. Catcher Ron Hassey's homer and three RBIs buoyed Oakland in a 7–5 win in the first game. Davis, still hampered by his hamstring, allowed three runs in five innings but gained credit for the win. Moore was roughed up for five runs in seven innings in the second game, a 5–1 Baltimore Orioles win. Billy Beane, who had been part of the right-field committee, became the 10th A's player to go on the DL. Beane's malady was left wrist tendinitis.

The A's were staggering, with La Russa lucky to field a healthy team for nine full innings. They lost 4–2 on Saturday, June 17. Matt Young, making his first major league appearance since undergoing reconstructive elbow surgery in the fall of 1988, lasted only three and two-thirds innings. Lansford had to leave after four and a half innings when his left hamstring tightened up on him.

Oakland lost by the same score on Sunday. It was the A's first three-game losing streak since the previous August. Lansford and his hamstring and Dave Henderson and his hypothermic bat spent the day on the bench. That Eckersley threw off the mound before the game was more tease than solace. The A's needed a spark. Meanwhile, in a seemingly unrelated development, Yankees outfielder Rickey Henderson reacted to rumors that the Giants were interested in obtaining his services. "They can't trade me unless I approve it," he told New York writers. "Right now, I ain't approving any trade."

♦ ♦ ♦ ♦

It didn't happen often—maybe once a season if that. But starting Monday, June 19, the Giants and A's were scheduled to play a three-game series at home at the same time. A Bay Area baseball fanatic could, with little effort and relatively modest expense, watch two games in one day, each featuring a home team that had the best record in its league.

Well, except for Monday, when both teams played at night. The Giants beat Houston 3–2 with newly acquired Bedrosian nailing down the save in his first game with the team. They drew a crowd of 22,386. At the Coliseum even Stewart was powerless to stop the A's skid. He was chased after allowing six runs in three and two-thirds innings in a 6–4 loss to Detroit, for which 38,607 fans had purchased tickets. It was Oakland's fourth consecutive loss. On the bright side, Canseco hit off a tee for the first time since the surgery on his left hand.

The A's had a 12:15 start the following day. The announced crowd of 30,184 (the American League counted all tickets sold in their attendance figures; the National League counted only tickets used) pushed their attendance over the 1 million mark on the earliest date in team history. Those fans got their money's worth. McGwire cracked a three-run home run (his 15th) and smashed a double off the left-field wall as the A's broke their four-game losing streak with a 6–4 win. Catcher Terry Steinbach added a two-run homer as Oakland increased its division lead to two games over Kansas City.

La Russa could be intense. He could be narrowly focused. Ask him how he was doing before a game, and he would unfailingly answer, "I'll let you know in three hours." But he also understood that he was part of a much bigger team. Thoughtful and articulate (he did his radio pregame show without a professional sidekick or a script), he often was asked about big-picture issues related to baseball and sometimes sports in general. He typically gave a question as much love as it deserved. After the game he was asked about the unique daily double available to Bay Area sports fans with both local baseball teams at the head of their respective classes. "If we're still saying the same things in September, it has more meaning," he said. "Right now it means a little. But it's too early to pat any team on the back—ours or theirs. If I didn't have a wife and two kids, I'd go see [the Giants] play tonight. But I asked, and they said no."

He missed a good one. Pitching in front of a crowd of 21,074, Garrelts threw seven and one-third scoreless innings as the Giants topped Houston 4–0, boosting their lead over the Astros to three games. Giants starters had compiled a 1.43 ERA over the first 11 games of the homestand.

Wednesday was a huge day. This time the Giants played the day game. Reuschel tossed seven and one-third innings of shutout ball, throwing just 67 pitches (53 strikes), lowering his ERA to 2.04, and leaving only because he felt a twinge in his groin. Bedrosian mopped up with one and two-thirds innings of hitless relief as the Giants muted Houston 2–0, making Reuschel the majors' first 12-game winner. San Francisco pitchers had 11 shutouts (10 combined), tied for the major league lead. Moreover, it gave the Giants a 10–2 record for the homestand, the first time they'd won 10 games on a homestand since 1966. They led the Astros by four games.

The good news wasn't limited to the game itself. Dravecky threw a 15-minute batting practice session that went so well he was scheduled to accompany the team on its next road trip and continue throwing BP. From the outside looking in, it seemed he was sailing past every milestone with ease. "For the most part, that's how it seemed," Dravecky said 24 years later. "Then all of a sudden in a couple of simulated games, I hit a brick wall. I wasn't throwing as hard as I wanted to. I remember going into the outfield and playing long toss with Atlee and telling him how frustrated I was. He said, 'Let's just air this thing out. Sooner or later you've got to test it. Just let it go.' I got loose and I started airing it out and I thought, *Holy smokes, this is feeling good.* I felt like a couple of adhesions had popped. I had complete freedom in my motion. He said, 'I don't know what just happened, but you're throwing good.' I remember I went up to [pitching coach] Norm [Sherry] and said, 'I want to do a bullpen.' I wanted to do it right then and there. He said, 'No, let's wait for the appropriate time.' Gosh, from there it went really fast."

Meanwhile, the Oakland Coliseum was abuzz with remarkable news: Rickey Henderson was coming home. A's general manager Sandy Alderson sent relievers Greg Cadaret and Eric Plunk and outfielder Polonia to the Yankees for Henderson. Though just 30 years old, he was already the fourth-leading base stealer in baseball history and owned a major-league-record 36 home runs to lead off a game. There was some risk involved. Henderson was making $2.12 million in the final year of a five-year contract. He had asked the Yankees for a three-year, $8.6 million deal, which the team deemed too rich. If the A's couldn't re-sign him at season's end, he would wind up being a prohibitively expensive rent-a-player.

Even after nearly a quarter-century, La Russa remembered well when Alderson alerted him they had a chance to trade for Henderson. "I was incredulous," La Russa said. "Mostly because you're grinding with what you have. The thought of having him on our team? I said, 'Are you kidding me?' He said, 'No. I think we've got a shot.' My first 10 years in the league, I was in Chicago, and he's in Oakland. I go to Oakland; he's in New York. The most dangerous player of our generation, I mean this guy was the player that managers, coaches, teams feared the most in a close game. I told the coaching staff. [The reaction was,] 'This can't possibly be true.' And sooner rather than later we had him. There's the old axiom, which is almost always true, nobody's perfect…Then we got Rickey, and then I think we were perfect."

"When you add a player of that caliber to the mix, that's a big, big, big, big deal," Dave Stewart said. "It was a surprise to all of us. Nobody knew what was going on except for the owner, Sandy Alderson, and probably Tony. We went from a low-budget Rickey [Polonia] to the real deal." Added Eckersley in retrospect: "When we got Rickey, I was like, how did we do that? Polonia was doing his thing. You're thinking, maybe he's enough. He's a little bit wild. You couldn't guarantee what he would do. We gave away two good bullpen arms [for Henderson], and I still thought it was a steal."

An Oakland Coliseum security guard whose station was just outside the A's clubhouse, chuckled at the news. "It'll be just like when he was here last time," the guard said. "He'd show up with two minutes to spare—running."

All things considered, it was an extraordinary three-day run during which the Bay Area teams, the best each league had to offer, won five of six games; reported a combined attendance of 173,635 (the A's had 97,445; the Giants had 76,190)—more than half of what the 1979 A's had drawn in a full season; pulled off a pair of blockbuster trades; and gave Bay Area baseball fans a once-in-three-lifetimes experience.

◆ ◆ ◆ ◆

By the time Rickey Henderson's delayed flight landed at Oakland Airport, it was 3:40 in the afternoon of Thursday, June 22. The A's were hosting the Toronto Blue Jays in a twilight special at 5:10. He showed up—running—with minutes to spare. He missed the rehab sessions of disabled pitchers Eckersley and Welch. Eck looked especially sharp, with trainer Weinberg calling it the closer's "best day yet."

His return wasn't exactly the stuff of legend. He grounded out in each of his first two at-bats. He singled his third time up but was caught stealing (the ninth time he'd been nabbed in 34 tries). He popped out in the seventh and struck out swinging to end the bottom of the ninth and send the 2–2 game into extra innings. Though he reached on an infield single in the 12th, the Blue Jays' Fred McGriff had the game-winner, a two-run home run in the top of the 13th off Brian Snyder, who was called up from Tacoma, Washington, after the trade had left the A's two bodies short of a full roster.

The following afternoon La Russa hit fly balls to Canseco, who was expected to begin a rehab assignment at Single A Modesto, California, a 90-minute drive from Oakland. The manager saw flashes of the right fielder's athleticism but pronounced him far from being game ready. As for his knack of saying the wrong thing at the right time, Canseco was in midseason form. All-Star balloting figures continued to show him one of the three top vote-getters among American League outfielders despite the fact he had yet to play a game and that the All-Star Game was less than three weeks away. "If everything goes right," Canseco told reporters, "my first [major league] appearance would be in the All-Star Game. If I'm voted in, I don't want to disappoint my fans. If my hand holds up, it should be safe."

It figured that La Russa, manager of not only the A's but also the American League All-Star team, would have something to say about that. It took a few days, but he didn't disappoint. Friday night's game was a pie fight. Both starters, Oakland's Young and Toronto's Frank Wills, were knocked out after retiring just two batters. The first inning took 51 minutes. Oakland led 7–6 after the first but lost 10–8, cutting their lead over second-place Kansas City to one game. The A's were 0–2 in the Rickey 2.0 era.

Stewart rode to the rescue Saturday, improving his record to 12–3 with a four-hitter in a 7–1 A's victory. And for the second time in 1989, there was ill will between the teams. It began when Toronto starter (and Bay Area native) Dave Stieb hit McGwire with a pitch. Later in the game, reliever Steve Cummings plunked Lansford just above the left elbow, forcing the Oakland third baseman out of the game. "I didn't enjoy being scared twice," La Russa told the media afterward, "and I'm not enjoying it now."

Also on Saturday the A's announced a change in Canseco's itinerary. Instead of reporting to Modesto on Sunday, he would take batting practice in Oakland, then report to Double A Huntsville, Alabama, for his rehab.

On Sunday, June 25, four days after being acquired from the Yankees, Henderson officially showed up in Oakland. He walked twice, singled three times, stole three bases, scored twice, and drove in two runs in a 6–3 win. Davis (6–3) pitched seven innings, tying a season high. And the A's hit the road after a 4–3 homestand during which they stretched their lead from one and a half games to two and a half.

◆ ◆ ◆ ◆

As hot as the Giants were, minor league third baseman Williams was even hotter. He had 15 home runs since being demoted to Triple A Phoenix on May 1 and was leading the Pacific Coast League. Phoenix manager Gordie MacKenzie was getting used to fielding calls from out-of-town reporters asking about the Giants' wayward third baseman. "I really don't expect him to be around here much longer," MacKenzie said.

In San Diego, the Giants opened a six-game road trip on Friday, June 23, with an 8–7 win against the Padres. It gave the Giants a six-game win streak and maintained their four-game cushion over Houston. LaCoss got his first start of the season, allowing four runs in four innings. Bedrosian was better at the end of the game, earning a four-out save, his ninth. Clark homered—his 13th of the season and second in two games. Clark had another big hit Saturday with a two-run, eighth-inning triple off the Padres' closer Davis that gave San Francisco a 2–1 lead. The big blow came 13 days after Clark's walk-off homer against Davis at Candlestick Park. Clark admitted he had been sitting on a curve on that occasion. This time, the (Thinking Man's) Natural switched it up. "I knew he'd be thinking about the curveball," Clark said, "so I was looking for some kind of fastball. Thank goodness it was on the first pitch." Clark then scored on a sacrifice fly to make it 3–1, the final score.

Robinson (7–4) won his fourth consecutive start, and Bedrosian logged a one-pitch save. The Giants had won seven in a row. They finally lost on Sunday 10–7. Garrelts had a rare bad outing, getting lit up for six runs in two and two-thirds innings. Mitchell was the only bright spot for the Giants, socking an RBI double in the first inning and hitting a mammoth homer into the second deck in the third. "That's why the game took four hours," Craig said after it was mercifully over. "It took 20 minutes for Mitchell's ball to come down."

The Giants arrived in Houston the same time as tropical storm Allison. Thus their 4–3 win against the Astros was witnessed by a relatively intimate crowd of 11,616. A pair of pinch-hits turned the tide for the Giants in the seventh inning. Maldonado's double knocked in the tying run, and Ken Oberkfell's single scored the tie-breaker in a 4–3 win that restored their four-game lead in the NL West. But San Francisco turned in two duds to end the short trip. Bedrosian took his first false step as a Giant on Tuesday, June 27, serving up a go-ahead three-run home run to Craig Biggio in a 7–5 loss.

Craig held a pregame meeting with the team Wednesday during which he called the game the most important of the year. Whereupon the Giants went out and got beat 7–3, cutting their lead to two games. Mitchell wasn't even in the dugout; he was sent back to the Bay Area to have his knee examined at the Palo Alto Medical Clinic. Meanwhile, in Santa Clara the city council, replying to the stadium task force's request for a six-month extension in preparing a stadium proposal for the Giants, accused Lurie of using Santa Clara County to get a better deal in San Francisco.

The Giants concluded the month by splitting a pair of home games with the Chicago Cubs. The first, a 12–2 romp, was built upon a seven-run, second-inning rally during which Garrelts strained a hamstring while running out a triple. Garrelts had to leave the game. But the night was even more noteworthy for a baseball follies moment that occurred in the top of the sixth inning.

In 1989 Candlestick Park was similar to many parks of that era—with bullpen mounds just off the field of play. For years in San Francisco, relief pitchers and bullpen catchers sat on benches along the walls down the left- and right-field lines. That year enclosures had been built for the bullpen crew—behind the left-field fence for the visiting team and in the right-field corner for Giants personnel. They were small, cramped quarters that immediately became known as penalty boxes.

In the sixth inning of the Thursday, June 29, game and with the score 7–1 Giants, Chicago left fielder Mitch Webster grounded a base hit down the right-field line. The door to the Giants' penalty box faced toward home plate and was in the open position when Webster hit the ball. Lefferts, seated closest to the door, saw a problem developing. Webster's hit was headed his way. It was going to wind up entering the enclosure unless he did something *fast.*

Lefferts reached for the door and yanked it closed—but not before the ball rolled inside. The Giants inside the penalty box couldn't help themselves. They convulsed with laughter as an unaware Maldonado arrived on scene and began looking frantically for the baseball. Webster was awarded a ground-rule double, and ESPN had its play of the day.

◆ ◆ ◆ ◆

Before Oakland's June 26 game in Minnesota, La Russa finally addressed Canseco's fantasy of starting the All-Star Game without having played a major league game all season. "I don't think there's any doubt in my mind," said La Russa, who would, by virtue of leading his team to the pennant in 1988, pilot the American League All-Stars in Anaheim on July 11. "If he doesn't play in a major league game before that Tuesday, no. If he's ready before then and the fans speak, that's the way it goes."

Before the game Eckersley threw breaking balls for the first time since straining his rotator cuff on May 27. The A's could have used him during Monday's contest. McGwire's RBI single in the top of the ninth inning tied the game, sending it into extra innings. But Burns, Oakland's unheralded Swiss Army knife of a pitcher, served up a game-winning homer to the Twins' Kirby Puckett in the bottom of the 10th. The A's lost 4–3.

They lost again Tuesday and looked bad doing it. Reliever Gene Nelson, inheriting a 4–3 lead in the bottom of the sixth, got just one out while allowing six runs. The Twins scored eight times that inning and won in an 11–5 runaway. For the second consecutive game, center fielder Dave Henderson lost a fly ball in the Minneapolis Metrodome, a lousy baseball venue that featured a fabric ceiling that was almost the exact color of a game-ready baseball. Lansford uncharacteristically allowed a Puckett grounder to scoot between his feet. It was that kind of night.

And it was that kind of series. Frank Viola outdueled Stewart in the finale, a 2–0 Twins win. The A's, who had a major league-best 50–31 road record in 1988, had lost six in a row away from home. That Eckersley enjoyed another satisfactory side session and that Canseco was 1-for-4 in his first game at Huntsville was of small consolation.

However, the latter gave La Russa another opportunity to address the absurdity of Canseco's desire to play in the All-Star Game. "I think it's a risk," La Russa said. "It's a risk for us. It's a risk for the American League. Who wins? The fans? The big thing that he is supposed to be doing is getting ready to help us win the division."

Chapter 6

The Stars Come Out

The Chicago Cubs were in third place, four games above .500 and two and a half games off the pace with the mighty New York Mets between them and the surprising first-place Montreal Expos. The Cubs had made just one postseason appearance in the previous 43 years (in 1984) and had encored that season with finishes of fourth, fifth, sixth, and fourth. So if you weren't a dreamer or a psychic, you weren't looking at their series with the Giants with anything more than a casual interest.

And yet having split the first two games of their four-game series against Chicago at Candlestick Park, the Giants opened July by sending 40-year-old Rick Reuschel against the Cubs' promising 23-year-old right-hander, Greg Maddux. The meeting of the ages resulted in a terrific pitchers duel. Reuschel threw his first complete game of the season, allowing three runs and striking out nine. For his trouble he was charged with his first loss since April 28, and his record fell to 12–3.

Maddux allowed two runs in seven and two-thirds innings and was replaced in the bottom of the eighth inning by Mitch Williams with two out, runners at the corners, and Will Clark striding to the plate. Twice before in 1989 the two men had squared off in late-game situations, and both times the Cubs were leading by a run with the Giants' tying run at third base. Both times Clark had found a way to get a run home (albeit once on an error). This time Williams threw two fastballs, and Clark fouled off both. On the 0–2 pitch, Williams threw a curve. Clark popped it to shortstop, and the rally died. Williams navigated the ninth inning to secure a 3–2 Cubs win and earn his 20th save, one off the National League lead. Clark's remarks to reporters after the game, however, indicated he was building a mental book on Williams. "He hides the ball real well with his motion," Clark said, "kind of slips it in on you. He's just funky. Still I had three good hacks to beat him."

Save for a pinch-hit appearance in which he walked, Kevin Mitchell sat out Saturday's game with a sore left knee. An MRI showed no ligament damage. Mitchell was back in the lineup Sunday, but the Giants quickly fell behind 3–0. Not only was Mike LaCoss pulled after allowing three runs on eight hits in three and one-third innings, but he was booed to the dugout. Chicago starter Rick Sutcliffe had the Giants down 3–1 in the bottom of the eighth. But the Giants' dynamic duo came to the rescue. First, Clark singled home a run to make it a 3–2. Then Mitchell muscled Sutcliffe's first pitch over the right-field fence, giving the Giants the lead and a 4–3 win.

◆ ◆ ◆ ◆

Dave Stewart made it four wins in a row for the A's on the first game of a seven-game homestand on Monday, July 3, throwing eight scoreless innings in a 1–0 win against the Kansas City Royals. Stewart retired 20 batters in a row at one point and became the American League's first 13-game winner. Still rallying from his slow start, Dave Parker drove in the game's only run off tough-luck loser Mark Gubicza. Relievers Todd Burns and Rick Honeycutt combined to retire all three batters they faced.

As far as the A's top reliever, his glacial recovery had seemed dead in the water. "I hate to say this," Dennis Eckersley told reporters after a disheartening batting practice session on July 1, "but it hurts." The official diagnosis was a strained right shoulder. But pitchers' arms can sometimes be maddeningly difficult to diagnose. A fitness fanatic with an ever present tan, flowing black hair, and a twinkle in his eye, Eck looked like he was 25. But he was 34, and his right arm had logged 3,160 professional innings (not including spring training). If no one else was articulating their darkest fears, Eckersley was thinking them.

On the afternoon of the Fourth of July, Eckersley climbed atop the pitcher's mound at the Oakland Coliseum and began to warm up. The crowd consisted of maybe a couple dozen intent onlookers. It included A's manager Tony La Russa, general manager Sandy Alderson, pitching coach Dave Duncan, and coaches Tommie Reynolds and Merv Rettenmund. It wasn't a real game. In Eckersley's mind it might have been bigger.

Sidelined since May 27 with strained muscles around his rotator cuff, Eckersley had been slowly trying to strengthen his shoulder with bullpen sessions. His last one had gone particularly poorly. He had felt pain. Then he felt doubts. Now hours before the regularly scheduled home game against Kansas City, Eckersley would throw a simulated game against teammates Ron Hassey, Lance Blankenship, and Jamie Quirk. His pitch count was set at 35.

To everyone's relief, it went well. There was no pain. No one was saying he was ready to come off the disabled list. Duncan wouldn't even put a timetable on his return. But Eckersley was buoyant. "After what I felt Saturday, I felt great today," he said. "I wish I was sharper than I am, but I guess I should just be happy that I feel good...I've always complained that the stress [of relieving] is really killing me. Now I crave it."

Twenty-four years later, Eckersley asked: "I said that? I guess that's like anytime something is taken away from you. You start to miss it. I knew there was something wrong. I strengthened it and made it through the season. But my arm wasn't the same. I wasn't throwing very well, but I got them out. At the end of season when we went to the White House, I couldn't even turn the radio dial. Believe me, I wasn't as good as I could have been. Thank God we won."

There were fireworks in the main event. Kansas City clubbed the A's 10–1. Bo Jackson hit a pair of home runs, giving him 20 to go with 20 stolen bases 81 games into the 162-game season. It was possible Jose Canseco wouldn't be the only Mr. 40–40 for long.

In the summer of 1989, Jackson seemed capable of anything. He won the 1985 Heisman Trophy as a tailback at Auburn and then decided he wanted to play baseball. He was a September call-up for the Royals in 1986, hitting .207 and striking out 34 times in 82 at-bats. He stuck for a full season in 1987, improving incrementally. He was still a work in progress as a baseball player, striking out too much and struggling to translate his staggering athleticism to the grand old game. It was after that season that Jackson decided to play for the NFL's Oakland Raiders as a "hobby."

For the next four years he was a physical phenomenon. Neither words nor numbers can adequately describe him. He could demolish bombastic linebacker Brian Bosworth at the goal line. He could throw out speedster Harold Reynolds at the plate with a hissing strike from the shadow of the center-field wall. He could gain 950 yards while playing just 11 games of a 16-game NFL season. He could run up and down an outfield wall after making a sprinting catch.

He began putting it all together in the 1989 baseball season. He was hitting for power, knocking in runs, and stealing bases. Yes, he would lead the majors with 172 strikeouts and he would commit eight errors, a big number for an outfielder. But his impact plays—the stunning throws, the awesome power, the blinding speed— influenced the winning and losing of games in a way that defied quantification. He was on a pace to equal Canseco's groundbreaking 40–40 season. American League West rivals had no choice but to take him, and the Royals, seriously.

The Royals outslugged the A's again on Wednesday 12–9, knocking them out of first place, despite Mark McGwire's 100th career home run and five RBIs. McGwire, who snapped a streak of 45 consecutive at-bats without a dinger, still became the second fastest to 100 home runs in major league history in terms of at-bats. Only Ralph Kiner surpassed him. Secondary to the game, if only slightly, final All-Star voting totals were announced, and three A's position players had made the team—McGwire, catcher Terry Steinbach, and, of course, Canseco.

The debate flared anew. Canseco pushed back against La Russa's assertion that it would be more in line with Canseco's professional mission to forgo the All-Star Game and prepare for the second half of the season. "I don't think it's in Tony's jurisdiction to decide whether or not I play in the All-Star Game," Canseco told reporters. Alderson backed his manager with a more pragmatic assessment. "Will [Canseco] be activated on this homestand?" he asked rhetorically. "Unlikely. If he's not activated for the homestand, will he be activated to allow him to play in the All-Star Game? No."

The following day the A's finally defeated the Royals to retake the division lead from the California Angels. Mike Moore (11–5) struck out 12 in seven shutout innings during the 3–1 victory. He and Stewart were added to the AL All-Star team. It was the first appointment for each, and an overdue honor for Stewart, who had won 20 games in 1987 and 21 in '88. At the time Stewart declared happily, "It's about time, ain't it? I don't care if I pitch or not." More than 24 years later, Stewart denied he spent much time dwelling on how underappreciated he seemed to be.

"I didn't think about it, no," he said. "I actually never thought about it. I didn't get picked for the All-Star Game because I pitched on the Sundays before the game. That's what Tony [La Russa] always told me. I took it for that. Obviously I should have made at least four years, the years I won 20. The Cy Young, after the first year, I think there was somebody who won it, maybe [Frank] Viola, who didn't win as many games as me. After a while that just became a joke as far as I was concerned. I can't honestly say that I started the year saying I'd win a Cy Young. Every year I came into it thinking, *I'm going to try to pitch as many innings as I can, and if I pitch enough innings, I have a chance to win 20.* I knew if I did that, we'd have a pretty good chance to be someplace close to the playoffs. That's all you ask."

As for his first All-Star Game? "I had a good time," he said. "I really did. I don't know why it worked out the way it did in 1989. I don't know how to put it. Some things you expect. Some things you don't expect. The only things I expected were the things I was capable of controlling—innings pitched and wins."

The biggest All-Star decision on Thursday was issued by the American League. Canseco would not play. On a more practical level, Eckersley threw 40 pitches before the game. "Things are looking up," he told reporters afterward. There were three games (one more series) until the All-Star break. The A's led the division by a half-game over the Angels. They were closing in on a feat that fell somewhere between unlikely and unthinkable. Having lost Canseco, McGwire, Gene Nelson, Walt Weiss, Bob Welch, Storm Davis, and Eckersley to disabling injuries and having weathered sluggish starts from Dave Henderson and Parker, they still had a chance to lead the AL West at the break.

La Russa had come to spring training with a plan. He wanted to combat any complacency that might have set in after the A's 104-win season in 1988. Maybe the stunning World Series loss to the Dodgers in '88 and the wave of injuries in '89 had been his ally in that regard. He was on the lookout for what he called "mental comfort." Could the unwanted adversity have helped him keep that scourge out of the A's clubhouse? "Absolutely," Eckersley said. "Looking back now—that's what Tony was concerned about. Psychologically, Tony was always pushing buttons, getting ahead of everything."

Then three games before the All-Star Game that La Russa would manage, the A's stumbled. Just a bit, but enough to make you wonder if all that drama and all that grinding through one close game after another was catching up to them. On Friday, July 7, Davis allowed six runs in eight innings and committed a two-base throwing error in a 6–3 loss to the Texas Rangers. The defeat knocked Oakland out of first place.

On Saturday Stewart threw eight strong innings and left with a 4–2 lead. But Burns gave up a pair of runs in the top of the ninth, Matt Young allowed two batters to reach in the 10th, and Nelson served up the run-scoring single that gave Texas a 5–4 win. It was the sixth blown save in 19 opportunities by the Oakland bullpen since Eckersley's injury. Coupled with the Angels' win over the Minnesota Twins, it dropped the A's to one and a half games out of first.

The A's managed to launch into the All-Star break on a positive note, a 7–1 win that kept them in second place, one and a half games out of first. Welch allowed a single unearned run in six and one-third innings to win his 10th game. Honeycutt notched his 11th save. McGwire nailed his 17th home run. Eckersley threw for 40 minutes on the side and reported no pain. And La Russa signed a three-year contract extension through 1992. "I don't think there's a better job than this in baseball," he said.

◆ ◆ ◆ ◆

The first half of the season was winding down, but Mitchell was not. The Giants opened a road trip in Pittsburgh on July 4, and after four innings, the score was tied 1–1. Batting with two out and no one on in the fifth, Mitchell changed that in a hurry, sending an 0–2 pitch from Randy Kramer far over the center-field fence in Three Rivers Stadium. The blast was estimated at 436 feet. Like many of his home runs in 1989, it seemed a shame it should only count for one run.

It seemed even more of a shame when San Francisco starter Don Robinson coughed up four runs in the bottom of the inning, decisive runs in the Pirates' 5–3 win. For all he'd done since joining the Giants on August 31, 1987—helping clinch a division title and getting to within one win of the World Series in 1987; going 10–5 with six saves and a 2.45 ERA as almost every other Giants pitcher succumbed to some kind of injury in 1988; holding down a spot in the rotation for a team leading its division by two and a half games in 1989—there was one thing Robinson hadn't done well: pitch well against his former team.

He'd won a game against them in relief in 1988 but had allowed two runs in one and one-third innings while doing so. The 1989 season was shaping up as a disaster when it came to pitching against the team with which he'd spent his first 13½ professional seasons. Robinson was 0–3 with an 11.25 ERA against the Pirates and 7–3 with a 2.21 ERA against everyone else. "I want to beat these guys pretty bad," he said after the game. "I can't seem to go five innings against them."

Mitchell, though, had no problem beating up on the Bucs. He was hit by a pitch from Bob Walk in his first at-bat the following day. He later admitted he thought about paying a visit to the mound. "I think the old me would have," he said. Instead he took his frustrations out on Walk in a more practical way, belting his 28th home run of the season. The Giants triumphed 6–4 with Trevor Wilson holding the Pirates to one run on two hits in seven innings to earn his first major league win. The only downer on the day was that Dave Dravecky's scheduled simulated game was rained out.

The National League filled out its All-Star roster on Thursday, July 6. Reuschel was the only Giant added. He joined Mitchell and Clark, who were voted in by the fans. It was presumed Reuschel would show up for the game in Anaheim; he'd skipped the 1988 All-Star Game to get married.

Two men who could conceivably have merited consideration lifted the Giants to a 2–1 win against the Pirates that day. Robby Thompson (.277, league-leading 59 runs) tied the game with a home run in the eighth inning, and Brett Butler (.297, 49 runs, 15 stolen bases) won it with a home run in the 10th. On the medical front, Dravecky traveled to Cleveland to have his arm examined. No new tumor was detected. His improbable comeback was still on track.

From Pittsburgh the Giants traveled to St. Louis. The change of scenery mattered not to Mitchell. He pounded his 29th home run on Friday, July 7, in a 6–4 loss. He hammered two more in an 8–5 victory on Saturday, giving him 31 and making him just the 12th player in the All-Star Game era to surpass 30 before the break. His three RBIs gave him 80, tying his career high and giving him 15 more than any other major leaguer. Having rejoined the team, Dravecky finally logged a simulated game, throwing 60 pitches.

The final game of the first half was nobody's idea of fun. The brutal St. Louis heat was magnified by the first-generation artificial turf in Busch Stadium. A thermometer placed on the field registered 110 degrees. The Giants trailed 2–0 when "Goose" Gossage came in to pitch the bottom of the sixth. To this point he had been everything the Giants could reasonably have hoped for when they claimed him off waivers in the season's second week. He was not the fearsome, awe-inspiring

Goose of his prime, but he was effective with a 2–1 record, three saves, a 1.64 ERA, and 19 strikeouts in 33 innings. But he melted down on that sweltering day along the Mississippi River, facing five batters, giving up two doubles, two singles, and walking opposing pitcher Joe Magrane on four pitches. He was charged with four runs. The Giants tried to fight back but fell 6–4. They hit the break in first place, two games up on Houston.

◆ ◆ ◆ ◆

Mitchell was swarmed by reporters at the All-Star workout in Anaheim the day before the game. His 31 home runs and 80 RBIs had him on a historic pace, which if maintained would give him 58 homers (a National League record) and 151 RBIs (the most in the majors since 1962). He was a new face with an amazing story, a grandmother who loved him like a son and whom he adored and respected. The national media couldn't get enough of him.

McGwire watched the commotion from a distance, thinking, *Better you than me.* Two years prior to the 1987 All-Star Game in Oakland, the fresh face and prodigious home total belonged to Big Mac. Just a rookie, he was laying waste to AL pitching, ducking national attention almost as relentlessly as he was attracting it. The day he was named to the AL team that summer, a group of local reporters caught up with him in the A's clubhouse before a game. Whatever he might have been feeling inside, his message to the media was subdued. "I don't know if I'm ready for all this," he said with a nervous laugh.

Two years later, he was certain he hadn't been. "To tell you the truth," he said the day before the 1989 All-Star Game, "I didn't have time to have fun in '87. It's very much suffocating. Your life is never the same after that. Expectations are so great it's unbelievable. I'd just tell [Mitchell], don't let people take your time. Try to keep the interviews to a minimum."

McGwire had the physical qualities of a home-run champion—he finished 1987 with 49, 11 more than the previous rookie record—but the personality of someone who preferred to let his work speak for itself. It was simply the way he was wired. Mitchell reveled in the attention. He was a people person and suddenly was surrounded by hundreds of people with cameras and notebooks wanting to know all about him. "There are a lot of distractions in the world," Mitchell said. "This is not that much of a distraction. The reporters have been good to me, and I have no problem with it. The game's not pressure. I've been through a lot of pressure. This is not pressure at all."

When the national media was done talking with Mitchell, they sought out other players to talk about Mitchell. Surprisingly, it was Reuschel, a man of few words, who uncorked the quote of the day. "Well," Big Daddy said, "you want to make sure you're not sitting in the john when he comes up."

La Russa had some decisions to make. The first was to convince Canseco, who had planned to come to Anaheim and work out, that he would be better off doing his work in Oakland. Then it was onto the AL's batting order. It can be tricky to build an All-Star lineup when most of the players bat third or fourth on their own team. La Russa decided it would be a good idea to start the game off with a (potential) bang. He made Jackson the leadoff hitter.

While La Russa could be accused of being unconventional, he could not be accused of playing favorites where the batting order was concerned. When it came to the two Athletics in the starting lineup, he penciled in McGwire eighth and Steinbach ninth. "Thanks a lot," McGwire said, jokingly. "The last time I batted eighth I might have been five." La Russa dished it right back, "Hey, they're lucky they're not batting 10th and 11th."

However, La Russa's choice for starting pitcher, Stewart, did draw some charges of favoritism. Rangers pitcher Nolan Ryan was having a terrific season by any standard. At 42, he was 10–4 with a 2.91 ERA and 148 strikeouts in 126⅔ innings. Stewart was 13–4 with a 3.24 ERA. What's more, Ryan was a fan favorite in Anaheim, where he had pitched eight seasons for the Angels, setting a major league record with 383 strikeouts in 1973 and throwing four no-hitters. That made him the sentimental choice to start. La Russa made what he considered the logical choice.

Dodgers manager Tommy Lasorda selected Reuschel to start for the National League. There was a nice symmetry to the matchup of starting pitchers. Both had been released—Reuschel by the Yankees in 1983 and Stewart by the Phillies in 1986. Both had enjoyed their best seasons after resurrecting their careers. And, of course, both called the Bay Area home. The All-Star Game pitching matchup would be a battle of the Bay—at least for one inning.

Stewart struggled in the top of the first inning. He served up a single to leadoff batter Ozzie Smith, but that was remedied quickly enough when Smith was caught stealing with Tony Gwynn at the plate. Gwynn, however, worked a walk and advanced to second on Clark's ground out. Then it was Mitchell time. Mitchell singled to center field to score Gwynn for a 1–0 lead. After moving to second on a walk to Eric Davis, Mitchell scored on Howard Johnson's base hit. Stewart managed to wiggle out of the inning with no further damage, but the American League returned to their dugout down 2–0.

On Monday, Reuschel had observed during a group interview that what he did best—throw low fastballs—played to the strength of many of the American League hitters. "So it should be interesting," he said.

Jackson was first up and took a fastball low for ball one. In the NBC broadcast booth, Vin Scully was trying to have a nice conversation with Ronald Reagan. The former president was talking about Jackson's remarkable "hobby" of playing pro football when Reuschel threw another low fastball. Jackson golfed it on a searing low arc far beyond the center-field fence. "He's remarkable," Scully said, interrupting the 40th president of the United States, "and look at that one! Bo Jackson says hello."

The buzz had barely subsided when the next batter, Wade Boggs, tagged another Reuschel pitch for a more pedestrian home run to left-center field. On two swings, the American League had tied the game. Reuschel settled down, inducing four ground balls, one of which scooted through the infield for a single, and escaped further damage.

And that was it for the Bay Area's best starting pitchers, who left with similar 1-2-3 outings—one inning, two runs, three hits. It was a much quieter evening for the other A's and Giants. McGwire and Steinbach each went 1-for-3. Moore threw a scoreless inning. Mitchell had two hits, and Clark went 0-for-2.

Jackson turned the game into his own highlight reel with the booming home run; a running catch in left field as his hat flew off; outrunning the relay on what could have been an inning-ending double-play grounder, allowing a run to score; stealing second base and continuing to third when the throw went into center field; and lining a single to center for his second hit of the game. The American League won 5–3 for its first back-to-back All-Star triumphs since Dwight Eisenhower was president. Ryan ultimately got the moment in the spotlight that Anaheim fans had hoped for, earning the win with two scoreless innings that featured three strikeouts. Jackson, the first player since Willie Mays in 1960 to homer and steal a base in the same All-Star Game, deservedly earned MVP honors.

While Jackson was demonstrating his jaw-dropping combination of speed and power on All-Star Tuesday, Canseco was doing the same in the Bay Area. Only Canseco was doing it from inside his new Porsche. Traveling an estimated

65 miles per hour on rural, winding Crow Canyon Road in Contra Costa County, Canseco was pulled over and ticketed by a California Highway Patrol officer. It was the second time he had been pulled over in the Porsche, which still had its paper license plates. He also was charged with not having his driver's license, not having proof of insurance, and not wearing a seat belt. He in turn accused the "lady police officer" of having "an attitude problem." "I'm impervious to it now," Alderson told the *San Jose Mercury News*. "When you drive a car like that, you don't even have to be speeding to get stopped."

Canseco took batting practice at the Coliseum on Wednesday, July 12, the day after the All-Star Game. He was ready to return. So was Eckersley. La Russa was anxious for the return of his stalwarts so he could field a complete team. That included newcomer Rickey Henderson, who had been fabulous since rejoining the A's, batting .413 and scoring 22 runs in 17 games. But Oakland had gone 8–9 during that stretch.

The A's opened the second half in Toronto on Thursday, July 13, under the retractable roof of the major league's newest stadium, the SkyDome. Canseco, batting sixth, played as if he hadn't missed a day. He singled, homered, stole a base, scored twice, and knocked in three runs as the A's romped 11–7. Even though it wasn't a save situation, La Russa had Eckersley pitch the ninth. "It's not like we forgot how good [Canseco] is," La Russa told reporters after the game, "but it's nice to be reminded. When you talk about Jose and you talk about Eck, you're talking about superstars. They're not like the rest of us."

Welch was off his game on Friday, giving up four runs, eight hits, and issuing five walks in seven innings as the Blue Jays won 4–1. The teams resumed their unpleasantries in the fifth inning when Welch hit the incendiary George Bell in the biceps with a pitch. It was the eighth hit batsmen in 10 games between the teams. Bell stared down the A's dugout and barked at Welch. Parker, a mountain of a man at 6'5" and 230 pounds, sauntered onto the field as what he termed a "peacemaker." Toronto won again Saturday despite Canseco's second home run in three games. But the A's gained a series split Sunday with a 6–2 victory. Steinbach hit his second career grand slam in support of Moore (12–5), who allowed a single unearned run in six innings.

Back in the states, the head of the California Police Chiefs Association felt compelled to write an open letter to Canseco that somehow wound up in the hands of multiple news organizations. "You have blamed your cars, the police, and your celebrity status," the letter read. "You are apparently a victim in your own mind."

Monday, July 17, found the A's in Detroit, where they lost on Chet Lemon's game-winning single off Honeycutt in the bottom of the ninth inning. But they actually gained ground in the division race by virtue of the Angels' doubleheader loss in Toronto. Oakland was just .001 out of first place. Canseco was hitless in the game and was 1-for-15 since his first game back. "My shoulder's tired, my arm's tired, both wrists are tired," he said to writers. "Your mind says do this, your body says, 'no.'"

Oakland rebounded to win Tuesday with Parker belting a three-run homer. It was the 299th home run of his career and pushed him past 1,300 career RBIs. By that point it was apparent that Parker would not equal the career numbers and achievements of Willie Stargell, the man to whom he was compared when he joined the Pirates in 1973. But the guy who inspired the nickname "Cobra" had little for which to apologize.

In 11 years with Pittsburgh, Parker helped the Bucs to the 1979 World Series title, was voted MVP in 1978, played in four All-Star Games, and won three Gold Gloves and two batting titles. He was MVP of the 1979 All-Star Game in which he had a hit, knocked in a run, and made two phenomenal throws from right field in a 7–6 National League victory.

He gained notoriety when he testified at the infamous Pittsburgh drug trials in 1985 that he had purchased cocaine. ("I took responsibility for my participation in that," he told the *Pittsburgh Tribune-Review* in 2009.) He began rehabilitating his character after signing as a free agent with his hometown Cincinnati Reds before the 1984 season. In four years in Cincinnati, he averaged 27 homers and 108 RBIs with two top five finishes in the MVP voting.

The A's acquired him in a trade after the 1987 season. He was okay in 1988—12 homers and 55 RBIs in 101 games. He got off to a poor start in 1989, hitting .196 through May 11. He woke up quickly. Between his low point on May 11 and his 299th home run on July 18, he hit .308 with 12 home runs and 45 RBIs in 56 games. That was good news for the A's.

That same day also brought horrible news. Donnie Moore, the Angels' relief pitcher who gave up Dave Henderson's stunning home run in the 1986 playoffs, had argued with his wife at their Anaheim home, shot her three times (she survived), and then killed himself. Moore's agent, Dave Pinter, told reporters his client "could not live with himself after Henderson hit the home run. He kept blaming himself."

It appeared there were other factors. There were reports that Moore and his wife had marital and financial problems. Injuries had robbed Moore of his effectiveness, and he was released twice in a 10-month period, by the Angels in August 1988 and by the Triple A Omaha Royals on June 12, 1989.

Oakland's Wednesday, July 19, game was rained out in Detroit. Reporters looking for a story sought out Dave Henderson. "Baseball's not life and death," he told writers. "I wish I could have told [Moore] that before. There's a connection, of course. It's a sad moment."

♦ ♦ ♦ ♦

Over the course of a baseball season, certain statistical oddities occur that tickle the brain. The Giants opened the second half on Thursday, July 13, by taking a 3–2 decision against the Pirates on Clark's game-winning single in the bottom of the 13th inning. Robinson finally held his own against his former team, allowing two runs in six and two-thirds innings. But the star of the game was rookie reliever Jeff Brantley, who threw four shutout innings to get the win. Not only did it boost his record to 5–0, it also meant he had received credit for five of the Giants' past six victories. Of course, there was a flip side to that brain tickler. In the past 15 games, only one Giants starter, rookie Wilson, had received credit for a win.

Not even All-Star starter Reuschel could buck that trend. He was roughed up for five runs in five innings in a 7–4 loss Friday, making him 0–4 against his (and Robinson's) former team since being traded to the Giants. It was later learned that Reuschel had tweaked his groin to the extent that he might miss a start or two. That news took some of the sparkle off two happier developments. Mitchell hit his 32nd home run, and the Giants surpassed the 1 million mark in attendance on their 44th home date.

It took erstwhile closer LaCoss to restore some polish to the rotation. He pitched six strong innings in an 8–3 win Saturday. Fresh off the disabled list, Scott Garrelts followed up with six dominant innings Sunday, allowing an unearned run on two hits in a 3–1 victory. San Francisco led the Houston Astros by three games in the National League West.

The St. Louis Cardinals followed the Pirates into Candlestick and never had much of a chance. They surged to a 4–0 lead after the first inning of the first game of the series, but the Giants roared back with seven runs in the second with three scoring on Thompson's bases-loaded triple. Even without Mitchell, who sat after taking a cortisone shot for his inflamed lower back, the Giants won 8–4. There was an 8–2 win in San Francisco that day as well, as the board of supervisors endorsed a plan for a downtown baseball stadium.

Before Tuesday night's contest, Dravecky threw 100 pitches in a simulated game. It was almost impossible at that point not to regard his comeback as an inevitability, the feel-good moment of the summer. Every milestone he passed thumbed its nose at logic. It wasn't supposed to be that easy. Dravecky didn't seem as good as new. He seemed better.

The Giants beat the Cardinals 7–3 on Tuesday on the strength of another three-run triple, a wind-tortured fly ball off the bat of Kirt Manwaring. Mitchell sat again, but who needed him when they had the power of Roger Craig's positive thinking? The Giants were now 33–15 in maligned Candlestick Park, the best home record in the league.

On Wednesday Mitchell sat again, and the Giants won again, completing a sweep, running their win streak to five games and extending their lead over the second-place Astros to four and a half games. Candy Maldonado homered and had three RBIs, and Brantley picked up for the ineffective Wilson and gained his sixth win. Wilson, another of the Giants' talented young pitchers who tended to think a little too much, brooded after the game. "You guys try to figure me out," he told reporters, "and I can't even do it."

♦ ♦ ♦ ♦

To call the Baltimore Orioles the surprise team of 1989 would have been a criminal understatement. The O's opened the 1988 season with 21 consecutive losses. They were so bad they became a national fascination. They fired manager Cal Ripken Sr. six games into the streak, replacing him with Frank Robinson, who presided over 15 additional defeats.

They were no basket of fruit even after they broke into the win column for the first time with a 9–0 victory against the White Sox in Chicago. Subtract their grotesque start, and they were still 32 games under .500 for the season. Even the most charitable predictions regarding the 1989 Orioles had them doubling, perhaps even tripling their April 1988 total of one win.

A week into the season's second half, Baltimore led the AL East by seven and a half games over the New York Yankees. Yes, it helped that no other team in the division had a winning record. But first place is first place, no matter how you do the math. In other words, the Orioles were nobody's pushover. Then they came to Oakland, where the A's pushed them around.

Stewart won the opener of a four-game series on Thursday, July 20, throwing seven effective innings. Eckersley pitched a 1-2-3 ninth inning with two strikeouts. Canseco had three hits, and the A's won 5–2. "Tonight," third baseman Carney Lansford said, "it felt like last year's team." It was a theme that would carry throughout the weekend.

The A's trailed the Friday night game 2–1 in the bottom of the ninth, but Dave Henderson scored on a wild pitch, and Rickey Henderson singled home the game-winning run as the A's triumphed 3–2. Moore improved to 13–5 with a 143-pitch complete game. It was Welch's turn Saturday. He earned his 11th win, allowing one run in seven innings as the A's triumphed 3–1. Canseco homered for the second consecutive game, and Eckersley worked a spotless ninth. La Russa won his 288th game as A's manager, tying Dick Williams for the team's Oakland record. "It seems like some pieces are falling into place," he said after the game.

The A's completed a sweep on Sunday, winning a 3–2 nail-biter. Davis started and won, Eckersley logged his 17th save, and Canseco homered into the second deck in left field—no pedestrian feat in the spacious Coliseum. It was Oakland's fifth consecutive win. Yet the streak had not drawn the A's any closer to the division-leading Angels, who maintained their percentage points lead by sweeping the Detroit Tigers in Anaheim. As it happened, the Angels were headed for Oakland for games Monday, Tuesday, and Wednesday. "It's not just another series," Eckersley said.

As it turned out, the A's fared better against the AL East leader than the AL West leader. Nelson entered a 3–3 tie in the Monday night, July 24, game but served up solo home runs to Chili Davis and Jack Howell in a 5–4 loss. The A's had nine hits and drew four walks but grounded into double plays in each of the first four innings. The A's had by then hit into 108 double plays, the most in the majors. There were no ifs and buts in the Tuesday night game, which was witnessed by the A's fourth consecutive sellout crowd (an Oakland record). Chuck Finley and reliever Greg Minton combined on a six-hit shutout to outduel Stewart in a 4–0 Angels victory. It gave California a seven-game win streak and a two-game lead.

The A's salvaged the series finale on Wednesday, thanks to Dave Henderson. Hendu had three hits, drove in two runs, and crashed into the wall catching Brian Downing's two-out, bases-loaded drive to preserve a 5–4 lead in the top of the seventh inning. It was the kind of game that underscored that the A's—while a team of stars—were also an ensemble of savvy and accomplished veterans, any one of whom could take over a ballgame.

On the team's off day, two of those veterans made news. Rickey Henderson, whose contract was up at the end of year, conceded to reporters: "I might take less and just stay here. My agent doesn't like to hear that." Henderson had a .369 average with 32 runs, 18 RBIs, and 16 stolen bases in 30 games since joining the A's. He was a superstar outlier, so gifted and prized that he could set the top of the market for baseball contracts.

The same day Welch and his wife welcomed their first child, son Dillon Robert. Within hours Welch's mother passed away after a long illness. One day after his son's birth and hours after his mother's death, Welch stood alone on the Coliseum pitcher's mound in the thick of a divisional race, the urgency of which must have been difficult for him to appreciate. Nonetheless, he contributed seven good innings in a game the A's won 8–7 against the Seattle Mariners in 11 innings. Welch left the game with a 6–3 lead but was denied a win when Eckersley surrendered a tying two-run homer to Darnell Coles in the eighth inning. "There's no justice," La Russa said afterward. "This game is heartless."

Veteran baseball observers have noted that the best baseball team in the modern (post-1900) era lost 36 games, and that the worst team won 36 games. Thus, the observation that there are 72 games during a season where the outcome is almost preordained. Oakland's Saturday, July 29, game was one of those. Seattle won 14–6, and Davis was driven from the game after one-third of an inning and charged with seven runs. A's pitchers walked 13 batters, tying a franchise record. Rickey Henderson scored four runs and tied a team record with five stolen bases.

Stewart restored order Sunday, becoming the first AL pitcher to 15 wins as the A's won 5–3. Eckersley converted a four-out save, his 18th. The win pulled the A's to within one and a half games of the Angels, a deficit they closed to a half-game on Monday night with a 3–2 win against the visiting White Sox. That game was the antithesis of the 72-game preordained-outcome model. Oakland trailed 2–1 entering the bottom of the ninth. Facing White Sox closer Bobby Thigpen,

Steinbach walked on four pitches. Then on an 0–1 pitch, Tony Phillips clubbed a game-winning home run to give the A's a stunning victory.

Weiss came off the DL to return to the lineup (Glenn Hubbard was released to make room on the roster), and the A's were finally whole with no players on the disabled list. Moore improved to 14–5 with his second complete game in his last three starts. But the story was Phillips' walk-off blast on a night when the Angels blew a 5–0 lead and lost to Seattle. "It jolted us," La Russa said. "There's a lot of juice in that clubhouse today."

◆ ◆ ◆ ◆

The Giants' five-game win streak died hard at Wrigley Field on Thursday, July 20, and it died ugly. LaCoss figured to be a bright spot, throwing seven shutout innings to start the game, but he had to leave with shoulder stiffness. Craig turned to closer Steve Bedrosian to protect a 3–0 lead over the final two innings. Bedrosian pitched a scoreless eighth but allowed three runs in the ninth, blowing the save and sending the game into extra innings. In the 11th inning, rookie reliever Randy McCament gave up a walk-off double to Cubs pitcher Les Lancaster, a career .071 hitter.

Garrelts evened the series on Friday with another impressive outing, giving up three runs (one earned) in seven and two-thirds innings. His 2.52 ERA was 10th in the National League. Craig had an observation: "When he starts, he pitches," he said. "When he relieves, he throws."

In Phoenix, Matt Williams hit yet another home run, giving him 25 in the 13 weeks since he had been sent down. General manager Al Rosen and vice president of baseball operations Bob Kennedy had traveled to see Williams play in person, but there didn't appear to be any urgency to bring him back to the majors.

The weekend was a washout for the Giants, as they lost 5–2 on Saturday and 9–5 on Sunday. In particular they had trouble with Chicago's second-year first baseman Mark Grace, who went 7-for-16 in the series and finished the season hitting .386 against San Francisco with 12 RBIs in 12 games. The Giants had lost three games off their lead while in Chicago. Suddenly, there was urgency. After Sunday's loss they recalled Williams, who left Phoenix after hitting 26 home runs in 76 games. "This might be a good shot in the arm for us," Craig told reporters.

Speaking of which, Dravecky made his first rehab start in a seven-inning game for Single A San Jose and threw a shutout. He cautioned reporters who had made a special trip to cover the game, "This does not mean I will pitch in the big leagues.

But it's a giant step toward that goal." And in a transaction that would take on added meaning in due time, the Blue Jays released former Giants catcher Bob Brenly.

From Chicago the Giants headed for Atlanta, where Reuschel and three relievers stopped the bleeding, combining to blank the Braves 2–0. The only runs were supplied courtesy of Mitchell's 33rd home run. LaCoss' second consecutive strong start helped the Giants to a 5–4 win Tuesday, allowing them to gain a game on Houston.

But the Giants lost Wednesday when Jose Uribe's error opened the door for a three-run homer by Giants nemesis Dale Murphy that erased a 3–0 San Francisco lead. The Giants edged back ahead 4–3, but Bedrosian had another rough outing, allowing two runs that handed the Braves a 5–4 win. Murphy really went off Thursday, hitting two three-run homers in the sixth inning, part of a 10-run rally that gave Atlanta a 10–1 victory. Murphy was a fabulous player, a back-to-back MVP winner, a seven-time All-Star. But he was otherworldly against the Giants. His homers in the series finale were the 52nd and 53rd of his career against San Francisco since his major league debut on September 13, 1976—15 more than any other Giants opponent over that time.

While his team was being battered by the Braves, Giants owner Bob Lurie, appearing at a news conference, announced he had signed a memorandum of agreement with San Francisco mayor Art Agnos and Spectacor Management to build a $115 million stadium at Second and King Streets in San Francisco, pending voter approval in November. In doing so Lurie passed on a proposal from a South Bay task force for a site near the Great America amusement park in Santa Clara, near where the San Francisco 49ers had just moved into a new training facility. Reporters quizzed Lurie about parking and traffic—legitimate questions regarding that part of town—and weather, a legitimate question regarding any site in San Francisco. "If I thought the weather was bad, the parking was bad, and the traffic was bad," Lurie said, "I wouldn't be standing here telling you how elated I am."

When it opened in 1965, the Astrodome elated the people of Houston. The world's first enclosed baseball/football stadium, it was billed as the Eighth Wonder of the World. Nearly a quarter-century later, it was regarded as a dark, cavernous expanse of dead air where home runs went to die. The Giants opened their series with the Astros there with a 3–2 win on Friday, July 28. Pitching with a brace designed to protect a stretched ligament in his right knee, Robinson threw a seven-hitter for just the fifth complete game by a San Francisco pitcher. Clark broke a 2–2 tie with a solo homer in the seventh inning. The lead was back to three games.

Away from the stagnant confines of the Astrodome, Dravecky, pitching for Single A San Jose, threw a complete-game eight-hitter against Reno. The Giants began discussions with Brenly's agent Tom Reich. And the Astros, in another transaction that would soon resonate with San Francisco fans, released former Giants pitcher Bob Knepper.

As it had in Chicago, the weekend went poorly for the Giants. Houston eased to wins of 8–1, on the strength of four home runs and Mark Portugal's three-hitter, and 6–2 as Mike Scott became the major leagues' first 17-game winner. The lead was down to a single game. Said Houston first baseman Glenn Davis, "Man for man, we have a better ballclub than they do."

Chapter 7

Dravecky's Comeback

I t didn't take Matt Williams long to start paying dividends. The young third baseman, who had made the team despite finishing spring training on an 0-for-18 skid, was sent down on May 1 with a .130 average and was recalled July 23 after hitting 26 home runs in 76 games at Triple A. His first seven games back with the Giants were a mixed bag. He batted .261, a marked improvement over his first 25 games of the season. But five of his six hits were singles. He had one double—but no home runs and only one RBI.

The Giants needed a lift as they reached Los Angeles with a 4–7 record on what was becoming a hellish 14-game road trip. They had been outscored 56–32, had seen closer Steve Bedrosian blow two saves, and had lost three and a half games off their four-and-a-half-game division lead.

Their first game against the Dodgers was no easy assignment. Like Atlanta Braves slugger Dale Murphy, pitcher Fernando Valenzuela had tormented the Giants. His 14–16 career record against San Francisco was somewhat misleading; since his major league debut on September 15, 1980, no pitcher had recorded more victories over the Giants, thrown as many shutouts (four), or compiled a better ERA than Valenzuela's 2.93 (minimum 150 innings pitched).

Through four innings of the Tuesday, August 1 game, Valenzuela and the Dodgers led the Giants 1–0. Leading off the top of the fifth, Williams launched a home run to left-center field to tie the game. The Giants scratched out two more runs in the sixth. When Valenzuela was lifted for a pinch-hitter in the bottom of the seventh inning, the Giants held a 3–2 lead. Williams led off the ninth with a double that sparked a two-run rally. The Giants won 5–2. "He's a changed man," Kevin Mitchell said of Williams. "And you could see it," Will Clark said, backing up Mitchell's assessment 24 years later. "When he had been sent down, he was not a happy camper. But to his credit, he basically said, 'Next time I come back up there, I'm going to do it to where they can't send me back down.' And he did."

The Giants fortunes seemed unchanged even in victory. Winning pitcher Scott Garrelts had to leave the game in the sixth inning with a sore elbow. And it was determined that Rick Reuschel's sore groin would cost him at least one start. It was beginning to look like the plague of 1988 all over again for the pitching staff. Reuschel was placed on the 15-day disabled list. And starting pitcher Atlee Hammaker injured his left knee while running the bases. He had to be carried off the field and was placed on the 21-day DL after the game. He was headed for arthroscopic surgery to repair cartilage damage and a four-week recovery.

Mitchell gave San Francisco a 3–0 lead with a first-inning homer in the series finale Thursday night, but the Dodgers scored the game's final six runs. The team's sick bay was bulging at the seams. Second baseman Robby Thompson had to sit out with his chronically balky back. Replacement Ken Oberkfell made two errors that led to a pair of unearned runs. The Giants finished the road trip 5–9. Perhaps the only saving grace was that they still held a one-game lead over the Houston Astros, who would be waiting for them at Candlestick Park on Monday night.

◆ ◆ ◆

Tony Phillips ended July with a walk-off dinger for the A's, and it was no surprise it gave the team a boost. The unexpected benefit was that Phillips' game-ending home run off Chicago White Sox closer Bobby Thigpen seemed to inspire the team's pitchers most of all. For starters, it made a winner of Mike Moore, who on Tuesday, August 1, was named the American League's Pitcher of the Month for July based on his 5–0 record and 2.30 ERA. That evening Curt Young and three relievers combined on a six-hit shutout. The 2–0 win enabled Oakland to leapfrog the California Angels, who had lost to the Mariners in Seattle, and reclaim first place.

The following night Storm Davis and two relievers teamed for a seven-hit shutout and another 2–0 win. The A's had won four in a row, allowing five runs in the process. That streak unraveled in uncharacteristic fashion on the final day of the homestand as Carney Lansford committed two errors, and Terry Steinbach added another. The miscues led to two unearned runs in a 6–4 loss.

Something had to give as the A's began a 10-game road trip in Seattle on Friday, August 4. It had been two months since Dave Stewart won consecutive starts, which he was endeavoring to do in the cement echo chamber known as the Kingdome. On the other hand, he had won 10 consecutive starts against the Mariners. Buoyed by back-to-back two-run doubles by Jose Canseco and Dave Parker in the third inning, Stewart (16–6) pitched himself and the A's to a 5–3 win. Dennis Eckersley closed it out for his 20th save.

Emotions ran hot the following night as the Mariners exacted their revenge with an 11–5 win. Moore was angry with himself after allowing six runs (and three home runs) in five innings. The A's were upset with the M's after Seattle reliever Mike Jackson plunked Steinbach with a pitch in the top of the seventh. It came three batters after Parker's 300th home run and it marked the third Oakland player hit by a pitch in the series' first two games. It wasn't difficult to guess what would happen next. Sure enough, in the bottom of the inning, A's reliever Jim Corsi drilled Harold Reynolds, causing both benches to empty.

One week after the Mariners had driven him to cover in the first inning, Davis threw seven shutout innings in a 2–1 win Sunday. Eckersley finished up for his save No. 21. Despite having missed more than six of the season's 14 weeks, and by his own admission pitching at less than 100 percent, Eck was tied for fifth in the league—only five saves behind leader Doug Jones of the Cleveland Indians.

Still struggling with his emotional equilibrium after the birth of his first child and the death of his mother within hours on July 27–28, Bob Welch struggled in the series finale in Seattle, allowing five runs and 11 hits in seven innings. "It's been a battle to be focused," he told reporters after the 5–1 loss. "I had the most wonderful thing happen in my life, and the next day I experienced the saddest thing I've ever had to deal with."

The A's had excelled in extra-inning games in 1988, winning 14 of 19. They, however, lost their first eight of 1989 before snapping the streak against Seattle on July 28. In the first game of a three-game set in Chicago, they made it two in a row with a 3–2 win against the White Sox. Stan Javier scored on Ozzie Guillen's throwing error in the top of the 10th inning to make a winner of reliever Rick Honeycutt. Stewart deserved special mention after throwing 133 pitches on three days' rest, holding the White Sox to two runs in eight innings.

But the A's dropped another overtime affair Wednesday. Mark McGwire gave Oakland a 1–0 lead in the fourth inning with his 20th home run and first in 62 at-bats—a fallow streak during which he batted .177 with three RBIs. The White Sox scored single runs in the fourth and sixth to lead 2–1, but Ron Hassey reached Thigpen for a game-tying single in the top of the ninth. Four A's relievers strung together four and one-third scoreless innings from the sixth inning through the 10th. The fifth, Corsi, gave up a game-winning single to Carlton Fisk in the bottom of the 11th. Davis threw six shutout innings (giving him 18 consecutive scoreless innings) in a 4–1 win Thursday, enabling Oakland to win the series and keep pace with the Angels—their next opponent.

In 1989 the American League had 14 teams to the National League's 12. So while the NL played an unbalanced schedule with teams playing the majority of their games against division rivals, AL clubs played 12 games against every other team in the league regardless of geography. It was all about the math of a 162-game season. But it created some unsatisfying scheduling quirks in the AL. While the National League pitted division rivals exclusively during the final weeks of the season, the American League, which featured at least one interdivisional game every day, didn't have that luxury. The A's and Angels were running first and second in the AL West. It wasn't out of the question that the Golden State rivals might battle down to the wire in a race that would beg for a late-season showdown. But that delicious scenario was not to be. When the A's arrived in Anaheim on August 10, it was for a three-game set that would conclude the season series between the two teams. After their game of Sunday, August 13, the A's and Angels would be done with each other until spring training of 1990.

The A's were at their methodical best in winning the first two games in Anaheim to establish a two-game lead in the division. Moore threw an eight-hit shutout with eight strikeouts in the first game, improving to 15–6. The same guy who averaged 14 losses during seven seasons in Seattle ranked third in the majors in wins and second with a 2.38 ERA. His perseverance had paid off. That same day, Canseco also paid off…$729 for his two speeding tickets in Alameda County.

Welch won his 12th game on Saturday, August 12, aided by four innings of shutout relief by Todd Burns. McGwire hit his 21st home run in the 8–3 victory that gave the A's a two-game lead in the division. Stewart and Bert Blyleven, two veteran warhorses, tangled in the third game. Stewart struck out nine and allowed four runs in eight innings. Blyleven was a tick better, allowing three runs in seven innings while striking out six. The game ended in a flurry of high heat and flailing lumber. Canseco and Dave Henderson had been withheld from the starting lineup, a decision by manager Tony La Russa likely dictated as much by Blyleven's devilish curveball, which was in its 20th year of frustrating right-handed major league hitters, as with their need for a day off. But La Russa called on them in the ninth inning with Angels hard-throwing closer Bryan Harvey on the mound, one out, and Javier on third base representing the tying run. Harvey struck out Canseco looking and whiffed Henderson swinging to preserve the Halos' 4–3 win.

◆ ◆ ◆ ◆

Clark's first major league at-bat came against Houston. Showing no respect for his elders, the 22-year-old Clark ripped a home run off 39-year-old Nolan Ryan. It was the first of a half-dozen homers Clark would hit off Ryan over the next three years. In the thick of a hot division race on August 10, 1987, Clark pounded a pitch from Houston's Dave Meads into the upper deck at Candlestick Park, giving the Giants a walk-off 6–5 win.

Later he came up in the seventh inning of a 2–2 tie with the Giants and Astros separated by one game in the standings. Swinging at reliever Danny Darwin's first pitch, Clark sent the ball soaring over the right-field fence for a 4–2 Giants lead. It was his 19th home run against Houston since his major league debut, five more than any other player during that time. That ended the scoring for the game. Robinson threw a three-hitter for his second complete game in three starts—both against the Astros. The Giants' lead was two games.

They were busy off the field as well. Needing able-bodied starters more than aging late relievers, the Giants released "Goose" Gossage and signed old friend Bob Knepper, recently released by the Astros. And in Tucson, Arizona, Dave Dravecky sailed through another rehab start, throwing a seven-hit complete game for Triple A Phoenix.

With Mike Scott set to start for Houston on Saturday, the Giants knew they'd have to be on their game. So did Giants fans. Scott and the Giants had a complicated relationship. Scott struggled through six big league seasons, compiling a 29–44 record and a 4.45 ERA. Then he was taught the split-finger fastball by none other than the current Giants manager. "Al Rosen—when he was [general manager] with Houston—he sent Mike Scott to me in the wintertime to work on the split-finger," Roger Craig said. "Once he got it, he was unbelievable."

Scott went 18–8 in 1985. In 1986 he went 18–10 with a major league-leading 2.22 ERA, pitched the Astros to a division championship, won the clinching game with a no-hitter against the Giants—where Rosen was now the GM and Craig the manager—and won the Cy Young. Craig and others began to suspect there was more to Scott's success than the splitter. They thought Scott was scuffing the baseball, an old act of gamesmanship that caused the ball to dip and dive unlike one with a smooth surface. Craig began pressing his case late in the 1987 season.

On September 7 of that year, Scott beat the Giants in the Astrodome, retiring the final 26 batters. Craig was certain Scott was using sandpaper on the ball and made his accusatory case so vociferously that he was ejected. "I'll do something about it [even] if I get thrown out of every game," the Giants manager pledged to writers.

"I'll never forget that game in Houston," Craig said in 2013. "I think it was [home-plate umpire] Charlie Williams, I told him before the game, 'When you throw a ball back to him before he makes a pitch, he's already got the ball scuffed.' It happened. He hadn't thrown a pitch, and I went out and said, 'I want to look at that ball.' He'd scuffed the ball. It had a scuff on it. He dropped his sandpaper. [Astros second baseman] Bill Doran came up right on the edge of the mound and put it down his shirt. [Umpire] Bruce Froemming was right there. Apparently he didn't see it."

Scott, however, was on notice. When Knepper joined the Giants after being released by the Astros, he told Craig [as Craig recalled it], "Mike Scott is scared to death to pitch against you." Nine days after Craig had been ejected in 1987, the Astros came to Candlestick, and Scott was confronted not only by Craig's eagle eyes, but also the scratchy sound of several thousand spectators rubbing sheets of sandpaper together and issuing taunting, sing-song cries of "Cheeeea-ter!" The Giants won 7–1, driving Scott from the game in the sixth inning.

Come 1989, Scott continued to struggle against the Giants. And San Francisco fans continued packing sandpaper whenever he pitched at Candlestick Park. On Saturday, August 5, Scott held the Giants scoreless through two innings. But leadoff man Brett Butler, battling a 10-for-64 slump, kicked off the scoring by tucking a solo home run inside the right-field foul pole in the bottom of the third. Pat Sheridan and Terry Kennedy drove in runs in the fourth to make it 3–0 San Francisco. The announced crowd of 33,736 was sandpapering itself into a frothy fit. Butler led off the fifth with a double. Thompson bunted him to third, and Clark scored him with a double to left-center field. Houston manager Art Howe insructed Scott to intentionally walk Mitchell before coming out to relieve him. The Giants went on to score four runs in the inning. Scott finished with an unsightly line: six runs on eight hits in four and one-third innings. In five starts against the Giants since Craig's 1987 ejection, Scott was 2–2 with a 4.99 ERA.

The beneficiary of the Giants' offense was Mike LaCoss, another of those Giants pitchers who struggled against his former team. LaCoss began his major league career with the Reds in 1978. He pitched in Cincinnati for four years before being waived. The Astros claimed him, and he pitched in Houston for three seasons. He left Houston as a free agent after 1984, signing with Kansas City. Demoted to Triple A Omaha in August, LaCoss wasn't around for the Royals' World Series triumph over the St. Louis Cardinals.

Released by the Royals, he found a new home and new life with the Giants. But he struggled against the Astros, going 1–5 with a 4.82 ERA in 11 games. In his 12th appearance against the Astros since he'd left Houston, he blanked them on four hits in seven innings of work.

On Sunday the Giants tossed another Houston expatriate, Knepper, at the Astros. Knepper had cut his teeth with the Giants, winning 47 games in his first five big league seasons before being traded to Houston. He was an All-Star twice during his eight-plus seasons there. He was back where he'd started, facing the team he'd just left. He pitched well, allowing two runs in six innings and leaving with the game tied 2–2. "Aside from the playoff game in 1986, this was the most emotional game I've ever pitched," he said afterward. The Astros scored a run in the eighth and won 3–2. The Giants' division lead was down to two games.

There was other news that Sunday, which almost overshadowed the game. Dravecky's three rehab starts had gone so well that his fourth and final outing was scrubbed. He would start for the Giants against the Reds on Thursday. It would be his first major league appearance since May 28, 1988. "I was hitting all my pitch counts," Dravecky recalled 24 years later. "My pitch counts were 75, 100, and then unlimited. The first game, it was the second game of a doubleheader, so it was only seven innings. I had 76 pitches in a complete game. The second game I had a

100-pitch limit and I threw a complete game in 93 pitches. The last game I think I threw less than 100 and had another complete game. That was pretty amazing."

Within 24 hours of the announcement, the Giants received 45 requests for media credentials for Dravecky's comeback game from national outlets such as *Time* magazine, *Newsweek*, NBC's *Today*, and all three network evening news shows. It was becoming apparent that Dravecky's return was going to be more than emotional window dressing to the Giants season. They really needed another starting pitcher. Garrelts strained his back during batting practice before the Monday, August 7 home game against the Reds. Rookie reliever Jeff Brantley was pressed into duty, becoming the 14th pitcher to start a game for the 1989 Giants. He was battered for five runs in four and one-third innings as Cincinnati romped 10–2. Another rookie starter, Russ Swan, took the mound on Tuesday. He lasted one and two-thirds innings, during which he gave up five runs and three homers. The Reds pounded the Giants again 10–4. San Francisco's lead was down to one game.

Between Tuesday night's 10:05 PM final out and Wednesday afternoon's 1:08 PM first pitch, Mitchell and Clark reported to a photo studio to pose for a souvenir Pacific Sock Exchange poster. Dressed in business suits, wearing eye black, and hefting bats on their shoulders, the National League's two top RBI producers stood surrounded by crazed stockbrokers with apparent madness (and a sheaf of papers) in the air. It's the type of opportunity you cash in on when you're swinging the baseball world by its tail and you have no idea how long the magic will continue.

The flip side was Mitchell was dragging when he arrived at Candlestick Park for the game against Cincinnati. You couldn't have proven it by Reds pitchers. Mitchell belted a two-run home run off starter Rick Mahler in the bottom of the first inning to key a three-run San Francisco rally. He was intentionally walked his second time up and drew another walk in his next plate appearance. His fourth time up he had his bat broken by Reds reliever Norm Charlton yet still managed to muscle the ball over the left-field fence for another two-run homer. Twenty-four years later, Clark recalled it vividly. "He hit it off the end of the bat," Clark said, "and you know when you hit a ball off the end of the bat with a wood bat, it generally does break. I remember the piece of the bat going flying out into the field, and the ball just kept going, and going, and going. It was a home run. I was like, 'Oh, I haven't seen that one before.'"

Mitchell's four RBIs in the Giants' 10–1 win gave him 100 for the year. Robinson completed his third consecutive start. The Caveman walloped his third home run of the year for good measure. The afternoon start and the remarkably quick pace of the game—it took just 2:10—left plenty of time for players and fans alike to find their way home and get a good night's sleep. They would need it. Thursday, August 10, was going to be a special day.

Here's how nervous Dravecky was the morning of his comeback game: he overslept. His wife, Jan, had to wake him and tell him it was almost time to go the ballpark. On the drive to Candlestick Park with teammate Garrelts, Dravecky felt a preternatural calm. He felt it in the clubhouse as he got dressed and while warming up in the bullpen. He felt so calm that it began to concern him.

It had only been 10 months since doctors had cut a cancerous tumor out of his upper left arm, taking half his deltoid muscle with it. It had been little more than nine months since Dravecky lay on his couch and watched Orel Hershiser record the final out of the 1988 World Series and thought to himself that he might never get that kind of chance again. Around the same time, mid-October of 1988, Dravecky, a man of faith, stood up in church and gave thanks to God that his surgery had gone well. He told the congregation that if he never resumed his baseball career, that was fine with him. At that point Dravecky choked up and had to stop speaking.

The hour of his second chance had arrived. Dravecky was bathed in loud ovations when he first appeared on the field in uniform, when he began his warm-up session in the bullpen, and when his name was announced as part of the starting lineup. "I was very much aware of the crowd," Dravecky said in 2013. "It started when I went into the bullpen to warm up. I got a standing ovation. I look at [catcher] Terry Kennedy and grabbed my shirt and started pumping my heart. I pointed to my throat trying to let him know that my heart was in my throat. He nodded and did the same thing. You realized something much bigger was going on here. I was floored by it."

Craig recalled being out in the bullpen with Dravecky for that warm-up session. "Oh my God," Craig said in the summer of 2013. "That was unbelievable, amazing. He went down to the bullpen to warm up and he got a standing ovation. When he walked back to the dugout, he got another standing ovation. I was walking with him and I said, 'Dave you go ahead. I've got to do something.' I wanted to stay back and watch it because it was all for him."

As game time drew nearer, the Giants became increasingly quiet. No one had ever been through something like that. No one was sure what to say. Dravecky noticed the awkward silence. So he said to his teammates something he made a habit of telling them late in close games: "Everybody on your bellies." In essence he was telling them: "Do whatever you have to do to win this game."

It broke the tension. When the Giants trotted onto the field for the start of the game, the crowd of 34,810 made a sound different than is typically heard at a baseball game. "You have to do extraordinary things to get that reaction from baseball fans," Kennedy would tell writers afterward. "You've got to retire, hit a sudden-death home run, or you've got to get cancer."

"Put it this way: it was a noise that wouldn't end," Will Clark said in 2013. "It reverberated for not one inning but for a bunch of innings. I remember taking the field that day. I had goose bumps. And I hadn't had goose bumps like that since my first at-bat as a rookie. Just talking about it now, the same thing. That emotional lift, you could see in the team. You literally could see it on everybody's face. You could see it in the way they went about playing the game. There was no possible way on the face of the planet that we were going to lose that game. We were going to do whatever it took to win that ballgame right there."

Before he threw his first pitch, Dravecky took a quick moment to drink in the scene. "It was absolutely amazing how at peace I was," he said. "The doctors saying, outside of a miracle I'd never pitch. To be there when nobody thought I'd ever get back, including myself. It's been well chronicled about my faith; I guess I was just overwhelmed with thankfulness. I felt as though through all the doctors and nurses and therapists and trainers that participated, that God used all of that to give me another chance. So I stood on the mound overwhelmed with thankfulness. It gave me great peace. When it came time to pitch, my heart was in my throat. After I threw the first pitch, it was game on. I felt like, this is fun again. I'm back in the saddle."

That first pitch, to leadoff hitter Luis Quinones, was a ball. Dravecky went to a 2–2 count and then retired the Reds shortstop on a fly ball to Butler in center field. He retired shortstop Jeff Richardson and center fielder Eric Davis on grounders to third baseman Williams. Three up, three down in 10 pitches. The comeback was off to a good start.

Scott Scudder was the starter for Cincinnati. It's unlikely he could have comprehended the communal kismet he was up against. He opened the game wild, walking Clark and Mitchell in the first inning before getting Williams on a foul pop-up.

Dravecky survived a one-out double by Joel Youngblood in the second. Pat Sheridan led off the bottom of the second with a triple off Scudder. Kennedy drove

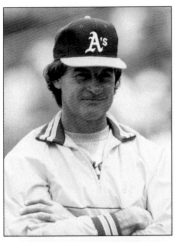

Left: A's manager Tony La Russa, who pushed all the right buttons in 1989, watches his team before a June game against the Baltimore Orioles. (Getty Images)

Below: The Bash Brothers, Mark McGwire (25) and Jose Canseco (33), combined to hit 50 home runs during the 1989 season.

Bottom: Acquired during a midseason trade with the New York Yankees, Rickey Henderson was known for his speed on the base path. (Getty Images)

Known as the Pacific Sock Exchange, Will Clark, the National League MVP runner-up that season, and Kevin Mitchell, the NL MVP, pose together in 1989. (Getty Images)

An inspiration to fans and teammates, Dave Dravecky warms up before pitching against the Cincinnati Reds on August 10, 1989, a game that marked his major league return after having a cancerous tumor removed from his throwing arm.

Jose Canseco marvels at his 484-foot, third-inning home run against Toronto Blue Jays pitcher Mike Flanagan during Game 4 of the 1989 American League Championship Series.

Closer Dennis Eckersley, who labored through a shoulder injury during 1989, celebrates the Game 4 victory of the contentious American League Championship Series against the Toronto Blue Jays.

Former teammates on the Dodgers and Mets, Chicago Cubs manager Don Zimmer and Giants manager Roger Craig joke before Game 1 of the 1989 National League Championship Series.

Will Clark acknowledges his teammates in the dugout, following his bases-loaded single off Chicago Cubs reliever Mitch Williams to win the National League Championship Series.

A section of the Bay Bridge, which supported about 250,000 vehicles a day, was destroyed by the Loma Prieta earthquake on October 17, 1989.

The earthquake ravaged the double-deck section on I-880 highway known as the Cypress Structure. (Getty Images)

The A's stare in disbelief after the earthquake strikes Candlestick Park prior to Game 3, forcing a delay in the World Series.

Measuring 6.9 on the Richter scale, the Loma Prieta earthquake leveled block after block of houses in the Marina District. (Getty Images)

Two days after the earthquake, Steve Bedrosian, acquired during the middle of the season to bolster the much-maligned bullpen, jokingly wears a construction helmet to the Giants' first practice since the disaster.

Because of the long layoff in the World Series, Oakland native Dave Stewart, the Game 1 starter, is also able to start Game 3 for the A's.

From left to right: Rickey Henderson, Dave Stewart, and Carney Lansford raise the World Series trophy during a muted celebration in Jack London Square.

him in with a ground ball out. Dravecky had a 1–0 lead. The Giants added a run in the third when Williams' double drove in Clark, and two more in the fifth when Williams homered with Mitchell on base. Kismet led 4–0. Dravecky was not only healthy and effective, he was dominating. After Youngblood's double he retired 17 of 18 batters through the seventh inning. He took a one-hitter into the eighth. "He pitched phenomenal," Clark said, "like he hadn't even stepped off the field."

"And you know what, it felt like that," Dravecky said. "It was the weirdest feeling. When I was back in uniform and stepped on the mound that first time, it felt like I'd never left. I was blown away by that. It was really, really strange."

Dravecky ran into trouble in the eighth. Todd Benzinger led off with a single. Two batters later Scott Madison doubled, putting runners on second and third. Dravecky struck out Ron Oester, batting for Scudder. On a 2–1 pitch, Quinones hit a three-run home run over the left-field fence. Suddenly, the special day had gone off script. It was 4–3, a one-run game. Craig, who managed based on equal parts intuition and empirical evidence, allowed Dravecky to continue. Dravecky retired Richardson on a ground ball to end the inning. With Bedrosian warming up in the bullpen, his day was over. But not until his teammates shoved him back onto the field to take a reluctant curtain call.

Bedrosian got Davis to ground out to open the ninth and then retired Herm Winningham and Ken Griffey Sr. on swinging third strikes to end the game. What followed was a transcendent moment that went beyond the Giants' season and their position in the standings. It was uplifting, joyous. Fair or not, fans had nominated Dravecky their valorous proxy. He was the guy who had handled a dire situation in the stoic manner we'd like to imagine ourselves using to deal with the same circumstance. As *San Francisco Chronicle* columnist Lowell Cohn wrote, "It was as if he beat cancer for all of us." By pitching so well in his return, he validated our faith in him and—by extension—ourselves.

The Giants and 49ers shared Candlestick Park. Each team had its own locker room. Because they had more players, the 49ers had a larger area. There was so much interest in this game and so many media members that the Giants held a special postgame interview session in the 49ers' empty locker room. When Dravecky finally arrived, he noticed a boy at the back of the room. It was six-year-old Alex Vlahos of nearby Hillsborough, a T-cell leukemia patient Dravecky had befriended during his own cancer treatment. Dravecky waved the boy to the front of the room and sat him on his lap for much of the interview session.

Vlahos had become a cause celebre even before the game. KNBR, the Giants' flagship radio station, had pledged $5 for each pitch Dravecky threw in his comeback game to a fund to offset the cost of Vlahos' bone marrow transplant. Dravecky threw 92 pitches, and the A's matched the pledge. As Dravecky sat before the microphones, the cameras, the huge clot of media in the aftermath of his comeback game, little Alex at his side, two things were apparent. One, he had been promoted to a higher calling in the eyes of Giants fans, baseball fans, and fans of the human condition. And two, from the outside looking in, he seemed to be okay with that. "I don't think I was aware of it," he said in 2013. "I realize, looking back, that what was going on in my life was bigger than baseball. It really was about putting the game in perspective. But then I had no clue. I was trying to survive."

His teammates were in awe. "I was working off Dave Dravecky's adrenaline," Bedrosian said after the game. "I'm proud of him and proud to have been a witness to it."

"If this is a movie," Mike Krukow told reporters, "he plays Dave Dravecky. Nobody else can do it. Nobody else has done what he's done. I told people he would never pitch another game. Never. It still doesn't make sense. I mean, it can't happen." Said Craig: "I've seen a lot in baseball. Five World Series. I saw Don Larsen throw a perfect game. But I don't think I've ever seen any game that had as much drama as this game today."

If any team was ripe for a letdown, it was the Giants in the wake of Dravecky's comeback game, but Williams refused to let it happen. When Williams came to bat in the bottom of the first inning of the Giants' Friday, August 11, game against the Dodgers, the bases were loaded with one out. He sent Tim Belcher's 2–2 pitch whistling over the left-field fence for a grand slam and a 4–0 San Francisco lead. In the bottom of the third during his next time up, he hammered an 0–1 delivery over the left-center-field fence. By the time the inning was over, Belcher was history, and the Giants led 8–1. It was a huge night for the middle of the order. Mitchell belted his 37th home run and drove in two. Clark had three hits and scored two runs. LaCoss pitched a sturdy seven innings in the Giants' 10–2 win. Coupled with Houston's loss, it put San Francisco four games up.

Sunday was a big day for Kelly Downs, who had spent two months at Triple A Phoenix, trying to tweak his delivery to take stress off his right shoulder. His first major league appearance since May 1 went as well as could be expected. He held the Dodgers to one run in six and two-thirds innings and left with a 2–1 lead.

But the Dodgers scored the tying run in the eighth inning, sending the game into extra innings. L.A. scratched out a run in the 12th against Don Robinson, making a between-starts relief appearance for the second time in 12 days. The Dodgers took the game 3–2 and the series 2–1. The Giants then took a three-game lead to Montreal and Dravecky's next start.

◆ ◆ ◆ ◆

It was difficult to know what to make of Davis. As a 20-year-old, Davis made the Baltimore Orioles in 1982, dragging the designation "the Next Jim Palmer" behind him. In his first four seasons, he did a passable imitation of the future Hall of Famer and underwear model, going 45–28 with a 3.66 ERA and helping the O's to the 1983 World Series championship. But after a 9–12 season in 1986, he was traded to San Diego. And late in the 1987 season, the Padres dealt him to Oakland.

He was indisputably effective during his time with the A's, but he rarely pitched—or was allowed to pitch—deep into a game. In his first year in Oakland in 1988, he went 16–7 with a 3.70 ERA. But he had just one complete game and averaged less than six and one-third innings per start. That left the bullpen to record the final eight outs. Through 21 starts in 1989, his average innings-per-start was less than five and one-third, and his ERA was up to 4.92. And yet he was 12–5.

Davis improved to 13–5 on Tuesday, August 15, opening a six-game homestand by beating Cleveland 5–2, pitching six innings and allowing one run. He was aided by home runs from Canseco and Rickey Henderson, and a high-wire save by Eckersley, who escaped a bases-loaded jam of his own creation for his 24th save. The bullpen that consistently came to Davis' rescue failed Moore on Wednesday. After throwing 104 pitches in five and two-thirds innings, Moore left with a 3–2 lead. But Gene Nelson allowed the tying run to score in the seventh, and Honeycutt gave up three in the eighth, thus disappointing the crowd of 29,502, which pushed the A's past 2 million in attendance for the second year in a row and the second time in franchise history. The 6–3 Cleveland win whittled the A's lead in the American League West to a half-game.

Three players were on their game in the series finale on Thursday. Welch threw eight shutout innings. Dave Henderson hit a solo home run in the bottom of the fifth. And Eckersley threw a scoreless 10-pitch ninth inning as Oakland beat Cleveland starter John Farrell 1–0 on one of the best days of his career (eight innings, four hits, 11 strikeouts). Friday, August 18, was an up-and-down day for

Stewart. Hours before his start against the Minnesota Twins, he was honored at Oakland City Square by civic officials and community leaders for his charitable work. Then came the game. Stewart allowed four runs—all in the first inning. That's all Minnesota needed as they edged the A's 4–3, knocking Oakland out of first place by two percentage points.

Then Davis did something he had never done: pitch a 10-inning complete game. He fell behind 4–0 after four innings, but held the Twins scoreless on three hits over the final six innings. Meanwhile, the A's offense began chipping away at the deficit. McGwire hit his 22nd home run to cut the Minnesota lead to 4–1. Rickey Henderson added a solo shot in the sixth as did Parker, who left the team following the game after learning that his father had died. A quintessential Rickey Rally tied it in the eighth. Henderson bunted for a single, stole second and third, and scored on a single by Canseco, who had been pulled over by police that day for having excess tint on the windows of his Porsche. Lansford not only won the game with a walk-off single in the 10th, but he also extended his hit streak to 15 games. Lansford, the 1981 American League batting champ, was now hitting .332, third in the league and just seven points behind leader Wade Boggs.

Sunday's game was no contest. Moore threw eight scoreless innings in a 5–0 Oakland victory. In so doing he tied Stewart for the league lead in wins and lowered his ERA to a league-leading 2.30. Those who enjoyed keeping one eye on the finish line couldn't help but notice the A's had four pitchers who could be considered viable Cy Young candidates: Moore and Stewart, who were on pace for 22 wins; Davis, on pace for 19; and Welch, on target for 18.

When it came to individual achievement, manager La Russa was not exactly an eyes-on-the-horizon guy. "My biggest pet peeve right now would be to get into a discussion on who will win the Cy Young," he said to reporters. "That's real counterproductive. It's like: who will win the division? The team that plays the best will win—same with the Cy Young."

♦ ♦ ♦ ♦

The morning of Tuesday, August 15, a member of the Giants public relations staff received a phone call in his Montreal hotel room. It was from a member of Ron Howard's movie company. There was interest in putting Dravecky's story on the big screen. As it happened, Dravecky was to start later that night in the first game of a nine-game road trip. He picked up where he'd left off in San Francisco, throwing strikes and getting outs early in the count. When he took the mound for the bottom of the sixth inning, he was working on a three-hit shutout. The Giants led 3–0 thanks in large part to a two-run homer by Williams, his seventh since rejoining the team on July 23.

Dravecky's second pitch of the inning was hit for a home run by Damaso Garcia. Dravecky went to 2–2 on Andres Galarraga and then hit the Expos slugger with a pitch. That brought Tim Raines to the plate as the potential tying run. It wasn't an ideal situation, but Dravecky had fared well against Raines during their respective careers. In 50 career plate appearances against Dravecky, the switch-hitting Raines was batting .209, 95 points below his career average.

Dravecky got the sign from Kennedy and settled into the stretch position. He lifted his right knee and pushed off the pitching rubber with his left foot, generating momentum to home plate. He drew back his left arm and propelled it forward to make the pitch. The ball squirted out of his hand and dribbled across the first base line in the direction of the Montreal dugout. That odd sight was accompanied by a loud snap. Dravecky flung himself to the ground, grabbing his left arm with his right hand and writhing in pain. "I had no advance notice of anything wrong," he said later to reporters. "There was a snap, and I knew it was something bad."

Intent on pursuing what he thought was an unusual wild pitch, Kennedy didn't realize at first what had happened. Clark was only too aware. He rushed from first base to Dravecky's side. "You could see he was in so much pain," Clark said after the game. "He was sweating up a storm, and all he could do was sit there and shake." Craig vividly recalled the scene 24 years later. "I heard the crack of his arm," Craig said. "I wasn't that nimble, but I was the first one [from the dugout] to the mound. I remember he was flat on his back with his head facing home plate. He said, 'Skip, we have to win this game.'"

Dravecky was taken from the field on a stretcher and driven to Queen Elizabeth Hospital, where his arm was placed in a protective wrap. The Giants went on to win 3–2, but the postgame locker room was funereal. Dravecky had come to symbolize more than a teammate coming back from cancer surgery. He had gone from the euphoria of his comeback game to one of the most gruesome injuries anyone on the team had ever seen. "It's a crying shame," Clark said in the postgame locker room. "Dave's first start changed the meaning of the season for us because it's not just about baseball. It's about life." Said Craig in 2013: "His teammates loved him before anything happened. Then after what he went through... He sacrificed his arm to keep us in contention and win. You talk about leading by example. It was miraculous."

As the Giants were losing to Montreal on Wednesday, Dravecky was making his way back to San Francisco. He was going on very little sleep. Doctors had told him to sleep sitting up so he wouldn't accidentally roll over on his broken arm. But he found that difficult. When he stepped off the plane at Gate 75 at San Francisco Airport on Wednesday night, he was greeted by legions of reporters—16 TV cameras, nearly a dozen radio stations (some of which covered the event live), several photographers, and newspaper reporters from as far away as Philadelphia. "There was a ton of media," he recalled in 2013. "And it was unbelievable how many fans came to the airport. I got off the plane and I couldn't wait to see my wife, and there were all these people there. I was overwhelmed by the support."

Attention quickly turned to the spot in the humerus where the break had occurred, the same spot that had been frozen with liquid nitrogen during surgery to ensure than any remaining cancerous cells had been killed. Dr. George Muschler, the surgeon, said he had warned Dravecky he could be at risk of a fracture in that area for up to two years after surgery. "We were aware of the sensitivity of the bone," Dravecky told the throng of reporters before leaving for the Palo Alto Medical Clinic's Sports Medicine Center. "But there was no added emphasis of caution. Once we passed through the danger zone—somewhere around four to six months—we were confident to go ahead."

Dr. Gordon Campbell, the Giants' head of medical services, told reporters it was further proof that modern medicine wasn't an exact science. "After his cancer surgery and all his months of rehabilitation, most of us thought his bone would be strong enough to handle the stress," Campbell said. "But we were wrong, and it's possible the bone had not returned to its normal state."

The Giants PR staff was inundated by another wave of requests for interviews from outlets as varied as *20/20* to Joan Rivers' new talk show. But on one of the most difficult nights of his life, Dravecky already had answered the biggest question anyone could have asked. "I certainly hope that in the next six to eight weeks the bone will heal," he said, "and I can start thinking of playing again."

The Pacific Sock Exchange was in fine fashion for the final game in Montreal, a 10–5 Giants rout. Clark singled, doubled, swatted his 19th home run, and drove in four runs. He was batting .342. Mitchell connected for his 39th home run. Knepper got the win but in an unfamiliar role—with five innings of shutout relief. The Giants left Canada as they had entered it, three games up on Houston.

A change of venue did little to cool off Clark. He had three more hits and another home run as the Giants opened a weekend set in Philadelphia with a 5–2 win on Friday, August 18. In bumping his average to .345, he overtook Tony Gwynn to lead the National League batting race. There also was good news on the pitching front. Reuschel came off the disabled list to win his 14th game with six solid innings.

On Saturday, the Giants were dealt some payback for the Bedrosian trade. Terry Mulholland, one of two young pitchers the Giants gave up to acquire the Phillies' closer, threw a two-hit shutout against his old mates in a 1–0 win. Making matters worse, Bedrosian was called on in the bottom of the ninth to face Ricky Jordan with the bases loaded. Jordan lined a game-winning single to right field. It was a disappointing night in many respects, especially given that it wasted a terrific start by Downs, who allowed one run in eight innings and got hung with the loss for his trouble.

San Francisco ran into another red hot expatriate on Sunday. Dennis Cook held the Giants to one run in six and two-thirds innings. And another San Francisco starting pitcher came off the disabled list as if he'd never missed a beat as Garrelts threw six shutout innings. Offensively, it was a frustrating afternoon. The Giants had no trouble getting runners on base. They had great difficulty bringing them home. Through eight innings they stranded 11 runners. Down to their last out in the ninth, they trailed 2–1 with the bases loaded and Ernest Riles at the plate. Riles had been a quiet contributor through 123 games. Now he faced Roger McDowell, who was acquired by the Phillies just hours after they had dealt Bedrosian to the Giants. McDowell had been conspicuously successful since coming to Philadelphia, going 2–0 with 10 saves in 12 chances and posting a 1.17 ERA. Riles made some noise, driving a McDowell delivery over the right-field wall. The Giants went on to win 5–2.

Craig decided to keep Riles' bat in the lineup for the first game in New York, starting him in right field. It was a risky move. Riles had never started a game in the outfield at the major league level. But Craig was frustrated with the team's offensive black hole. Candy Maldonado was still looking for his lost stroke. Tracy Jones had played so poorly he'd been traded for Sheridan, whom Craig was reluctant to hit against left-handers. The Riles experiment was among many things that went wrong in a 4–1 loss to the Mets. He was indecisive on two balls that fell for doubles and was charged with an error. The Giants struck out 11 times. The team's play was so lackluster that Craig thought something needed to be said. "I decided in the seventh inning to have a meeting," he told writers after the game. "We got to 20 games over .500 and we're playing .500 ever since. We've got to play with more intensity and fire."

Nothing said intensity and fire quite like a Mitchell home run. On Tuesday, Mitchell's 40th of the season drove in three runs and gave the Giants a 4–0 lead in the top of the sixth. That was more than Knepper needed. He tossed a four-hitter in a 5–0 win. The next day Reuschel, Craig Lefferts, and Bedrosian combined on another shutout in another 5–0 win. Williams doubled and homered. The back-to-back whitewashes coincided with two Houston losses. The lead, one and a half games when Craig gave his speech, was back up to three and a half.

◆ ◆ ◆ ◆

Because of a rainout on July 19, the A's had to start their road trip to Texas, Kansas City, New York, and Milwaukee in…Detroit. It was a one-game matinee that wasn't on the original schedule, and the Tigers were having a miserable season, sitting 30 games under .500. Thus the game was played in virtual privacy, before 6,197 fans, the Tigers' worst home crowd since 1983. That limited crowd saw McGwire clobber a two-run home run in the A's four-run rally in the first inning. It was his 12th home run in 77 career at-bats in Tiger Stadium. Lansford extended his hit streak to 17 games. Coupled with the Angels loss at Kansas City, the 6–1 win returned Oakland to first place.

Clubhouse manager Steve Vucinich had a little something waiting for the A's when they got to the visiting locker room at Arlington Stadium before their Tuesday, August 22, game against the Texas Rangers. It was a sign reading: "Bob Welch goes for No. 14 tonight." It was a subtle reminder that there was a game to be played. It was timely given the excitement over what might happen during the game. Ryan, the Rangers starter, needed six strikeouts to become the first major league pitcher to reach 5,000 for his career. It was a national story and a pleasant local diversion. The Rangers had shown some early foot in 1989, leading the division as late as May 4. They were still on the fringes of the race at the All-Star break, trailing by five and a half games. They had stagnated since the break, going 18–18 and dropping another four games off the pace.

So Welch went for No. 14 and got it with eight shutout innings. Eckersley pitched the ninth for his 26th save. And the A's bumped their lead to two games over the Angels. Ryan bagged his milestone and then some. The 42-year-old marvel struck out 13 in a complete game. He got Rickey Henderson swinging for No. 5,000, much to the delight of the crowd of 42,869, which included Rangers owner George W. Bush and baseball commissioner Bart Giamatti.

There had been some good-natured banter before the game between A's players, wondering which of them would be the 5,000th whiff immortalized in highlight clips for years to come. Rickey played the moment just right, telling the press, "If you ain't struck out against Nolan, you ain't struck out against nobody. I can't feel badly about it because nobody could hit that pitch. I'm honored to be part of the record. I'm happy he got it and I'm happy we won."

Major news involving another record holder would rock the national pastime on Wednesday, August 23. It was reported that Pete Rose, Reds manager, Cincinnati icon, and leading hit-maker in baseball history, had agreed to a suspension from baseball. Under investigation since spring training for betting on baseball, Rose agreed to the ban as a compromise with Commissioner Giamatti. In exchange, Giamatti agreed to halt the probe, which had grown into a scathing, damning 225-page report. In addition, Rose would be spared an admission of guilt.

Giamatti scheduled a news conference in New York for Thursday morning at 9:00 AM. Rose, who was away from the Reds to be with his wife after the birth of their daughter, spent part of Wednesday night hawking memorabilia on cable TV. He called a news conference at Riverfront Stadium for 10:00 the following morning. The two events could hardly have been more different. Giamatti made his case with righteous eloquence. "The matter of Mr. Rose is now closed," he said. "It will be debated and discussed. Let no one think that it did not hurt baseball. The hurt will pass, however, as the great glory of the game asserts itself and a resilient institution goes forward. Let it also be clear that no one individual is superior to the game."

Rose had the right to apply for reinstatement after one year. Giamatti was noncommittal when asked whether Rose might eventually be welcomed back into baseball. "I cannot say what my inclination would be after one year toward an application for reinstatement," the commissioner said in a statement that a little more than one week later took on haunting overtones.

Rose cut straight to the boilerplate denials he would issue over the next 15 years. "I made some mistakes and I think I'm being punished for those mistakes," he said in Cincinnati. "However, the settlement is fair, especially the wording that says

I never bet on baseball. It's something I told the commissioner back in February, and I've told you people the past four months."

Rose's problems weren't over. He seemed headed from one rundown to another. His agreement with Giamatti had halted baseball's probe. And the FBI announced it had dropped its investigation of the Hit King, but the investigation of a Cincinnati federal grand jury into Rose's alleged income tax violations would continue.

As baseball drama was playing out in New York and Cincinnati, the A's were enduring a streak-busting kind of day. They lost to the Rangers 6–2, ending their five-game win streak. Davis saw his personal five-game win streak snapped. And Lansford took an 0-fer, ending his hit streak at 19 games. It was just one of those forgettable days even after the game. The typically genial Lansford, believing some comments he had made about Texas closer Jeff Russell had been taken out of context, announced he was boycotting the media immediately and for the rest of the season.

To the extent the A's had been watching the scoreboard, they'd been looking first to see how the Angels had done. But with nine wins in 10 games, the Royals had thrust themselves back into the race, pulling to within four and a half games of Oakland. And were they happy to see the A's roll into Kansas City. Mark Gubicza and two relievers combined on a five-hitter on Friday, August 25, as the Royals won for the 10th time in 11 games. They were then within three and a half games of the A's, whose lead over the Angels was down to one game. On Saturday, Bret Saberhagen shackled the A's with a four-hit shutout. It was nothing to be ashamed of—Saberhagen was 16–5 (13–1 since May 24). The Royals were legitimately hot, having won 11 out of 12. It was getting crowded at the top of the AL West with Oakland leading California by one game and Kansas City by two and a half.

Welch was on a bit of a roll himself. He stopped the skid on Sunday with eight shutout innings in a 6–0 win. Welch improved to 15–7 and had thrown 24 consecutive scoreless innings. It was off to the Big Apple. Canseco announced the A's presence in batting practice before their Monday, August 28, game against the Yankees, putting on an awesome power display despite wearing tape on his sore left wrist. By the time the night was over, the Yankees had stars in their eyes. Stewart won his 18th game to lead the majors. Eckersley earned his 28th save, putting him just two off the AL lead. Canseco had two hits and an RBI. Parker doubled, homered, and drove in two runs. Rickey Henderson went 2-for-5 in his return to the Bronx. But the guy who most enjoyed the A's 7–3 victory was probably shortstop Walt Weiss, who grew up in nearby Suffern, New York, and who had upwards of 75 friends and family in the stands. Weiss doubled and homered. The A's gained a half-game on the idle Angels.

Oakland really cranked up the offense in a 19–5 win Tuesday night. Canseco seemed to be in the middle of everything with two singles, two homers (including a three-run 442-foot bolt of lightning in the A's 10-run rally in the fifth), and five RBIs. With the Angels dropping a doubleheader in Boston, Oakland's lead doubled to three games. Canseco also found himself in the crosshairs of the California Department of Motor Vehicles, which sent him a letter advising him that with one more moving violation, his license could be suspended. "Basically," said a DMV spokesman, "you're talking speeding and going through stop signs."

Canseco brought his stay in the Bronx to a crashing climax Wednesday with a three-run home run and four RBIs. It went for naught as the A's lost 8–5 with Moore enduring a rare bad outing. But it gave Canseco an impressive line for the three-game series: 8-for-15, one double, three homers, and 10 RBIs. And one "nolo contendre." Attorney Robert Shapiro announced Wednesday that Canseco had decided to plead no contest to possessing a gun during an April visit to the UCSF medical campus. As conditions of the plea, Canseco received three years unsupervised probation and was ordered to do 80 hours of community work and take 100 underprivileged kids to a baseball game. "He suggested it, and the court accepted," Shapiro said. "And he's not going to have a gun. And the gun that he had is going to be destroyed."

◆ ◆ ◆ ◆

Wearing a plastic brace on his upper left arm, Dravecky was back at Candlestick Park on Friday, August 25, as the Giants opened a weekend series against the Expos. It had only been 15 days since his uplifting return to baseball, but it seemed a lifetime had passed in the interim. He repeated what he had been saying almost from the moment he broke his arm: he was optimistic he would pitch again.

The Giants could have used him. Downs fell to 2–5, allowing four runs in four innings. San Francisco walked seven, and errors by Thompson and Oberkfell led to eight earned runs. The Expos romped 12–2. Dravecky appeared on the field before Saturday's game, accepting a check for $115,000 raised by 2,000 donors for six-year-old leukemia patient Vlahos, who was in need of a bone marrow transplant. It was yet another example of how Dravecky was changing the focus of the season for the Giants and their fans.

Garrelts was brilliant in the main event, taking a one-hitter into the eighth inning before giving up three runs in the Giants' 8–3 win. Garrelts (10–3) was 4–0 with a 1.37 ERA since coming off the disabled list. Craig said he was pitching "as good as anyone in the league." On that day he was better than Mark Langston, an impending free agent. Believing this might be their year, the Expos had acquired Langston from Seattle for three players, including Randy Johnson. The Giants power hitters were in fine fashion. Mitchell had a two-run single, Clark had a two-run double, and Williams continued blazing away at opposing pitchers with a three-run home run in the bottom of the first inning.

A grand slam by Montreal's Galarraga broke up a tight game Sunday. The Giants lost 6–3. They were still moseying along at a win one/lose one pace that frustrated Craig. But the Astros seemed incapable of making a run. The lead remained four games. The malaise continued on Monday, August 28. The Phillies roughed up Reuschel for seven runs in two and one-third innings. And another member of the Bedrosian trade came back to haunt the Giants. Third baseman Charlie Hayes hit two doubles, a home run, scored three runs, and drove in four.

Another Phillies player with local roots did in the Giants on Tuesday. Von Hayes, who played baseball at Saint Mary's College in the East Bay, had a career night with three home runs and six RBIs as Philadelphia romped 6–1. "You've got to take the good with the bad," Craig said to reporters, "and right now we're not too good."

They perked up Wednesday, at least for one at-bat. Clark came to the plate in the fifth inning with the Giants trailing 1–0, runners on first and second, and facing former teammate Mulholland. Clark sliced a double to left field, scoring both runners. When shortstop Dickie Thon committed a throwing error on the relay from the outfield, Clark scored as well. It was all the offense the Giants could manage. Thanks to a solid outing by Downs and Bedrosian's 18th save, it was all they needed to win 3–2.

There was no game on the final day of the month, but there was a happy development for Giants fans. The team promoted catcher Bob Brenly from Triple A Phoenix in time to make him eligible for the postseason roster. The fan favorite was back in town. "Anything I'm asked to do, or not do, is fine with me," he told writers. "If I can help them out even a little, I'll be happy because they made it fun for me to come to the ballpark again."

Chapter 8

The Homestretch

Baseball fans were still coming to grips with the fact that Pete Rose had been banned from the game he had personified when commissioner Bart Giamatti died of a heart attack on September 1. The Yale-educated Giamatti was an anachronism when he assumed baseball's commissionership, an idealist in a realm obsessed with money, a romantic in an autocrat's clothing. It was he who wrote in the oft-quoted essay, "The Green Fields of the Mind": "It breaks your heart. It is designed to break your heart. The game begins in the spring, when everything else begins again, and it blossoms in the summer, filling the afternoons and evenings, and then as soon as the chill rains come, it stops and leaves you to face the fall alone. You count on it, rely on it to buffer the passage of time, to keep the memory of sunshine and high skies alive, and then just when the days are all twilight, when you need it most, it stops."

He was more the game's poet laureate than a commissioner, more Roger Kahn or David Halberstam than an executive authority. Yet in the first year of his commissionership he had been forced to channel Kenesaw Mountain Landis. Some friends and acquaintances believed his banishment of Rose, preceded by months of acrimony and investigation, had contributed to his death. "Bart was a very sensitive man," Dr. Frank Castiglione, a friend who had urged Giamatti to give up smoking, told *The Boston Globe*. "He loved baseball so much that having to [ban Rose] probably hurt him to the core. I'm sure that added to the tension and the stress."

The A's game that night in Milwaukee seemed one more indication that the baseball world was slightly off its axis. Down 3–2 to the Brewers, Oakland took a 4–3 lead on Mark McGwire's two-run home run in the sixth inning. After the Brewers tied it in the bottom of the sixth, Jose Canseco untied it with a solo home run in the seventh (his fourth homer in three games). Manager Tony La Russa called on Dennis Eckersley to record a rare six-out save. Eck got within one out of the finish line and then gave up a game-tying double to B.J. Surhoff in the bottom of the ninth. Todd Burns surrendered a bases-loaded single to Greg Vaughn in the 10th inning, and the A's lost 6–5.

The A's set about closing their road trip in impressive fashion with a 7–2 win on Saturday. Dave Stewart won his 19th game, retiring the final 18 batters in a five-hitter. He was within one game of his third consecutive 20-win season. "What I'm about to do hasn't been done in a long time," he told writers. "I'm feeling real proud about it." His left wrist still heavily taped, Canseco belted his fifth home run in four games. McGwire added his 26th of the season.

Meanwhile, baseball owners named Fay Vincent, Giamatti's second in command, as acting commissioner. His first few weeks on the job turned out to be as eventful and trying as his predecessor's last.

◆ ◆ ◆ ◆

The Giants had an open date on the final day of August. Kevin Mitchell took advantage of the small window of freedom to take a detour to his home in San Diego. He had tailed off on the Giants road trip and was hitting .186 with 15 strikeouts in his past 11 games. So he spent some time in his batting cage, hitting Wiffle balls.

On Friday, September 1, the Giants led the visiting Mets 2–0 in the bottom of the seventh. It had been a tight pitchers duel between Scott Garrelts and New York's Ron Darling. With two out and speedy leadoff man Brett Butler on second base, the Mets opted to walk left-hander Will Clark to get to Mitchell, giving Darling a righty-on-righty matchup.

Darling's first pitch to Mitchell went sailing out of the park for a three-run home run and a 5–0 lead in an eventual 7–1 San Francisco victory. That Darling would walk Clark to get to him "upset me a little bit," said Mitchell, whose homer was his 41st of the season. Garrelts improved his record to 11–3. Even more impressively, after allowing a single unearned run in eight innings, his ERA fell to 2.26, best in the majors.

Matt Williams was the game changer Saturday. In just his seventh start since being traded to the Mets, Frank Viola, the reigning American League Cy Young Award winner, walked Mitchell to put runners on first and second in the sixth inning of a 2–1 squeaker. Williams tagged Viola's second pitch for a three-run home run and a 5–1 lead. He would later add an RBI double. Rick Reuschel held the Mets to one run in eight innings to improve to 16–6.

But the biggest cheers from the 31,066 fans on hand that day were reserved for Bob Brenly, who was back in the Giants lineup. He received a standing ovation before his first at-bat and responded with an RBI double. "It was like I went home from the ballpark one day, erased four months of my life, and the next day I'm back," he told reporters. "Things haven't changed a bit." After being waived by the Toronto Blue Jays, Brenly wasn't acquired by the Giants for his quick bat or blazing speed. What San Francisco prized was his knowledge, perspective, and ability to keep those around him loose.

About his brief time in Toronto, he said: "I wanted to see all those [American League] parks. Now that I've seen them, I can get on with my career." And about his baseball philosophy: "I like to laugh. I like to hear funny things. I like to be around when people say funny things. There are enough bad things in life. You have to get your yuks where you can."

Saturday's win gave the Giants a five-game lead over the Houston Astros. Don Robinson's seven-hit shutout on Sunday boosted the lead to six games. Williams cracked a two-run home run, giving him 11 homers and 26 RBIs in his past 23 games. San Francisco was looking like destiny's pick as Western Division champions.

◆ ◆ ◆ ◆

Some among the Coliseum crowd of 32,697 on the night of Monday, September 4, already seemed to be looking forward to a Bay Bridge World Series. The Giants were playing in Cincinnati that day, their game running two hours ahead of Oakland's. So A's fans watching the hand-operated out-of-town scoreboard could track the Giants' incredible comeback from an 8–0 deficit after six innings to a 9–8 win. When the final score was posted, it was met with cheers.

The A's rocked Roger Clemens on Tuesday, scoring five runs and drawing five walks in his seven innings in a 13–1 Oakland win. At that point it was a trend bordering on tradition. La Russa's first game managing the A's was July 7, 1986, against the eventual American League champion Red Sox in Boston against Clemens, who was in the heart of what would be a Cy Young/MVP season. For obvious reasons La Russa wanted to make a statement in his first game. He tabbed Stewart as his starting pitcher, which marked the beginning of a beautiful professional friendship—and the beginning of a nightmare for Clemens. The A's won that game 6–4 behind Stewart. Counting Tuesday's flameout, Clemens was 0–5 in seven starts, with a 3.56 ERA against La Russa's A's. And that didn't include a no-decision in the 1988 American League Championship Series. On a more pragmatic level, the win boosted the A's lead over the Kansas City Royals to three and a half games, their biggest advantage of the season. Catcher Terry Steinbach homered for the second consecutive game and was feeling it. "It's in our hands," he told the media. "We're the ones with the lead."

The A's won the rubber match of the three-game series 7–5. Dave Parker turned a 2–1 deficit into a 5–2 lead with a grand slam in the bottom of the third inning. The game wasn't without its concerning moments. Carney Lansford left in the fourth after being hit in the elbow with a pitch. And Bob Welch left with an abdominal strain after five innings. (He still improved to 16–7.) On the plus side, the lead was now four and a half, and Oakland was 30 games over .500 for the first time in 1989.

The New York Yankees followed the Red Sox into Oakland, and Stewart took aim at his 20th win in the Friday, September 8, game. He had the audience, the A's 14th sellout of the season, which hiked the season attendance to 2,294,763. Both were team records. Stewart went the distance but allowed five runs—four more than the A's scored. It was a full day for Canseco, who began serving his 80 hours of community service related to his gun charges by appearing at Humana Hospital in San Leandro. After arriving 40 minutes late, he met with patients and did volunteer chores.

The following day he resumed his assault on Yankees pitching, homering in support of Moore's four-hit shutout. It was Oakland's 19th shutout, second in team history only to the 1972 world champions. Both Hendersons, Dave and Rickey, hit their 11th home run. It was interesting timing on Rickey's part. The *New York Post* reported in its Saturday edition that the Yankees were interested in signing him if he chose to become a free agent at season's end.

Storm Davis improved to 17–6 in the series closer. Parker hit his 20th home run. And Canseco found yet another way to straddle the line between athlete and celebrity. It was announced on Sunday, September 10, that at some point in the coming days, Canseco would have a 1-900 line (900-234-JOSE) that fans could call to get daily personal updates from Mr. 40–40 himself. The cost would be $2, plus $1 for every additional minute.

For the second time in 1989, a scheduling anomaly had the A's and Giants both playing home games on the same dates—Tuesday, September 12 and Wednesday, September 13. As was the case when both teams played at home on three dates in June, both the A's and the Giants had the best records in their respective leagues.

The A's raced to a 5–0 lead against Milwaukee after two innings on Tuesday night, but Welch couldn't hold it. He wasn't charged with the 7–6 loss. That distinction went to reliever Matt Young, but Welch took blame for it after the game. Canseco hit his 14th home run, his seventh in 11 games. Whose market was it? It was difficult to tell by Tuesday's games. The A's outdrew the Giants 23,862 to 11,077. (Both teams played at night.) But the Giants telecast topped the A's, according to the Nielsen and Arbitron ratings.

Stewart went for his 20th win for the second time on Wednesday afternoon and seemed in good hands when Eckersley came on to protect a 6–4 lead in the bottom of the ninth. But Surhoff singled with one out, and Vaughn followed with a game-tying home run. The A's won on Dave Henderson's solo homer in the bottom of the ninth. But having suffered just his fourth blown save in 33 chances, Eckersley was disconsolate afterward. "It's the worst you can feel after winning the game," he told reporters. On the bright side, the A's outdrew the Giants again, 21,246 to 13,827.

♦ ♦ ♦ ♦

If the final game of their homestand made the Giants appear to be destiny's darlings, the first game of their road trip left little doubt. They landed in Cincinnati with a six-game lead over Houston. Six innings into their Monday, September 4, game they trailed 8–0. Manager Roger Craig decided not to fight it, but instead to use it as an opportunity to rest his regulars. Mitchell, suffering from a sprained left wrist, had already been given the day off. Second baseman Robby Thompson, lifted for a pinch-hitter in the top of the sixth, joined him on the bench. So did center fielder Butler and shortstop Jose Uribe, who were pulled before the bottom of the inning. Clark and catcher Terry Kennedy both homered in the seventh to cut the Reds lead to 8–2, and both were replaced after the Giants' turn at bat.

Reds starter Tim Leary had struggled since being acquired from the Los Angeles Dodgers in mid-July, going 2–5 with a 4.62 ERA. But he appeared to be on his game against the Giants, taking a five-hitter and a six-run lead into the eighth. There he retired the first two hitters before giving up a ground ball single to Ernest Riles. The next batter was September call-up Mike Laga, who had replaced Clark. He lifted an 0–1 pitch over the right-field wall for a two-run home run. The Reds' lead was down to 8–4. Ernie Camacho came on in relief for the Giants and struck out the side in the bottom of the eighth. In the tidy span of 14 pitches, the Giants were back in their dugout and ready to hit.

Greg Litton led off the top of the ninth inning, pinch-hitting for Pat Sheridan, the sixth San Francisco starter to be removed from the game. Litton grounded a single off hard-throwing Reds reliever Norm Charlton. Candy Maldonado, hitting for Camacho, lined to second for the first out, but Donell Nixon grounded a base hit into center field, with Litton stopping at second. Craig sent Brenly up to hit for right fielder Jim Weaver, and Brenly nubbed a ball to the left side. Reds third baseman Chris Sabo couldn't make a play; it was ruled an error. The bases were loaded.

The Giants had scored two moral victories. They had chased Charlton from the game, and they had brought the potential tying run to plate. Meanwhile, in the visitors' clubhouse, those Giants who had been pulled from the game were gathered around a radio, scarcely believing what they were hearing. Kennedy, caught up in the moment, told everyone in the room, "I'm buying the whole team dinner if we win this game."

In his 10th game since officially replacing Rose as manager of the Reds, Tommy Helms called on John Franco to stop the bleeding. Craig called on yet another pinch-hitter, his fourth of the inning and seventh of the game. Veteran Chris Speier, who had already announced his retirement effective at season's end, hit for shortstop Mike Benjamin. He worked the count full and then grounded a single to center, scoring Litton. The Reds' lead was 8–5. Bill Bathe was next. He also worked the count full and singled to center. Nixon and Brenly scored, and Speier moved to second. The Reds' lead was 8–7.

Helms popped out of the Cincinnati dugout once again, replacing Franco with Rob Dibble. It was an interesting move, considering the next San Francisco batter, left-hand batter Riles, would be spared the southpaw Franco and would hit instead against a right-hander. Then again, maybe nothing could have changed the improbable course of events.

Riles singled to score Speier with the tying run. Garrelts, running for Bathe, scooted to third. Laga, who had averaged just 54 at-bats over his seven major league seasons, was next. He was playing his first major league game of the season since being called up from Triple A. He capped the game of his life with a single to right, scoring Garrelts with the run that gave the Giants their first lead of the game 9–8.

Bedrosian made it interesting in the bottom of the ninth, loading the bases before getting the final two outs. Craig still got a chuckle out of the whole Humm Baby episode 24 years later. "A lot of guys got big hits," he said. "Mike Laga got a really big hit in that game. When it was over and we had won, one of the writers asked me, 'How did you do that?' I said, 'You don't know how good I am, do you?' I was just giving the regulars some time off. Everything went right. It was just one of those things that very seldom ever happen."

While the madness was playing out in Cincinnati, the Astros blew a 5–4 lead and lost to the Dodgers. The Giants led the National League West by seven games with 25 to play. The brief two-game series ended on a down note for San Francisco, which lost 6–5 on Tuesday. Mike LaCoss (7–10) was strafed (five runs in four innings pitched) for the third consecutive start. But Williams, playing shortstop in place of Uribe and batting cleanup in place of Mitchell, still out with his wrist, homered for the 12th time in 25 games.

Off the field is where a lot of the baseball season plays out beyond the view of the fans. The things that happen there are shared experience for the players, coaches, and managers and can affect the camaraderie and morale—or lack of it—on a team. The Giants' third-base coach, Bill Fahey, was a genial presence. He never asked for credit and never shied away from the inevitable second-guess. His nickname was Pooch, and he didn't seem to mind. Giants players had been ragging him over his new flattop haircut. They disliked it so much that they collected $5,000 and dared him to shave his head. Pooch did. An Associated Press photographer got a shot of Fahey with his hat over his heart during the national anthem and his bald, white pate shining like a full moon. It went out over the wire to all corners of the country, giving the Giants players the kind of laugh that money can't buy.

The Giants moved on to Atlanta, where the Braves were out of contention—as evidenced by the crowd of 2,735 at the Wednesday, September 6, game. The Giants won in a 7–2 walkover that night with Garrelts throwing an eight-hitter and lowering his major league-leading ERA to 2.19. "I'm just trying to stay in a groove and keep things as simple as possible," he told reporters. "When I start to think about it, that's usually when I get into trouble."

Clark knocked in two runs to reach 100 RBIs for the season. With Mitchell at 114, it marked the sixth time two Giants had knocked in 100 runs in the same season since the team moved West and the first time since Willie McCovey and Dick Dietz had done so in 1970. The Pacific Sock Exchange struck again Thursday in a 7–5 Giants win. Clark tied the game with a two-run triple in the seventh inning. In his second game back from his wrist problem, Mitchell homered for an insurance run in the ninth. The Giants headed for Houston with a seven-game lead over the Astros and San Diego Padres.

It was the Astros' last, best chance to get back into the race, and they jumped the Giants on Friday, September 8, winning 5–2. Houston's Mark Portugal pitched well into the seventh inning and hit his first career homer. He improved to 4–1 with two of those wins against San Francisco. The Giants weren't as concerned with an incipient Giant killer as they were about their starter, Robinson. The Caveman not only allowed four runs in five innings, but he also left with a sore left knee and hamstring. It was not an insignificant development, given his problems with his right knee, for which he had been wearing a brace.

Off the field, Mitchell responded to a civil suit filed in San Diego the previous day, charging him with beating his former girlfriend and threatening her with a gun on September 11, 1988, in Foster City, just south of Candlestick Park. He had been faced with criminal charges during spring training that were dropped after he agreed on July 14 to enter a domestic violence diversion program. It was unsettling given that Mitchell's formative years were spent around gangs and guns. "I've got nothing to hide," he told the media. "I thought everything was supposed to have been shut down, and now this pops up."

Houston won again Saturday, 4–1. Mike Scott was on his game, throwing a three-hitter to become the National League's first pitcher to 19 wins. Craig displayed a baseball with an apparent scuff mark after the game, but home-plate umpire Bob Engel saw no cause for action. "I just go out and pitch and wait to hear 'em gripe,"

Scott said. "I love it." Astros manager Art Howe was loving it, too. "Are we planting a little doubt in their minds?" He asked reporters. "What do you think?"

The Giants thought not. They took the final game of the series, but it seemed like more than one win, given the manner in which they won it. Craig started Bob Knepper, who had been released by the Astros on July 28 and picked up by San Francisco on August 4. Knepper was booed loudly by the Astrodome crowd of 26,004. Either impervious to the crowd or inspired by it, Knepper held his former team to two runs in six innings to improve to 3–1 since joining the Giants. Sheridan provided him early support with a three-run double in the top of the first inning. It was a big blow for a couple of reasons. One, Williams, such a huge contributor since returning from the minors, went 0-for-4 and was in an 0-for-19 funk. And two, Mitchell left in the eighth inning after aggravating his left wrist. The Giants returned to San Francisco leading the National League West by six games over Houston and San Diego.

◆ ◆ ◆ ◆

The A's arrived in Boston in good shape—three and a half games ahead of Kansas City and poised to start 17-game-winners Moore and Davis and 16-game-winner Welch against the Red Sox. It was a three-game series of which manager La Russa said afterward, "We got what we deserved here." Moore, who had been scuffling since being named the American League Pitcher of the Month for August, lasted just three and two-thirds innings in the first game, on Friday, September 15. The A's underrated defense committed three errors. The Red Sox won 7–2, and Clemens recorded his second win against the A's in 13 career appearances.

Oakland committed three more errors in a 5–2 loss Saturday. Davis allowed five runs in five and one-third innings. It all fell apart for the A's in Sunday's 7–6 loss. First, Welch lasted just four innings, allowing five runs. A's batters struck out 14 times, tying a season high. Canseco was tossed by home-plate umpire John Hirschbeck after arguing a called third strike (his fourth whiff) in the top of the ninth. McGwire, who came into the game with a .224 average, homered twice. But he committed a throwing error with the bases loaded. As providence would have it, the A's already had scheduled a team get-together in Cleveland on Sunday night. Suddenly they had something to talk about. "The mood was: in that [Boston] series we didn't play very well, so we got beat." La Russa told reporters, recapping the meeting. "We've still got our edge, so let's play that edge."

The A's won on Monday, September 18, but it wasn't the satisfying streak-buster it could have been. Stewart, in his third try for his 20th win, pitched brilliantly for eight innings, handing off a 2–1 lead to Eckersley in the ninth. For the second time in six days, Eckersley denied Stewart his 20th win by blowing a save. This time he coughed up a leadoff home run to Brook Jacoby on an 0–2 pitch.

Dave Henderson and Tony Phillips stroked RBI singles in the 10th, giving the A's a victory they needed, and Eckersley a win he would rather not have received. Stewart, the ultimate team player, struggled to reach the high road. "I'm glad we won," he told reporters, "but how many chances am I going to get?" Twenty-four years later, the blown saves still haunted Eckersley, who recalled them in detail. "I did it twice," he said. "One was Greg Vaughn. The other was Jacoby. In Cleveland. On an 0–2 pitch. And they had champagne in the clubhouse waiting for [Stewart's] 20th. I don't blame him [for being upset]. That's the life of a closer. The older you got, the worse it got."

During spring training in 2013, Eckersley and Stewart ran into each other in Florida. They went to dinner with former A's trainer Barry Weinberg. The subject of the two blown saves in 1989 came up. "I never realized how badly he felt," Stewart said. "Eck was talking about blowing the saves trying to get my 20th win. He even said, 'I think I probably cost you a Cy Young that year.' Coming out of August, I had 19 wins. Tony [La Russa] was trying to save innings and pitches for the playoffs. Hell, I just wanted to win games."

Eckersley's lament over the Cy Young was no doubt heartfelt. But it's not likely his two blown saves were difference-makers in the balloting for the award. Winner Bret Saberhagen of Kansas City finished 23–6. With two more wins, Stewart would have had 23. But he had three more losses, and his ERA was 1.16 higher than Saberhagen's. Like the Giants' Juan Marichal in the 1960s, Stewart had a succession of outstanding years, but he was always trumped by someone having, in the eyes of Cy Young voters, a measurably better year.

On Tuesday night, September 19, Moore held the Indians to an unearned run in eight innings to achieve his career-high 18th win. On Wednesday, Rickey Henderson belted his 40th career leadoff home run to start the contest, Davis won his 18th game despite throwing just five innings, and Eckersley recorded his 30th save. But all was not sweetness and light off the field. La Russa had become aware of Canseco's 1-900 line, which was by then operational. "I saw the commercial when we were in Boston and I thought, *This is ridiculous*," the A's manager told the press. "I wouldn't have done this. What's the point of it?"

The A's were rolling. They were stacked with big-time players, enough so that only a handful had to have a big game for the team to win. On Thursday, September 21, they began a four-game series at the Metrodome with a 2–1 win against the Minnesota Twins. Welch allowed one run in seven and two-thirds innings. McGwire doubled and scored the first run in the third inning and blasted a Rick Aguilera pitch 453 feet for the second run. The following night, Stewart finally nailed down his 20th win. He allowed two runs in seven innings and left with a 5–2 lead. Eckersley, who had blown Stewart's previous two attempts at No. 20, had pitched four of the previous five games and was given the night off. So Gene Nelson wrapped up with two scoreless innings. Stewart had his 100th career win and his third consecutive season of 20.

On Sunday, Oakland's magic number fell to three. Davis won his 19th game. McGwire hammered two homers (No. 30 and 31), becoming the second player (behind Canseco) to hit at least 30 homers in his first three full major league seasons. La Russa, always the in-the-moment pragmatist, cautioned against assuming anything. "I don't think that would be a very smart, very healthy thing for our ballclub," he said after his team turned an 0–3 start into a 6–4 road trip. But some members of the team couldn't help themselves when questioned by reporters. "We're just taking it for granted that we're going to clinch it," Stewart said. "I can smell a championship," Davis said. Parker had won a World Series with the Pittsburgh Pirates in 1979. He knew how and why championships were won. "Let it come in kind of quietly," he said.

◆ ◆ ◆ ◆

The failed Garrelts-as-closer experiment seemed like a distant memory. The bespectacled right-hander with the nose-diving split-finger was mowing people down. So it was almost a shock when the Braves came to Candlestick Park on Monday, September 11, and jumped to a 2–0 lead after three innings. But Lonnie Smith's solo home run was Atlanta's last hurrah. Garrelts retired 16 of the final 17 batters he faced, finishing with seven strikeouts in eight innings. Meanwhile the Giants cobbled together just enough offense to squeak out a 3–2 win. Clark's RBI single broke a 2–2 tie in the bottom of the eighth inning, and Bedrosian breezed through a 1-2-3 ninth for his 20th save. Garrelts improved his record to 13–3. His

ERA actually inched up to 2.19, but that was still good enough to lead the majors. At 7–0 with a 1.26 ERA in his past nine starts, he was the hottest starter in baseball.

Mitchell sat out the game after receiving another cortisone shot in his wrist but returned with a bang on Tuesday. His 43rd home run helped the Giants build a 5–1 lead after seven innings. With Reuschel on the mound, the game seemed a lock. But the Braves fought back in the eighth against Kelly Downs and Bedrosian, scoring five runs. Dale Murphy—that man again—capped the rally with a go-ahead three-run homer. The Giants lost 6–5 and were reminded of destiny's fickle nature.

The Giants blew another lead Wednesday, a 5–2 advantage over the Reds. Craig Lefferts surrendered a tying three-run home run to Eric Davis in the eighth. The 5–5 tie held until the 13th inning, when Cincinnati scored twice off Randy McCament. But the Giants weren't finished tormenting the Reds just yet. In the bottom of the 13th, Litton slapped a two-run double into the right-field corner to tie the game, and Butler finished off the comeback with an RBI single to left field.

It was Brenly's turn to be the hero Thursday. His bloop single down the right-field line in the bottom of the 12th inning scored Clark with the winning run in a 4–3 victory against the Reds. It was the last game of the year between the division rivals, and they were ready for a break from one another. The Giants had won 10 of the 18 games between them. Actually, "survived" might be a more precise verb given that 11 of the 18 games had been decided by one run.

Clark was sizzling. He singled, doubled, and tripled in Thursday's game. He stole second base ahead of Brenly's game-winning hit. He scored twice, giving him 101 runs for the season. Thus he became the first Giants player to record back-to-back 100 run, 100 RBI-seasons since Willie Mays. In San Francisco, there was no higher standard than equaling something Mays had done. Not only was Clark playing with abandon, but he also was talking the same way. That the first four games of the homestand had drawn a modest average of 13,201 fans had not escaped him. "If people want to see a first-place ballclub, they better come out now," he said, "because they won't be able to get in to see the playoffs. I'm not anticipating anything. We're in first place, and I'm loving life."

The Astros had taken a shot at climbing back into the National League West race, falling short of the three-game sweep they needed to gain serious traction. On Friday night it was the Padres' turn. They came to Candlestick Park six games behind the Giants and riding a hot streak that had seen them win 19 of their previous 24 games. Thanks to a pair of botched bunts in the sixth inning, the Padres took the opener of the three-game series. Garry Templeton, trying to bunt a runner to second base in a 2–2 tie, fouled off the first pitch from Knepper. Given the swing-away sign by manager Jack McKeon, he doubled to drive in the tie-breaking run. The next batter, Benito Santiago, after failing to bunt Templeton to third, belted an 0–2 pitch for a two-run homer and a 5–3 San Diego lead that held up as the winning margin.

There was an intriguing subplot to the series. Competition for the NL batting crown had turned into a two-horse race. Tony Gwynn had three hits in the San Diego win Friday to pull slightly ahead of Clark, .341 to .339. The next closest batter was Atlanta's Smith at .317. So the issue would be decided by the two sweet-swinging lefties—quite possibly in San Diego in the final weekend of the season.

Saturday's game was postponed, only the 22nd rainout in the Giants' San Francisco history. That set up a Sunday doubleheader, after which both teams would have 12 games to play. Anything short of a sweep was going to make things tough for the Padres. Mitchell and Garrelts made sure there would be no San Diego sweep. Mitchell hit home runs No. 44 and 45, and Garrelts (14–3) won his eighth consecutive decision as the Giants won the opener 5–3. Bruce Hurst threw a five-hitter as the Padres took the nightcap 6–1. But everyone was aware of the real score. "Five up with 12 to play," Craig said. "It's going to be awfully tough for anybody to catch us now."

There was no game Monday, but there was news. The winner of the Giants' Willie Mac Award, named for Hall of Famer McCovey and voted on by the players to honor inspirational play, was announced. Everyone agreed that Dave Dravecky was a most deserving winner. The voting was an indication of relationships that would extend beyond baseball and well past 1989. "I have been quoted as saying on many occasions that cancer has been a blessing for me," Dravecky said in 2013. "I don't say that anymore. I hate cancer. I hate what it did to me. I don't like the fact that I'm an amputee. But what I've learned and the experience it's given me, I wouldn't trade for anything. What's a blessing is the byproduct, the lessons learned, growing up, really seeing the significance of relationships in life and beginning to look at relationships a lot different than I did as a young teen—cocky, arrogant, and full of himself. Life does that to us. As we get older, it seems to put things in perspective. You become more reflective, more aware of things that matter most. It's not about the stuff anymore, man. It's about the journey with others."

By Tuesday, September 19, the Dodgers had been eliminated from the NL West race. They were not going to defend their World Series title. Finishing at .500 was going to be difficult. In other words, Giants fans had the Dodgers right where they wanted them when Tommy Lasorda's crew pulled into Candlestick Park for a three-game series. The Giants won the first game as Laga's dream month continued. Sent up to pinch hit for the scuffling Williams with the bases loaded and the Giants trailing Orel Hershiser 2–0 in the fifth inning, Laga roped a three-run double to right field. Lefferts and Bedrosian threw two scoreless innings each to preserve the 3–2 win for LaCoss. Even with a win by San Diego and Houston, the Giants' magic number fell to seven.

And then: it happened again. Sixteen days after the Giants' comeback from an 8–0 deficit to beat the Reds in Cincinnati, they trailed the Dodgers 7–0 after five innings at home. Only this time, aside from employing four different right fielders, Craig kept his regulars in the game. In the sixth inning, they began chipping away at the L.A. lead. A Mitchell ground-out drove in one run. Riles followed with a two-run homer, and the Giants were within 7–3.

They still trailed by four entering the bottom of the ninth and facing Dodgers closer Jay Howell. Mitchell greeted Howell with his 46th home run. Riles singled and scored on Williams' double. Kennedy's single scored Williams, and that was all for Howell. The Giants were within 7–6. Mike Hartley, a September call-up making his fourth big league appearance, took the ball from Lasorda. Speier greeted him with a double, moving pinch-runner Benjamin to third base. Litton singled to score Benjamin and move Speier to third. The game was tied 7–7.

Lasorda yanked Hartley and called on John Tudor, a once-outstanding starting pitcher trying to come back from offseason elbow surgery. Butler polished off the comeback with a single to right, scoring Speier with the winning run. Seven Giants had batted in the inning, and none had made an out. "It's a crime to lose that one," moaned Lasorda to reporters.

The Giants won again on Thursday night but got a scare. Scoring on Mitchell's double in the bottom of the first inning, Clark injured his right leg sliding into Dodgers catcher Mike Scioscia. Clark left after the second inning, departed for X-rays, and returned to Candlestick by the eighth inning, expressing hope he would be back in the lineup shortly. "He basically buried me at home plate," Clark said in 2013, "as he had done to several other people."

Butler, who struck the decisive blow in Wednesday's comeback, delivered again Thursday, snapping a 2–2 tie in the bottom of the seventh inning with a two-run double. The Giants won 4–3, sweeping Los Angeles and cutting their magic number to five. What's more, the crowd of 24,896 boosted their season attendance to 1,934,717, breaking the San Francisco season record set two years earlier.

The Giants closed out their home schedule with three games against Houston, beginning on Friday, September 22. Houston's Portugal won the opener, his third victory of the year against San Francisco. It was Garrelts' first loss since June 25. But the Padres lost, too, reducing the Giants' magic number to four. San Francisco played without Clark, who rested his aching leg and saw his consecutive games streak come to an end at 320. Another Giant on the mend, Atlee Hammaker, threw his first simulated game since suffering a knee injury while running the bases in Los Angeles. Brenly, not the kind of teammate to let such a milestone pass quietly, presented the oft-injured Hammaker a game ball for most simulated games in a career.

Behind Reuschel's seven-hitter and Williams' tie-breaking two-run home run, the Giants beat the Astros on Saturday 3–1. The win reduced the Giants' magic number to three. Even better, for the 46,664 sandpaper-wielding Candlestick Park fans, 20-game-winner Scott took the loss. The Giants closed out their home schedule in style Sunday, eliminating Houston with a 10–2 win. It was a festive day that began with former Giants pitcher Vida Blue marrying Peggy Shannon on the Candlestick Park pitcher's mound. McCovey was the best man. Rev. Cecil Williams of San Francisco's Glide Memorial Church officiated. The game also featured Mitchell's 47th home run of the season and 100th of his career. Thompson cracked his 13th, a career high, and LaCoss tossed an eight-hit complete game. The magic number was two. Clinching, it appeared, would be a piece of (wedding) cake.

◆ ◆ ◆ ◆

The 1989 A's clinched the AL West in 1988 fashion on Wednesday night, September 27. Okay, technically, Moore, who threw seven innings of one-hit, shutout ball in the 5–0 clincher against the Texas Rangers, hadn't been on the team the previous season. But strong starting pitching was a hallmark of both the '88 and '89 Athletics. So was Canseco. He hit a monstrous two-run home run, estimated at 459 feet, off Jamie Moyer in the first inning. Set-up men Rick Honeycutt and Nelson were so good in relief of Moore that Eckersley wasn't needed. The end came at 9:44 PM when Rafael Palmeiro grounded out to McGwire. "It's better because of the way we had to win it," Parker told writers, comparing the 1989 title to the one earned in 1988. "We didn't have Jose, having his 40–40 year. We didn't have [Dave] Henderson having his kind of year. I think this is the best team I've played on in my 16 years."

La Russa harkened back to spring training, when the team gathered together for the first time since the final out of the 1988 World Series and how he'd kept an eye out for something that never materialized. "I came in with a bias," he said. "Anything that smelled of comfort, I and the coaching staff would be impatient with. There hasn't been much. I believe for a lot these guys it was a little sweeter because they had to dig deeper."

Caught up in the moment, Lansford relaxed his media ban. "To put us in a position close to first place when Jose came back," he said to reporters, "that's just a tribute to the belief of these players, the heart and depth of this team." Said infielder Mike Gallego: "Just put stars by everybody's name."

It was a quick turnaround, emotionally and otherwise, for the first pitch of Thursday's afternoon game. Oakland beat Texas 5–3 with Stewart throwing five shutout innings and earning his career high-tying 21st win. Pitching the following night against Kansas City, Davis wasn't as fortunate. Seeking his 20th win, he left after seven and one-third innings with a 3–2 lead. The A's blew the lead but won the game 4–3. Davis finished 19–7. "I'll take 19 wins every year," he said.

There was another member of the team trying to keep sharp by pursuing a personal goal. Lansford, who won the American League batting title during the strike-shortened 1981 season, was bearing down on league leader Kirby Puckett. With a 2-for-4 effort Friday night, Lansford raised his average to .338. Puckett was at .340.

For all intents and purposes, Saberhagen clinched the Cy Young on the final Saturday of the season, holding the A's to one run in eight innings while recording a career-high 13 strikeouts. The A's managed just four hits off Saberhagen, but Lansford got one of them in his three at-bats. He was at .338, .0005 behind Puckett. Also on Saturday the A's learned their playoff opponent: Toronto clinched the American League East.

It's a tried and true baseball tradition. On the final day of the season, pitchers tend to throw strikes, and batters tend to swing at the first pitch. It's a long grind from mid-February to early October, and teams that aren't headed for the postseason are typically ready to get things over with and head home. Another tradition: it seems at least one game on the schedule goes into extra innings. It took the A's 11 innings to beat the Royals. September call-up Chris Bando, younger brother of former A's captain Sal Bando, knocked in the winning run with a single in what was to be his final major league at-bat. Lansford's bid for the batting title was foiled. He went 0-for-3 to finish at .336 while Puckett went 2-for-5 to win his first crown at .339. Moore never got a chance to be foiled. La Russa was going to start Moore to give him a chance for his 20th win, but thought Welch had looked tired during his final start. So he decided to bypass Moore in the season finale to have him ready to pitch Game 2 of the ALCS with Welch getting pushed back in the postseason rotation.

Other numbers fell the A's way. Their 3.09 team ERA led the American League, making them the first team since the 1972–73 Baltimore Orioles to lead the league in consecutive seasons. Not coincidentally, the A's finished 80–14 when scoring three runs or less. And they were just the third team since the 1927 Yankees to have four 17-game winners.

♦ ♦ ♦ ♦

Clark returned to the lineup for the first game of the Giants' season-ending road trip, on Monday, September 25. But he wasn't right for the rest of the season and in some respects for the rest of his career. The Giants kicked off their trip by losing 5–2 to the Dodgers in Los Angeles. Clark was 0-for-4 with three strikeouts, and Robinson struggled on his sore right knee. In his first start in 12 days, he allowed four runs in five and two-thirds innings, falling to 12–11. Lefferts took a cortisone shot in his left (throwing) shoulder. Suddenly, it seemed as if the Giants were limping toward the finish line. On the bright side, with the Padres' loss to Cincinnati, the Giants clinched a tie for the division. The Giants lost again on Tuesday 2–1. They whiffed 11 times against Dodgers starter Ramon Martinez. That time there was no bright side, unless you counted Clark's 23rd home run of the year. The Padres beat Cincinnati. The Giants still hadn't clinched anything better than a tie.

Before Wednesday's game, Giants general manager Al Rosen walked through the clubhouse wearing a T-shirt that read, "Enough of this shit." Rosen's shirt displayed more fight than his team put up in losing 1–0 on a four-hitter (with another 11 strikeouts) by the Dodgers' Tim Belcher. Dispirited, the Giants gathered in their clubhouse to monitor the Padres-Reds game by radio from San Diego.

The Reds seemed poised to win 1–0 until the Padres scratched out a run in the bottom of the ninth inning. The game lurched along into the 13th inning with the Giants unsure what to do or what to feel. In the top of the 13th, Cincinnati's

Davis doubled home the tie-breaking run. Charlton shrugged off a leadoff single by Gwynn in the 13th, striking out Templeton to end the game and hand the Giants their second division title in three years. "If I had to use two words to describe this club," Craig told writers in an uproarious clubhouse, "it would be consistency and character. The craziest thing about this is that the one time we get swept turns out to be the happiest night of the season."

Robinson wasn't around for the celebration. He had flown back to Pittsburgh to have his knee examined by specialists who had treated it during his time with the Pirates. The diagnosis ultimately was stretched ligaments and required cortisone shots. Since the Giants had Thursday, September 28, off, Craig treated the team to a pig roast on his ranch in Borrego Springs just outside San Diego. "It wasn't hard to tell that the last horse some of these guys were on was a rocking horse," Craig said.

It was off to Jack Murphy Stadium to decide the last bit of business in the NL West—who would win the batting title. Clark went 2-for-4 in Friday night's 7–2 win by the Giants while Gwynn went 1-for-5. Clark led him .334 to .331. Considering Clark's tender right leg, Craig gave his first basemen the option of sitting out the final two games. Clark would have none of that. "Why should I?" he said. "My job is to play. Ted Williams had a batting title wrapped up [in 1941], he had a .400 season wrapped up and he played. My job is to play—not to sit on a batting average."

LaCoss, a closer on Opening Day, evened his record at 10–10 with five tidy innings. Hammaker threw two scoreless innings in his first appearance since coming off the disabled list. Maybe the Giants would have enough pitchers to finish the season after all. On Saturday the Padres spanked Reuschel for eight runs in four innings in an 11–5 triumph. Clark went 1-for-4 while Gwynn went 3-for-4. Clark led going into the final game, .334 to .333. The batting race came down to the eighth inning of the final game. Gwynn singled to cap a 3-for-4 effort that trumped Clark's 1-for-4 outing as the Giants lost 3–0. When Gwynn reached first base after the hit that clinched his third consecutive batting title with a .336 average to Clark's .333, Clark shook his hand. "I'm a little disappointed," Clark acknowledged to reporters. "I lost to the best. You have to tip your hat to him."

Chapter 9

Postseason Friends and Foes

Roger Craig and Don Zimmer went *way* back—to the days of two eight-team leagues, three franchises in New York, real grass, black-and-white TV, and wool uniforms. Brooklyn Dodgers farmhands and then teammates on the big league club, they had been friends for 40 years. They won rings in 1955 when next year finally arrived in Brooklyn. They moved west with the franchise and won rings with the 1959 Los Angeles Dodgers. When the expansion New York Mets played their first game on April 11, 1962, Craig was the starting pitcher; Zimmer was the starting third baseman. Both were coaches for the San Diego Padres in 1972 when Zimmer was promoted to succeed Preston Gomez as manager 11 games into the season. When Zimmer found himself looking for work after the 1986 season, Craig hired him to coach third base for the 1987 Giants.

Zimmer was hired to manage the Cubs in 1988. Before the Cubbies' first game at Candlestick Park that year, Craig was asked about his old friend. "Go ask him what he learned from working for me," Craig said with a twinkle in his eye. Reporters dutifully trooped over to the Chicago dugout and did just that. Zimmer shot back with a smile, "Why don't you go ask him what *he* learned from *me?*"

Unafraid of playing hunches or thumbing their nose at convention, they were both seat-of-the-pants managers. Their teams split 12 games in 1989, going 3–3 in each city. Six games were decided by one run (with five of those by a 4–3 score). And the old friends would square off as managers in the National League Championship Series. "We'd played with the Dodgers in Brooklyn and L.A. and with the Mets a little bit," Craig said in 2013. "Zim was an outstanding manager. To manage against him, you have to be on your toes. He's a good, aggressive manager. I was with him as a pitching coach for a couple years. He was on top of everything. He wasn't afraid to do anything."

The American League Championship Series matchup was neither warm nor fuzzy. The A's had edged the Toronto Blue Jays 7–5 in the season series. But bad blood was a recurring theme. On May 2 at Toronto's Exhibition Stadium, George Bell had charged the mound after being hit by a Gene Nelson pitch. On June 24 in Oakland, A's manager Tony La Russa stewed after Mark McGwire and Carney Lansford were hit by pitches. On July 14 in Toronto's new SkyDome, Oakland's Bob Welch hit Bell in the biceps with a pitch. A staredown ensued.

Those confrontations were sparklers compared with the fireworks that soon lit up the postseason sky. The fun began in Oakland on Tuesday, October 3, with the 7–3 win against Toronto in Game 1. Dave Stewart had been managing a stiff shoulder over the latter stages of the season. He fell behind 3–1 after four innings. Dave Parker's RBI single off Blue Jays ace Dave Stieb cut the lead to 3–2 in the fifth inning. When McGwire led off the sixth with a home run, it was tied. One out later, Tony Phillips bunted for a hit. Toronto manager Cito Gaston had seen enough of Stieb. The call went to Jim Acker, who gave up an infield single to Mike Gallego and hit Rickey Henderson to load the bases with one out. Lansford grounded the first pitch he saw to shortstop Tony Fernandez. The Blue Jays had a shot at an inning-ending double play. Fernandez threw to second baseman Nelson Liriano for the force on Rickey Henderson. But Henderson had gotten a tremendous jump off first base. He was at second in a flash, and his hard slide unsettled Liriano, who threw wildly to first. Phillips and Gallego scored on the error to give the A's a 5–3 lead. Having pumped up the Oakland Coliseum crowd and his teammates, Henderson ran off the field pumping his fist.

The A's tacked on two more runs. Rickey Henderson scored one after walking, stealing second, going to third on a wild pitch, and scampering home on an infield single. The Blue Jays went hitless after the first batter of the fourth inning. Stewart wound up throwing eight gritty innings. "I struggled early and I was there for the decision," he told reporters afterward. "That's my story." But the story of the day was Rickey's slide. "Without a doubt, the play of the game," Lansford said. Added La Russa: "He got a great jump. He runs hard. He slides hard. And that's our style."

It seemed bigger than one win—in part because of the pitching matchups for the next three games: Mike Moore (19–11) vs. Todd Stottlemyre (7–7), Storm Davis (19–7) vs. Jimmy Key (13–14), and Welch (17–8) vs. Mike Flanagan (8–10). And it seemed bigger still because Rickey Henderson was at the top of his game—energized, engaged, and highly motivated. And when Henderson was at the top of his game, there was no stopping him. "He was on a mission that year," said Dennis Eckersley, who pitched a scoreless ninth inning in Game 1. "He was excited to come back. We got him right at the right time. He was incredible. After it's all over, he was the greatest player I ever played with."

While the A's were beating the Blue Jays in Oakland, the Giants were making hard decisions in Chicago. They already had decided that infielder Chris Speier would not be on the postseason roster; his career was over. On Tuesday, the day before the NLCS opener, Don Robinson threw 70 pitches without any pain in his right knee. He was included on the roster, as was Atlee Hammaker. Bob Knepper was the odd man out. Catcher Terry Kennedy needed a cortisone shot in his right shoulder. Kevin Mitchell was still nursing his left wrist. Will Clark's right leg was still feeling the effects of his September 21 collision with Mike Scioscia, as it would even two decades later. "It was sort of screwed up," Clark said. "And until this day, I've got a little issue here and there. I had to have my knee cleaned out after I retired. After that collision…put it this way, I remember playing against the Cubs and I had a brace on. I had MCL issues, so I was having to stabilize the knee. The shin got tore up. It looked like ground meat. The knee was the thing that bothered [me]."

There were two playoff games on the docket on Wednesday, October 4. The A's and Jays got the early start time, and Rickey Henderson picked right up where he'd left off Tuesday night. He had two singles. On two occasions he walked, stole second and third, and scored. He stole one base so decisively that Toronto catcher Ernie Whitt didn't even bother to throw. Henderson pulled up, tip-toeing into the bag. Parker hit the first postseason home run of his career and enjoyed every second of his home-run trot. Moore allowed a single unearned run in seven innings. Eckersley earned a two-inning save. It all added up to a decisive 6–3 win for the A's. The war of words afterward was more competitive than the first two games had been. "I'll tell you what. If I'm pitching, there would be some guys ducking," Blue Jays third baseman Kelly Gruber told the national media. "I mean Parker and I mean [Rickey] Henderson. I don't care for hotdogging. I don't play that way. I don't like it and I don't care if they know."

The A's knew. They didn't care. "I don't need to show [Whitt] up," Rickey Henderson answered back. "I can beat him. I don't believe he can throw me out. It's bad for my legs to slide when I don't have to or to go fast and stop right on the base. If they want me to slide just for the hell of it, you should have them say, 'Hey, Rickey, please slide next time.' Then I'll know to slide." Said Parker: "That's my trot. I'm not apologizing for my trot."

La Russa admitted the Oakland strategy for the first two games was "to push it." Whitt was an All-Star and, though he turned 37 during the 1989 season, he threw out 31 percent of would-be base stealers, equaling the American League average. But Henderson was not your average would-be base stealer. He swiped six bags in the first two games; the A's stole 10. They were burying the Blue Jays with their speed, athleticism, and attitude. It was almost incidental that Jose Canseco awoke the day of Game 2 with a migraine headache and didn't enter the game until the sixth inning. One could only wonder what would happen when the A's began to flaunt their power.

Then finally, it was the Giants' turn. They jumped to a 3–0 lead in their first at-bat against Cubs ace Greg Maddux. Clark doubled home one run, and Matt Williams doubled home two. But National League ERA champion Scott Garrelts gave most of that lead back, serving up a two-run home run to Cubs first baseman Mark Grace in the bottom of the first. Clark's solo home run in the third gave the Giants a 4–2 lead. Garrelts dished up a home run to Ryne Sandberg in the bottom of the inning.

The fourth inning inserted itself immediately into Giants lore. No. 7 hitter Pat Sheridan singled to lead off. Jose Uribe followed with a single to right field, with Sheridan moving to third. Uribe stole second while Garrelts was batting; the Giants pitcher struck out. Zimmer instructed Maddux to walk leadoff hitter Brett Butler. Maddux then retired Robby Thompson on a pop fly to shortstop. He was almost out of the jam.

Think of all the changes that have buffeted baseball since Clark strode to the plate with the bases loaded and two out in the fourth inning of that game. Wrigley Field was in just its second season of night baseball then. First-generation artificial turf has gone the way of the ash bat. Every stadium in Major League Baseball has been replaced or refurbished. The average MLB salary has risen from $512,000 to $3.4 million. And catchers and pitchers now put their gloves in front of their faces when meeting at the mound to prevent opponents from reading their lips.

With a wild Game 1 in danger of taking another zany turn, Zimmer went to the mound to consult with Maddux, a 23-year-old who had won a career-high 19 games with a career-low 2.95 ERA during the regular season. Clark stood in the on-deck circle with cleanup hitter Mitchell. Looking out at the Cubs conference, he could see Maddux telling Zimmer, "Fastball in." "Kevin and I were standing in the on-deck circle when I read his lips," Clark said. "I told Kevin, and Kevin went in and told some guys in the dugout. A little later it came out. Back then you tried to take advantage of anything possible. Wrigley's a small ballpark as far as you're right on top of the fans, and then you're on top of the field, so I'm sitting there, looking at Maddux talking to Zimmer, and he's about 60, 70 feet from me. So it's pretty easy to see." So was the first-pitch fastball. Clark smoked it over the right-field wall onto Sheffield Avenue for a grand slam and an 8–3 Giants lead.

When Clark came up in the top of the eighth inning, he was 4-for-4 with two home runs, a double, and six RBIs. Chicago reliever Steve Wilson pitched around him, walking him to put runners on first and second. Then Mitchell lined a three-run homer to left for the final runs in an 11–3 Giants win. Said Zimmer of Clark: "He had a hell of a week tonight."

Thursday, October 5, was an off day for the A's and Blue Jays. The ill will between the teams continued to percolate. Nearly as concerning for the A's and their fans was the prospect of a return to Oakland by the Raiders football team. The Raiders had played in Oakland from 1960–81 before relocating to Los Angeles. On August 26, 1989, they returned to the Coliseum for an exhibition game against the Houston Oilers that was regarded by many as a trial balloon to gauge the interest of a Sliver and Black homecoming. It was reported by the *Oakland Tribune* that the city had proposed an offer to Raiders owner Al Davis of $54.9 million in cash and five years guaranteed sellouts in a remodeled Coliseum.

Coliseum board president George Vukasin told reporters that A's management had "raised some questions in relation to the marketing aspect and how it might affect the A's. The questions relate to the total sports dollars throughout the Bay Area and how far those sports dollars can go." The Athletics' contract with the

Oakland Coliseum ran until 2000 but had provisions that would allow the team to void the agreement as early as 1991.

With the ALCS taking the day off, the Giants and Cubs had primetime to themselves. Rick Reuschel enjoyed it for all of 18 pitches. The National League's All-Star starter lasted two-thirds of an inning, allowing five runs on five hits before being lifted for Kelly Downs. Reuschel had been considerably better before the All-Star break (12–3, 2.12 ERA) than after (5–5, 4.61 ERA). It was a concerning downturn, doubly so for a 17-year veteran who had just turned 40. "I don't think his arm is tired," Craig told reporters. "But if it is, I'm going to have to make the decision to start somebody else." When writers asked if his arm was tired, Big Daddy gave a typically expansive Reuschelian answer: "No."

Cubs first baseman Grace had three hits and four RBIs in the Cubs' 9–5 victory, giving him a .750 average after two games. The Giants continued their power surge with Mitchell, Thompson, and Matt Williams all hitting home runs. But Clark went 1-for-4, sending his postseason average plummeting to .625.

Whitt got a measure of revenge in Game 3 of the ALCS on Friday, October 6, in Toronto. Not so much defensively—Rickey Henderson stole a base, giving Oakland 11 steals for the series. The A's only unsuccessful stolen base attempt was a result of pitcher John Cerruti's pickoff move in Game 2. But Whitt did cap a four-run fourth-inning rally by singling home the tie-breaking run that stood up as the winner in Toronto's 7–3 victory. Davis took the loss, giving up six runs in six and one-third innings. Of equal concern was the performance of reliever Rick Honeycutt, who faced three batters and allowed two hits and a bases-loaded walk. Honeycutt had faced six batters in the series with all six reaching base.

In San Francisco, where the Cubs and Giants worked out the day before Game 3 of the NLCS, talk turned to a pair of All-Stars—Clark, who'd had a nice two days in Chicago, and Cubs right fielder Andre Dawson, who had gone hitless in the first two games without getting a ball out of the infield in seven at-bats. Zimmer expressed concern over Dawson. As for Clark he told reporters, "It didn't take no genius to see he was going to hit." And why was that? "Because," Zimmer said, "he'd tell you."

In the summer of 2013, Clark tried to describe what it was like to be red hot at precisely the right time. "As a ballplayer you love getting to the point where you're like what we call 'locked in,'" he said. "You get a pitch and you just don't miss it. There are plenty of times over the course of a season where you get locked in. And you're hitting the ball hard, but they're not all falling. That whole playoffs, I don't know why, but they were falling in. There were other times over the course of my career I got locked in. That was the one time the bright lights of the playoffs were shining." Also reflecting in 2013, Dave Dravecky said, "When you looked at Will, the easiest way I could sum it up is: if someone gave me the ability to pick a team of eight guys and a pitcher, all eight guys would be Will Clark. I'll take eight of him all day long."

Game 4 of the ALCS was a benign affair through two scoreless innings. Then the haymakers began to fly. With one out in the top of the third inning, Oakland shortstop Walt Weiss grounded a double into the left-field corner. On Flanagan's 1–1 pitch to Rickey Henderson, Weiss swiped third for Oakland's 12th stolen base of the series. All Henderson had to do was hit a fly ball deep enough to score Weiss, and the A's would take the early lead. Henderson did that and more, lifting the 2–1 pitch over the center-field fence for a 2–0 advantage. Two batters later, Canseco tore into a Flanagan delivery and sent it rocketing into the fifth deck, a blast that left his teammates gape-mouthed in astonishment and scrambling to provide reporters with a frame of reference. "By far the longest I've ever seen," Parker said. "It's like Jay Johnstone said, 'Anything hit that far should have food served on it.'" The shot was estimated to be 484 feet, and it was the first to reach the SkyDome's fifth level. "It was hit so hard, I fell off the bench," Rickey Henderson said. Canseco said the homer was no better than his "10th or 11th best." Dennis Eckersley would have none of it. "I'm sure it was probably his longest," Eck said. "He's full of himself."

There was an odd vibe to the game. Announcer Bob Costas said the home run silenced the excitable crowd to such an extent that it seemed like a library. Canseco's blow felt symbolic and decisive, but it had decided nothing. Rickey Henderson hit a second home run, a two-run shot, for a 5–1 A's lead. But the Blue Jays kept chipping away, scoring two runs in the eighth—after another unsettling effort by Honeycutt—to cut the deficit to 6–5. Eckersley mitigated the damage in the eighth and pitched a scoreless ninth as the A's outlasted Toronto. "I'm exhausted," La Russa told writers. "That's why I asked Cito outside the interview room, 'Are you sure you want to do this for a living?'"

The biggest baseball crowd in Candlestick Park history, 62,065, was on its feet before Game 3 between the Giants and Cubs. On the one-year anniversary of his cancer surgery, Dravecky threw out the ceremonial first pitch—right-handed, of course. Then things got weird. Both starters were forced to leave with injuries—the Giants' Mike LaCoss with a sprained knee suffered while trying to field a bunt in the fourth inning and the Cubs' Rick Sutcliffe after injuring his right quad while running the bases in the seventh. Sutcliffe's pinch-runner, fellow pitcher Maddux, scored on a sacrifice fly to give Chicago a 4–3 lead.

Left-hander Paul Assenmacher relieved Sutcliffe to start the bottom of the seventh. He retired Donell Nixon on a fly ball. Butler followed with a single. Assenmacher missed with his first pitch to Thompson, bringing Zimmer out of the dugout for a pitching change. Les Lancaster, a right-hander, was summoned to finish the at-bat with the right-handed Thompson. Lancaster's first pitch was ball two. Craig flashed the hit-and-run sign. As Lancaster delivered, Butler took off for second base. Thompson pounded the pitch over the left-field fence. The Giants led 5–4.

That's how the game ended. Even after it was over, the weirdness continued. Lancaster, recounting his matchup with Thompson, unwittingly revealed that he'd been unaware of the count when he came into the game. Until reporters informed him otherwise, he thought Thompson's home run came on a 3–0 pitch instead of a 2–0 count. "I thought I would have to come in with a strike or I'd be facing Clark," he said.

Zimmer was asked why he had allowed the left-handed Assenmacher to throw even one pitch to right-handed Thompson, given that Thompson was 6-for-6 lifetime against Assenmacher? "I manage the way I want to manage," Zimmer said. "I bring in guys I want to bring in. That's what I did all season and that's what I did tonight."

Almost overlooked in the intrigue was that Thompson had snapped out of a long offensive slumber to become the game's difference maker. The Giants' second baseman, considered an All-Star candidate after a strong first half of the season, had slumped in the second. "This is a new season," said Thompson, one of those players you didn't fully appreciate unless you saw him play every day. "Everybody says I'm a scrapper. I may be lacking in talent sometimes, but deep down inside I have a big heart. I love to play the game. When I go between the white lines, I give 100 percent. When I leave the ballpark at night, I feel good about myself."

◆ ◆ ◆ ◆

Game 5 of the ALCS was an afternoon start—not that you could tell inside the hermetically sealed SkyDome. This was the 13th time the Blue Jays had played in their new stadium with the roof closed. They had won the first 11. Game 4 was their first loss.

Day, night, open, closed, it didn't matter to Rickey Henderson. He was a force of nature at that point. On the fifth pitch of the game from Stieb, Henderson walked. On the eighth pitch, he stole second base, his eighth steal of the series. On the 15th pitch, he scored on Canseco's single. The A's led 1–0. They would never trail.

Stewart wasn't dominant, but his damage control was impeccable early on. In the second, third, and fourth innings, the Blue Jays left a combined four runners in base, all in scoring position. Before the Blue Jays could break through, the A's added on. Terry Steinbach singled home one run, and Gallego squeezed home another in the seventh as Oakland boosted its lead to 4–0. Lloyd Moseby put Toronto on the board with a solo home run in the bottom of the eighth. When Bell led off the ninth with another home run, La Russa made the call for Eckersley to protect a 4–1 lead.

That prompted Toronto manager Gaston to make his own call. He asked umpires to check Eckersley's glove for a foreign object. Later Gaston contended Eckersley had taken something from his glove and stuck it inside his pants. La Russa rushed out. Pointed words were exchanged. A misunderstanding, La Russa explained 24 years after the incident. "What happened was, I found out later, that a kid in the clubhouse told Cito, 'Hey, there's something going on with Eck's glove,'" La Russa said. "And so Cito, now he's between a rock and a hard place. Cito I would rank, and everybody who knows him, would rank him as a terrific competitor but a classy guy. He's not going to be one of those guys who's a gamesman. But they're getting ready to get beat, and you get that piece of information. I think he's honor-bound to challenge. I remember telling Eck, 'I think he had to do it.' But he comes out there and [Eck] knows nothing, so…"

When order was restored—umpires found nothing untoward in Eckersley's glove—Tony Fernandez singled to center field. He stole second, went to third on Whitt's ground-out, and scored on a sacrifice fly by Gruber. The A's lead was a wafer-thin 4–3. No. 8 hitter Junior Felix, a 22-year-old rookie, was Toronto's last hope. He worked the count full. He fouled off a 3–2 pitch. On the seventh pitch of the at-bat, he swung through an Eckersley delivery. The A's were headed back to the World Series.

But the A's and Blue Jays weren't quite done with each other. Some Toronto players claimed that Eckersley flipped his middle finger in the direction of their dugout after the final out. More charges of hotdoggery were leveled. This wasn't the first time an opponent questioned the A's deportment. The fact is, if the A's were beating your favorite team, they were an easy team to dislike. Eckersley liked to punctuate his strikeouts by pointing at the plate. Rickey Henderson and Parker enjoyed their home-run trots. This was the apex of an opponent's A's-as-antiheros screed. After acknowledging to reporters his own reputation as "a hot dog and controversial," Bell said the A's had "the worst attitude I've ever seen in baseball." "That's putting it mildly," Whitt said. "You've just won the championship. Why rub our noses in it?"

"My memory of my 10 years with the A's," La Russa said in 2013, "the great majority of the games we played against Toronto and Minnesota were competitive, contested, and had a bunch of heroics. The difference is, maybe once did the aggression and the hot competition spark anything between us and the Twins. But with the Blue Jays, we had excitable guys, they had excitable guys. They were really talented. We had a lot of similarities. Pitchers on both sides had good stuff and were very aggressive in and out. Hitters on both sides dug in and let it fly. And there's a lot of aggressive base running. So it's impossible for sparks not to fly. I would say that there was a certain perception of arrogance with those A's clubs. The bashing, there wasn't a lot of that going on at the time. We had some big imposing pitchers and hitters. Stew staring. Eck: 'Yaaaah!' There were personalities up and down that team. So I can see a team like that beats you, it'll get under your skin."

Rickey Henderson was the obvious choice as series MVP. He hit .400, had a .609 on-base percentage, stole eight bases, scored eight runs, drew seven walks, hit two homers, and had five RBIs. He called it a dream come true. Never one to resort to overstatement when measured analysis was an option, La Russa told writers, "It has to be the best playoff series that anyone's ever played."

◆ ◆ ◆ ◆

Fifteen National League pitchers posted ERAs below 3.00 in 1989. Two of them started Game 4 of the NCLS—ERA champ Garrelts and Maddux. Both were gone before the fifth inning. The first half of the game was dramatic but hardly artful. The Cubs, hoping to even the best-of-seven series 2–2, led 1–0 and 2–1. The Giants, looking to take a commanding 3–1 lead in the series, came back to lead 3–2 and 4–2. The Cubs tied it 4–4 in the top of the fifth, after which both starting pitchers had been relieved.

Steve Wilson, who had taken over for Maddux in the fourth inning, began the bottom of the fifth. Clark sliced Wilson's first pitch down the left-field line for a double. Also swinging at the first pitch, Mitchell lined out to left field. That brought Williams to the plate.

In his previous at-bat, the right-handed Williams drove in two runs against the right-handed Maddux with a single. Wilson threw lefty. Williams had tremendous power numbers against left-handers in 1989 with nine home runs in 87 at-bats and a .644 slugging percentage. It seemed like a pivotal at-bat even before Wilson threw his first pitch, which Williams fouled off for strike one. "A new man" is what Mitchell called Williams when the latter was recalled from Triple A in late July. The numbers bore him out.

- In the first month of the season with the Giants, Williams hit .130 in 21 games with two home runs and five RBIs.

- In 76 games with Phoenix (slightly more than half a minor league season), he hit .320 with 26 home runs and 61 RBIs. He finished one homer shy of tying for the PCL lead in a league that featured future major league All-Stars Sandy Alomar Jr., Jay Buhner, and Carlos Baerga.

- In 63 games after rejoining the Giants, Williams—despite a .218 average—hit 16 homers (tied for second in the majors over that period) and drove in 45 runs (third in the National League).

- Including his first two at-bats in Game 4, he was 4-for-14 in the NLCS with a home run and seven RBIs.

"When you see Matt Williams and look at him even to this day," said Clark in 2013, "you go, man, he's a good athlete. You stand next to him. He's 6'3" and 220 pounds of just muscle. He's so put-together. He's launching balls left and right. But then on top of that—and this is first and foremost—he was the best third baseman I ever played with. Not only could he pick it over there, but he made my job so easy at first base, just chest-high throws, one after another from wherever it was on the field, whatever arm angle he had to throw."

Williams took Wilson's second pitch for a called strike. He was down in the count 0–2. Those who had watched Williams to that point in his career understood what 0–2 meant—strike three was on its way. But not that time. Williams took ball one and then ball two. He fouled off two pitches after that and took ball three. The count was full.

He fouled off four consecutive pitches after that. The game had slowed down. It had become a gripping battle of wills, a defining moment in two young careers and a contentious postseason game. Wilson dealt the 12th pitch of the at-bat. Williams pumped it over the left-field fence. The Giants led 6–4. Incredibly, there was no more scoring. In relief of Garrelts, Downs threw four shutout innings. Steve Bedrosian struck out Dawson with the bases loaded to end the game. The Giants were one win away from their first World Series since 1962. Wilson was in tears after the game. "Tomorrow will be another day," he said, without much conviction.

On the Giants' side, Craig called Williams' at-bat one of the greatest he had seen in 39 years in baseball. Williams acknowledged that when he was sent down in May he wasn't sure if he'd ever be back in the majors. "So yeah," he told reporters, "I'd say that's the best at-bat of my life."

Little did anyone suspect that Sunday night was just a warm-up act for Monday afternoon. Game 5 began at 12:07 PM in unusually warm weather. Indian summer is typically the best weather of the year in San Francisco. But these temperatures were historically high: 88 in San Francisco and 87 in Oakland. Some refer to such anomalous warm spells as earthquake weather.

The Cubs struck first in Game 5. Sandberg doubled off Giants starter Reuschel to score Jerome Walton for a 1–0 lead in the top of the third inning. Chicago starter Mike Bielecki, who won 18 games for the Cubs in 1989, retired the first 11 Giants before Clark singled with two out in the fourth. Bielecki struck out Mitchell to end the inning.

The Giants evened the score in the seventh when Clark tripled—he had then hit for the cycle in the series—and Mitchell fetched him home with a sacrifice fly. It was 1–1. As the game entered the bottom of the eighth, Bielecki seemed strong, working on a three-hitter with seven strikeouts and no walks. He got pinch-hitter Ken Oberkfell on a fly ball to left and then struck out Uribe for the second out.

Then came a tense, 10-pitch battle with Candy Maldonado, pinch-hitting for Reuschel. Maldonado fouled off two full-count pitches before taking ball four. Leadoff hitter Butler worked the count full before he, too, took ball four. Zimmer visited the mound with Mitch Williams warming up in the bullpen. He opted to stick with his starter. Thompson took four straight balls to load the bases. Zimmer re-emerged from the dugout. He lifted Bielecki after 131 pitches—only the third time all season Bielecki had been allowed to go past 117—and called for the Wild Thing.

As Williams jogged in from the bullpen, the Candlestick Park public-address system began filling the stadium with the jangly strains of "Wild Thing," the song popularized by English band the Troggs in 1966. The tune had been given a second life by the movie *Major League*, in which it had been the walk-in song for fictional Cleveland Indians closer Ricky Vaughn, played by Charlie Sheen. It seemed only natural that the song was appropriated as Williams' anthem at Wrigley Field. But here? Now? The song went on for about 15 seconds before it was interrupted by what sounded like a needle being raked back and forth across a vinyl record, a cacophonous noise that drew cheers from the Candlestick Park crowd. It wasn't an ill-advised homage after all. It was a mocking gesture.

Clark was focused on other things. "I remember he came in to warm up," Clark said. "I went over to speak to [hitting coach] Dusty [Baker]. I said, 'I'm looking fastball away. What do you think?' First thing—and I'll remember this till I die—Dusty said, 'He's got a lot better command than what people think. But I'd go with that fastball away, too.' So I said, 'All right, cool.' We were both on the same page."

In the NBC broadcast booth in the *Game of the Week* network's final telecast before CBS took over the rights to televise Major League Baseball in 1990, Vin Scully, ever the verbal artiste, set the scene. "Well, I guess we should have figured it would come down to this," he told viewers. "Will Clark with a chance to win it, the bases loaded, two out, and the Wild Thing, Mitch Williams, on the mound."

"I got up to home plate," Clark said, "and the first pitch [Williams] absolutely painted. Knee high, right on the outside corner. There was not much I could do with that ball, so…strike one." Clark got what he was looking for on the second pitch—a fastball away. "I fouled it off, just missed it," he said. "So now I'm in the hole 0–2. I remember backing out of the batter's box and taking a deep breath and I said, 'All right, we got a war on our hands now.'"

The third pitch was high and away. The fourth was another fastball, which Clark fouled off. "It was a high fastball and, oh God, it was 95, 96, I guess," he said. "It was letter high, and I fouled it straight back. And I stepped out of the batter's box again and said, 'Oh, Jesus. Whew!' I said, 'If I can get on top of that one, that'd be awesome.'"

The fifth pitch was a high front-door slider, which looped over Clark's right shoulder. Clark, a little in front of the pitch, fouled it back and then lurched across the plate off-balance. Scully, who had been letting the action speak for itself, stepped in with a maestro's touch. "In every important series," he said, as Clark backed out of the box, "there comes that very important moment, where it's difficult to breathe, difficult to swallow. This is that moment." Clark agreed. "Hard to breathe, yeah," Clark said. "I'm standing there and that's why I [exhaled] like that."

The seventh pitch was a searing fastball around the letters, one alpha dog at the top of his game challenging another. Somehow Clark got his top hand up to meet that pitch and drilled it up the middle. The crowd of 62,084, yet another San Francisco baseball record, went berserk. "I looked up," Clark said, "and the ball was headed right at second base. The one thing that went through my mind was, *Don't hit the bag! Don't hit the bag!* I didn't want it to ricochet right at [an infielder]. It missed hitting the bag by a few inches and went into center field, and, I mean, all hell was breaking loose. The fans were going crazy. Brett Butler was running on contact, so Candy Maldonado scored and Butler scored. Robby Thompson was on his way to third base, and Jerome Walton for some reason double-clutched. I think he had Robby Thompson dead to rights going to third base, and he double-clutched, and Robby made it into third. I was on first base and the first thing I thought about was, *I need to turn around and acknowledge my teammates.* I remember standing on first and pointing in the dugout like that, and everybody is right back at me. So it was pretty cool."

The drama wasn't over. Bedrosian retired the first two Cubs batters in the top of the ninth. Then he allowed three consecutive singles, the last of which drove in a run that cut the lead to 3–2. Sandberg, who had had a fine NLCS, came up with runners on first and second. He grounded Bedrosian's first pitch to Thompson at second base. Thompson threw to Clark at first, and the Giants had captured their first pennant in 27 years.

The Giants had barely reached the clubhouse when the gushing commenced. Not on the active roster but allowed be in uniform for the games, pitcher Mike Krukow sat on a training table in his baseball underwear, offering a soliloquy to a clot of reporters as he waxed eloquently about Clark. "It seems scenarios are written for him," Krukow said. "He comes into the game in weighty situations. If you were Bernard Malamud, you'd write this SOB up. Will Clark's a legend. I'm telling you right now—that single opened the eyes of a lot of people who had heard of him but never had a chance to see him play that much. What you do [in the postseason] is how you are judged by people in this game. I can tell you people I've played with who have had great careers but who didn't play well in this particular arena. And their careers were tainted by it. This is how you are judged."

His hair matted with champagne, Giants general manager Al Rosen said he didn't want to overstate the case "when you're in a state of euphoria like I'm in now. [Clark's] had a great series. He's a great player and he's going to be a Hall of Famer."

Perhaps the highest praise was offered by Williams. "I know I just got beat by the best," he said to the media. "I dropped down and threw him two of my best sliders. One of them started out behind his head. Any other hitter in the league probably bails out and strikes out on that pitch, but he just fouled them off. I got beat by a guy who's going to be in the Hall of Fame one day." Craig reflected 24 years later. "Every time I see Mitch Williams on MLB Network I still think about that. Will Clark is one of the best clutch hitters in tough situations that I've ever been around. He loved that atmosphere. Williams was one of the nastiest left-handers in baseball. He threw 97, 98 mph, and they didn't call him the Wild Thing for nothing."

And still the drama was not complete. Inactive but in uniform, Dravecky made his way to the dugout as Bedrosian set about closing out the clincher in the top of the ninth inning. "I walked into the dugout and I'm waiting for the end of the game," Dravecky said, "and Tom Seaver comes in. He was doing the game for TV. He sits down next to me and says, 'You're not going to go out there in that pile, are you?' And I said, 'Why wouldn't I? Those are my teammates. I want to be with them.' I paid no attention to him whatsoever."

On his way out to the celebratory scrum, a teammate inadvertently bumped Dravecky from behind, rebreaking his arm. "And next thing you know," Dravecky said, "[trainer] Mark Letendre has grabbed me and he's holding me up. I'm about to pass out because the pain is so intense. It was a moment of extreme stupidity. At the same time, it was a reminder of how severe the break was and the damage to the arm was. It was," he said, referring to his baseball career, "a nail in the coffin."

Chapter 10

La Russa's Second Chance

Tony La Russa was determined his second World Series experience would be different from his first. In 1988 his A's won the American League Championship Series six days before the start of the World Series. When La Russa suggested to his players a plan to ramp up their practices to stay sharp during the layoff, the players pushed back. "Not to show panic and lack of confidence, we let it go," La Russa recalled almost a quarter-century later.

Thus the A's went through their leisurely paces while the Los Angeles Dodgers were grinding through the final three games of their playoff series against the New York Mets. Dodgers hitters looked sharp during the 1988 World Series. A's hitters did not. "Virtually everybody on that [A's] team got one hit [in the series]," La Russa said. "Almost nobody got more than one hit. And if you watched how many times the ball was in the strike zone and guys fouled it off; our timing was off. We hadn't played seriously and hadn't practiced well enough. So what we felt when it was over was, *Man, we backed off.* The buck stops here. I didn't correct it."

There would be no leisurely run-up to the 1989 World Series for the A's. They closed out the Toronto Blue Jays on Sunday, October 8, once again six days before Game 1 of the World Series. When the team reconvened Tuesday, La Russa was not in the mood for give and take. His team had accepted the challenge of righting what went wrong in 1988. "It isn't that we lost to the Dodgers," he said. "We lost in five games. That was unacceptable."

So this time the A's left nothing to chance. La Russa reminded his players of their spring training vow. "We said, 'No regrets,'" La Russa said. "'We can't have what happened last time. Today we're going to work out. Wednesday, Thursday, we're going to schedule our pitchers to pitch and our hitters to have three at-bats. Look, fellas, this is our chance to stay sharp.' And Wednesday, our guys were digging in, fouling balls off. I mean, they were really working."

Thursday's intrasquad game was equally spirited. It ended with Dennis Eckersley scheduled to pitch against the heart of the Oakland order, starting with Jose Canseco. "I remember Jose got up, and he was pointing his bat to center field like he was Babe Ruth," Eckersley said. "I drilled him in the back, first pitch," said La Russa, picking up the story. "To this day I've never asked Eck…I don't want to know. Jose drops the bat and he starts walking toward the mound, and that's the end of practice. And nobody [in the press box] is noticing. They're writing their stories. Nobody saw it. It never got reported."

Eckersley understands how suspicious it must have looked. And in truth, he didn't mind if his teammates thought he had deliberately thrown at Canseco. But years later he swore it was an accident. "I didn't mean it," he said, "I tried to throw it in. I think [Canseco] thinks to this day that I hit him on purpose, but I didn't. It was great, though. It made me look like a bad ass. I looked like Studly Do-Right."

La Russa was so excited about his team's intensity that he had to pull over on his drive from Oakland to his East Bay home to calm down. "I went home and told [my wife] Elaine," La Russa said, "'I don't know what's going to happen in the World Series. But this club can't be more ready to play.'" Another thing happened while La Russa was driving home after one of the A's practices. He was listening to the radio and heard a report that Giants manager Roger Craig had suggested more intense pre-World Series workouts, but that his players had pushed back. "So they were making the same mistake that we did in '88," La Russa said. "I said, 'Holy smokes. Here's this really great team, and they're going to miss an edge.'"

An edge wouldn't have been the only thing missing from the Giants' first workout. Thinking Wednesday was an off day, Kevin Mitchell was in San Diego closing escrow on a house. "Sure I'm upset," Craig told reporters. "I made an announcement in front of the whole ballclub on Monday about the workout. He was right there when I said it. As much as I hate to do it at this time of year, I have to use some discipline. It wouldn't be fair to the other guys on this club if I didn't." Discipline came in the form of a fine. A contrite Mitchell was on time for Thursday's practice, where it came to light he had missed the team flight to Chicago for the start of the NLCS after spending the night in San Diego. "Whatever Craig gave me, I deserve it," he told the media. "I missed a practice and I let my teammates down."

Thursday was the day the Giants received their scouting report on the A's from scouts Charlie Fox, who managed San Francisco to the 1971 division title, and John Van Ornum. It also was the day the A's received a 75-page report on the Giants from scouts Ron Schueler and Jeff Scott. In any other year, the scouting reports would have received little or no notice. But this was 1989. Kirk Gibson's instantly historic 1988 home run off Eckersley was still fresh in the public consciousness. And to hear Gibson tell it, that home run was the product of the observation and intuition of a veteran scout named Mel Didier. "He had watched Dennis Eckersley for many years," Gibson said. "He came up to me [before the World Series] in his southern drawl, and said, 'Pardnuh, as sure as I'm standin' here breathin', you're goin' to see a 3–2 backdoor slider.'" So news of the scouting reports, even though the public might never be privy to a word of them, tickled the imagination. Did one of them contain a nugget of wisdom that would change the course of World Series history?

◆ ◆ ◆ ◆

The so-called Subway World Series wasn't a novel concept. There had been 15 intra-city battles for baseball's biggest prize, including five in a six-year stretch from 1951–56, matching the New York Yankees against either the New York Giants or Brooklyn Dodgers. But this was the first in 33 years and the first held west of the Rockies. It was only the second time in the 22 years the Giants and A's had shared the Bay Area that both teams reached the playoffs in the same season. It was a glorious novelty for some. For others it carried a deeper meaning.

Oakland third baseman Carney Lansford was from Santa Clara. "I know what it means to the fans for there to be a Bay Bridge World Series," he told reporters in 1989. "I grew up as a kid going and watching the Giants and A's play. One was not more favorite than the other. I pulled for both."

Two other A's players had a shared childhood experience—Eckersley, who grew up in Fremont, and Dave Stewart, who grew up in Oakland. Nearly a quarter-century later, both appreciate the Bay Bridge matchup even more than they did in real time. "That was big time for me, very special," Stewart said. "As a kid I grew up on the Giants. The A's didn't get to Oakland until 1968. My dad was a big Giants fan. That's the team I watched—Willie Mays, the Alou brothers, Orlando Cepeda, Willie McCovey, Mike McCormick, Juan Marichal, Gaylord Perry. Watching those guys growing up, that tradition stays with you. Even now, I root for the Giants and I root for the A's."

Eckersley kicks himself for not enjoying it more at the time. "I didn't have time to take it in," he said. "I'll always regret that at some level not being in the moment more. There's so much pressure you can't enjoy it. That whole Bay Area thing, I grew up there, went to watch the Giants at Candlestick. I talk about it now, but then I wasn't feeling it."

Even broadcaster Al Michaels, who would call the World Series for ABC, was excited. Born in Brooklyn, New York, Michaels had been the Giants' lead radio play-by-play man from 1974–76. "I've got to fess up," he told writers at the time. "It is something special for me. It's my old team and an area I grew to love immensely."

Almost overnight, the region was saturated with Bay Bridge Series souvenirs and apparel. The celebratory mood soured briefly when San Francisco mayor Art Agnos, asked about the traditional wager between political leaders of the World Series host cities, joked that there was nothing in Oakland he wanted. Oakland mayor Lionel Wilson took offense. But eventually the elected officials worked out their differences and agreed on a bet. The losing mayor would host the winning mayor and a group of children from the victorious city to dinner and a game the following season. At a news conference, they also unveiled a trophy modeled after the Bay Bridge, which would be awarded to the winning team. "This symbolizes regionalism," Agnos said. Said Wilson: "We're so close together. We're like brothers and sisters."

◆ ◆ ◆ ◆

On October 6, 1931, A's manager Connie Mack sent George Earnshaw to the mound to start Game 4 of the World Series against the St. Louis Cardinals. Earnshaw responded with a two-hit shutout to even the series at two games apiece. Those were high times for the Athletics, who were just two wins away from nabbing their third consecutive World Series. Earnshaw was coming off his third consecutive 20-win season. Lefty Grove was voted MVP after a 31–4 year in which he added five saves. Catcher Mickey Cochrane batted .349 and was such a popular star that 10 days after the final game of the 1931 World Series, in Commerce, Oklahoma, rabid baseball fan Mutt Mantle gave his newborn son Cochrane's first name.

Those high times didn't last. The A's lost the 1931 World Series to the Cardinals in seven games. Mack managed 19 more seasons but produced just five winning records and no pennant winners. Earnshaw's Game 4 gem stood until 1972 as the A's most recent home win in a World Series game. Fifty-eight years later, the A's were still waiting for their next World Series shutout.

None of which was on the mind of Stewart as he sat through the pregame pomp and pageantry before Game 1 of the Bay Bridge Series. The son of the late commissioner Bart Giamatti threw out the first pitch; the Yale Whiffenpoofs sang the national anthem. Stewart was simply focusing on giving his team a chance to win that day's game. If his right arm had been dragging during the latter stages of the season, you couldn't tell by Game 1. Stewart overcame his own throwing error to pitch a scoreless first inning. Giants starter Scott Garrelts matched him in the bottom of the frame, allowing just a one-out single by Lansford. Stewart sailed through a 1-2-3 second inning, striking out Matt Williams and Candy Maldonado.

As ready as it could possibly be—the way manager Tony La Russa saw it—the A's offense jumped to life in the bottom of the frame. Dave Henderson drew a leadoff walk. One out later Terry Steinbach singled Hendu to second. Swinging at the first pitch as Steinbach had done, Tony Phillips singled to right, scoring Henderson and putting runners at the corners. In the span of nine pitches, Garrelts was down 1–0 and in trouble. Walt Weiss followed with a ground ball to Will Clark at first. Breaking for home plate on contact, Steinbach should have been out, but San Francisco catcher Terry Kennedy couldn't handle Clark's low throw. It was 2–0, and the A's had runners on first and second.

Leadoff hitter Rickey Henderson worked the count full—a pick-your-poison count for opposing pitchers the way Henderson had been playing—before lining a single to right that scored Phillips. Garrelts got Lansford and Canseco to end the inning. But his third pitch of the third inning was smoked into the right-field bleachers by Dave Parker, giving Oakland a 4–0 lead. His third pitch of the fourth inning was tagged for a home run by Weiss. It was 5–0. Garrelts exited after the fourth inning, having allowed five runs on seven hits.

There was no stopping Stewart. He had just three 1-2-3 innings, but he retired the leadoff batter eight times in nine frames. Clark broke that spell with a single in the ninth. Mitchell followed with a single. Though they advanced on a passed ball, Stewart left them stranded, completing the first World Series shutout for the A's since Prohibition. And, for what it was worth, improving Oakland's 1989 record against the Giants to 9–1, including spring training games.

Afterward, Stewart navigated the inevitable questions about how his Earnshawian effort might impact his status as an underrated pitcher. La Russa informed those who didn't watch much A's baseball that what they had just seen was one of two things Stewart did best—start winning streaks and end losing streaks. Parker harkened back to his .194 average in April and his desire to prove to young bucks like Canseco that he wasn't "a senior statesman."

There wasn't much to be said in the Giants clubhouse. "I'll tell it like I see it," Clark told reporters. "They kicked our butts. This is the World Series. This ain't spring training. I'll guarantee that." Nearly 24 years later, La Russa echoed Clark's contention. "I would say if there was any kind of [spring training] carryover, it would be the slightest for a lot of reasons," La Russa said. "No. 1, they had a really solid club. Roger and his staff did a great job. They had a lot of really good players, good veterans, good young guys. They had won the National League championship. They had beaten the Cubs. We won in five [games], and they won it in five, too. So they had their magical season going. I don't think the spring training [games mattered]. I think they probably looked at us like we were a really good club. We looked at them like they were a really good club."

On a chilly Sunday night at the Coliseum, Game 2 was more competitive at least for three innings. Oakland took a 1–0 lead in the bottom of the first inning against Rick Reuschel on a Rickey Rally. Henderson drew a four-pitch walk to lead off, stole second on the second pitch to Lansford, and scored on Lansford's double. The Giants tied it off Mike Moore in the top of the third when Robby Thompson's sacrifice fly scored Jose Uribe.

The A's mounted the decisive rally in the bottom of the fourth inning, scoring four times in a dizzying span of five hitters. Canseco battled for 10 pitches against Reuschel before drawing a leadoff walk. The next batter, Parker, drove Canseco home with a double off the top of the wall in the right-field corner. Reuschel walked Dave Henderson, putting runners on first and second, and then struck out Mark McGwire on three pitches. Big Daddy missed with the first two pitches to Steinbach, but Steinbach didn't miss the third, slugging it over the left-field wall for a three-run homer and a 5–1 lead. Moore threw seven strong innings for the win. Rick Honeycutt and Eckersley mopped up in scoreless fashion. The World Series was looking like a walkover.

It was difficult to know which was more shocking—how well the A's were playing or how poorly the Giants were playing. Oakland's starting pitching had allowed one run in 16 innings. San Francisco's offense had scored once in two games, the first time that had happened in a World Series since 1950. San Francisco had nine hits, eight of them singles. Oakland hitters had 18 hits and had hit for the cycle. The designated hitter matchup was a reflection of the series at large. Oakland's Parker had a homer, double, and two RBIs. San Francisco's Ernest Riles was 0-for-7.

In addition to those problems, Clark looked and sounded like death warmed over. Injured in his collision with Mike Scioscia in September, his leg was aching. He also was battling tonsillitis. "There ain't no advantage to being down 2–0," he croaked after Game 2. "We just have to get back to the 'Stick." At that point a Giants public relations employee stepped between Clark and the assembled media. "Will's not feeling well," the PR guy said. "He's got to save his voice." Dressing one locker away, Bob Brenly smiled. "Gee," he said, "what a polite way to say 'Fuck off.'"

Rickey Henderson was late to Oakland's Monday workout at Candlestick Park, and Clark never made it to the Giants'. Asked about Clark's absence, Craig, snidely referencing Mitchell's absence from a pre-World Series workout, cracked to reporters, "He's in San Diego closing escrow on a house." The real reason was less interesting. The Giants had told Clark, suffering from tonsillitis, to stay home and get some rest.

La Russa announced that Bob Welch would start Game 3 and that Ron Hassey would catch him. Craig announced Don Robinson as his starting pitcher and said shortstop Uribe and right fielder Maldonado would be replaced in the lineup by third baseman Ken Oberkfell (with Williams moving to shortstop) and right fielder Pat Sheridan.

Everyone marveled at the gorgeous, calm weather at Candlestick Park. "This is beautiful," Giants hitting coach Dusty Baker remarked to the *San Jose Mercury News*. "This was probably the time of year they sold the property to [the Giants]." The forecast for Tuesday's Game 3 called for more unseasonably warm weather. The National Weather Service called for 65 degrees around game time with westerly winds of 10–20 mph subsiding throughout the evening. "We're definitely into a bit of a warming trend," an NWS spokesman said.

Chapter 11

15 Seconds of Terror

Will Clark had just run a sprint from the right-field line to center field. Tony La Russa was sitting in the visitors' dugout. Dave Dravecky was at his locker in the Giants clubhouse, chatting with Bob Knepper. Dave Stewart was "goofing off" in the A's training room with Rickey Henderson, Dave Henderson, Dave Parker, and team trainer Barry Weinberg. Roger Craig had just come in from infield practice and was changing his shirt in his office.

Game 3 of the World Series was a little more than 15 minutes from the first pitch. It was a do-or-die game for the Giants. A loss and they would trail the A's 3–0. In the history of the modern World Series (since 1903), none of the 15 teams that trailed 3–0 in a seven-game series had come back to win. Only two had managed to salvage a single game before being kicked to the curb. But a San Francisco win would make it a 2–1 Series, and that's where it got interesting. Of the 66 teams that trailed 2–1 in a seven-game World Series, 23 had come back to win. Since the end of World War II, it was basically a flip of the coin: 18 of 38 teams trailing 2–1 had won world championship rings.

So Game 3 was a highly anticipated affair. Perhaps Craig's lineup changes would jump-start the Giants offense. Maybe the A's would miss the booming bat of designated hitter Parker. (The DH would not be used at Candlestick Park, a National League venue.) Maybe the 'Stick's blustery winds and eccentric microclimates would work in the Giants' favor.

Commissioner Fay Vincent, on the job for just six weeks since the death of Bart Giamatti, was standing at his box seat near the Giants dugout talking with Willie Mays. Giants scheduled starting pitcher Don Robinson was in the clubhouse, strapping on the huge brace that would stabilize his right knee. Giants general manager Al Rosen was in his luxury box talking with Bill Walsh, the recently retired coach of the San Francisco 49ers. Chub Feeney, formerly the Giants general manager and National League president, was walking in through the right-field gate.

In the umpires' room, American League arbiters Al Clark and Rich Garcia were preparing to make the short walk up the steps through the double doors and onto the playing field. Inactive for the postseason, Giants infielder Chris Speier was on the field chatting with the Gatlin Brothers, the country music group that was to sing the national anthem. A's catcher Terry Steinbach, out of the lineup in favor of Ron Hassey, made sure he was in the A's dugout nice and early, so he could experience the pregame festivities. 49ers quarterback Joe Montana and his wife, Jennifer, who was holding their two-week-old son, were headed back to their seats where Joe's parents, brother, and sister were chatting with former 49ers receiver Dwight Clark. Broadcaster Al Michaels was in the ABC broadcast booth, preparing for the pregame show. Dennis Eckersley was in the bathroom in the A's clubhouse. "It was about intro time," he said, "so I was combing my hair." Oakland pitcher Curt Young was in limbo. Bob Welch was the scheduled starter, but he had strained his groin shagging fly balls during a workout. Uncertain if Welch would be able to go, La Russa had told Young, "You might be the one."

Benjamin Young, an employee at Candlestick Park, had volunteered to climb one of the stadium's light towers to untangle a decorative wind sock. He was 100 feet above the ground at precisely 5:04 PM.

♦ ♦ ♦ ♦

What they didn't know, what none of the 60,000-plus people either at Candlestick Park or headed that way knew, was that all hell was breaking loose nine miles northeast of Santa Cruz and several miles below the Earth's surface at that very moment.

166

The Pacific and North American tectonic plates are slabs of solid, miles-thick rock. Fused in place for years by unimaginable friction, they suddenly succumbed to awesome geologic forces, urging the plates to slide against one another. At 5:04 PM on Tuesday, October 17, 1989, a 22-foot section of the San Andreas Fault slipped with a spectacular grinding lurch, moving seven lateral feet before once again locking in place. The jolt sent more than 30 times the energy of the Hiroshima atom bomb pulsing up, down, and out.

Energy moving south smashed into Watsonville, then a town of 32,000, leveling an estimated 800 homes and 50 buildings. Bricks peeling off the Odd Fellows Building struck and killed a woman. The police communications center was rendered inoperable. A few miles east of Watsonville, Gilroy and Hollister were hammered with buildings and homes suffering structural damage. Energy moving west plowed through Santa Cruz, destroying 774 houses and 310 businesses. Thousands of other structures were damaged. With its unreinforced masonry, the Pacific Garden Mall was no match for nature's fury. Three of the six people who died in Santa Cruz as a result of the earthquake were killed when walls at the mall collapsed.

After roaring through Santa Cruz, the energy dove into the Pacific Ocean, creating an undersea landslide and sending an eight-inch-high tsunami south into Monterey Bay. Energy released to the north raced at a furious pace, covering the 60 miles between Santa Cruz and San Francisco in about 23 seconds. There were those who swore they heard it coming. "When it hit, I knew," Eckersley said. "I'm from the Bay Area. It sounded just like a train coming through the door. It scared you to death. The auxiliary lights came on. I said, 'Earthquake!' and I hauled ass into the parking lot."

"I was walking back toward the right-field line, and it sounded like those F-15s when they fly over," Clark said. "When I looked up, that's when the light standards were whipping back and forth. I said, 'Oh, this is not good.' You could literally see the wave coming through the stadium. It wasn't any fun."

"I remember being in the dugout and the stories after we beat them the first two games," La Russa said. "Roger [Craig] was a great motivator. I love Roger. He's a great competitor. He played in the old days when competition was competition, you know? After we beat them the first two games, I remember him quoted as saying, 'Hey, they had their way. But when they come to Candlestick with our fans, it's going to be different.' And I remember sitting there. Some guys are playing catch. Some guys are running sprints. And all of a sudden, I'm hearing this noise. I thought it was fans stamping their feet, getting ready. I thought, *Oh, this is going to be a tough night. We're just going to have to get through it.* That's my first impression: the fans. Roger, he called it. Then I saw the light standards [swaying], and I knew."

"I was sitting in my locker next to Bob Knepper," Dravecky said. "We had heard this rumble. He looked at me and said, 'Earthquake. Let's get out of here.' We ran out to the parking lot, me in a sling."

"We're watching smoke come out of the air vents," Stewart said. "It was tremors. We got the hell from underneath the stadium. It didn't seem like that much at first. Then we started hearing reports, and all the police officers came onto the field, and we realized this is not good."

"I just felt this rumbling," Craig said. "My ceiling was kind of cracking. I heard Don Robinson out in the clubhouse yell, 'Earthquake!' We went out to the parking lot because it was close. We were standing in the parking lot, and the asphalt was rolling under your feet with the aftershocks."

Benjamin Young spent 15 seconds clinging to the light standard, reeling back and forth at what must have seemed like the top of the world. "I hung on for dear life," he told a reporter shortly after safely reaching the ground. "I was so scared, I [vomited]. It was the most frightening thing I've ever experienced. The thing just swayed and swayed. I thought I was a goner."

Umpire Clark's legs buckled. The cinder block walls of the small umpires' room began to waver, inspiring Garcia to seek refuge under a table.

Feeney, nephew of onetime Giants owner Horace Stoneham and the Giants GM from 1950–69, moved west with the team in 1958. He loved the Bay Area so much he transferred the National League offices there from New York when he was appointed league president. He knew exactly what was happening the moment the ground began to undulate.

The Montanas were under the second-deck overhang. "It was moving," Joe told Scripps Howard News Service. "The only thing we could think of was to get somewhere we'd be safe if it fell." Speier grew up in Alameda. "It's an earthquake," he told the Gatlins, according to *The Orange County Register.* "Just relax and try to enjoy it."

In the ABC booth, Michaels understood what was happening immediately, but his message to the outside world was cut off when the network lost its connection to the stadium. "I tell you what," he said, "We're having an earth…" Years later Michaels told SI.com, "There's suddenly this noise—sounds like kids banging bats on the floor of the upper deck—and this movement. We start to move. I lived in California, so I know earthquakes and I know it's either a big jolt that subsides or a small jolt that builds. And so the lights in the booth went out. We couldn't hear the truck. We didn't know if we were on the air or not. [Analyst Tim] McCarver grabbed my left thigh and squeezed it…I mean, we were holding on. I felt for a moment we'd be pitched out onto the lower deck."

About the same time the ruinous waves of energy were buffeting Candlestick Park, they were rocking a double-deck portion of Oakland's I-880 freeway back and forth as if it was a child's toy. The top deck swayed one way while the bottom deck swung the other. It was part of the Nimitz Freeway, named after World War II Navy hero Chester Nimitz. In 1958 Nimitz had cut a ribbon to open the last section of the freeway, the double-deck section, which would become known locally as the Cypress Structure. This was a time before air bags, crumple zones, and widespread use of seatbelts. Auto fatalities were practically epidemic. Nimitz, according to a story in the *Oakland Tribune*, expressed the hope that the new freeway would "also be a 'safeway' helping to cut down on the tremendous loss of life on our highways." But part of the Cypress Structure had been built on soft mud. The shaking there was too intense and lasted too long for that part of the road. The supports separating the two roadways collapsed. The top deck came thundering down upon the lower deck. A massive dust cloud arose. An Oakland firefighter responding to the scene said it looked like the structure had been bombed.

Meanwhile, the eastern span of the 53-year-old Bay Bridge began jiggling and bouncing. The western span, which connects Yerba Buena Island and San Francisco, is a suspension bridge like the iconic Golden Gate Bridge a few miles to the west. But the old eastern span, which connected Oakland to the island, was a double-deck cantilever design with steel trusses crisscrossing up and over the roadway. As the eastern span rocked and creaked, the frame holding a 50-foot slab of the upper deck became so compromised that the roadway was left unsupported on one end. It swung down like a massive trap door with one end still hinged on the upper deck and the other slamming down upon the lower deck. Traveled by 250,000 vehicles a day, the busiest bridge in the Bay Area was instantly out of commission.

Even before they were finished tormenting Candlestick Park, the quake's waves rolled through San Francisco, causing sidewalks to buckle, power lines to snap, and gas lines to rupture. The earthquake announced itself to the Marina District in the estimation of one witness like the business end of a bullwhip. The Marina was especially susceptible to earthquake damage. Once a lagoon it had been filled with sand and rubble from the 1906 earthquake. As it shook, the ground began to liquefy with water oozing up through the fill to create a dense muddy mix that amplified the earthquake's energy. The Marina also was home to scores of "soft-story" homes and apartment buildings, residences built on top of first-floor garages that had no lateral bracing. Block after block of these buildings collapsed, sometimes with multiple floors pancaking to the ground. The smell of natural gas was pervasive.

More than two dozen fires were reported in San Francisco. The brick façade of a building at Sixth and Bluxome came tumbling to the ground, killing six people. San Francisco's double-deck Embarcadero Freeway, which extended along the city's waterfront north of the Bay Bridge, suffered heavy damage. Part of a terminal at San Francisco International Airport collapsed, and the airport shut down. Seventy-three windows in the I. Magnin department store in Union Square shattered, showering bystanders with broken glass. The clock at the Ferry Building stopped at 5:04, and the flagpole atop it listed crazily.

There wasn't much damage in neighboring Marin, Sonoma, and Contra Costa counties. A 400,000-gallon gasoline tank at the Union Oil refinery in Richmond sprung a leak. There were some ruptured gas lines and downed power lines in Alameda County. Compared to the disaster-scape around it, Candlestick Park was a fortress. When the shaking there finally subsided, a loud cheer arose. The stadium had escaped apparently unscathed. The distinctive cement canopy, which had undergone a seismic retrofit a few years earlier, held firm. The only damage was located around expansion joints, which were designed to allow the stadium to flex during a seismic event. It wasn't long before people inside the stadium learned that not everyone had been so lucky.

"After everything subsided," Will Clark said, "I got back to the dugout, and we had some policemen who were on the field, and their radios were just going crazy, talking about the fire that had already broken out in the Marina. And then somebody said something about the Bay Bridge had a collapse. So you knew that we're not playing this ballgame. People are wandering around on the field, completely lost. And the first thing I thought about was: *I've got to get my family out of the stands.*"

Not long after the earthquake, the stadium—like the rest of San Francisco— lost power. More than 1 million people spent the night without electricity. "We came back through that hallway that leads to right field," Eckersley said. "It was pitch black. We made our way onto the field to see what's happening. As soon as they said the Bay Bridge went down, I went, 'Oh, that's trouble.' Then more cops came in, and you knew this was serious."

Much of the crowd was standing around, wondering what would come next. Players and their families congregated on the field. There were no obvious signs that Candlestick Park would be unable to host a baseball game. But there was no chance of that happening. Official resources were needed elsewhere in the city. The stadium would need to be inspected for possible hidden damage. There was no power, and it was getting dark. Sunset would occur around 7:00 PM.

Vincent, after consulting with San Francisco police, postponed the game around 6:00 PM. Craig was hoping to provide a positive influence for fans. "Fay Vincent was talking to Tony and I after it happened," Craig said. "One of the TV cameramen told him that one section in center field moved down three or four inches. I said, 'We better get out of here. Maybe if the fans see us leave…'"

Pictures of the aftermath of the earthquake at Candlestick showed Steinbach trying to console his wife, Mary; Jose Canseco walking off the field hand-in-hand with his wife, Esther, clad in a red leather ensemble; Mike Krukow carrying his young son Chase. Clark found his parents and brother, and they headed home. Police, using bullhorns, asked fans to leave. Craig didn't have to be asked twice. Still wearing his uniform, the Giants manager piled 11 family members and friends into his pickup truck. Eight of the passengers sat in the bed, and Craig drove off into the gridlock around the stadium. "I got in my pickup truck. And as I was driving out, we were going about five mph to get out of there. Some of the fans were coming up," Craig said. "There was one guy with a bottle of wine. He said, 'You want a sip?' I took a little sip and gave it back to him. It took us a very long time to get home."

All the while the region continued to shake. After the Loma Prieta earthquake, which registered 6.9 on the Richter scale, 51 aftershocks struck in the following 24 hours with a couple measured in the mid-4s. Fires raged in the Marina District. First responders and volunteers alike risked their own lives in a desperate attempt to locate survivors on the Cypress Structure. With the Bay Bridge impassable and the roads clogged, it took the A's bus forever to get back to the Coliseum.

One Oakland player stayed in San Francisco. Welch and his wife lived in a rented two-story house in the Marina District. They liked it so much they bought a condo into which they planned to move after the World Series. They were desperate to get home. Their two-month-old son Dylan was being babysat. Unable to connect with their babysitter via landline, and in an age before widespread use of cell phones, they had no way of knowing if he was all right. It took them two hours to get home. Dylan was fine. Their new condo had been heavily damaged, but their rental was intact. They just wouldn't have electricity or heat for the foreseeable future. They were in good company. Among the displaced residents of the Marina was Joe DiMaggio.

Dravecky was similarly concerned about his kids, who were being cared for in Foster City, which like the Marina was built on a landfill. "All I remembered was getting to my wife, and my mom and dad were there, finally getting to them," he said. "We couldn't get in contact with our kids who were being babysat in Foster City. Word kept trickling in, the Bay Bridge, the lights are out. We were very concerned whether Foster City would have lights on."

For Stewart to get home, he had to pass by the collapsed portion of the Cypress Structure. Still wearing his baseball pants, he found himself drawn to the rescue efforts there that night and for many nights thereafter. He would park at the corner of 18th and Adeline streets. The police recognized him and allowed him inside the disaster zone. He almost always showed up with something for the firemen and police working on the freeway. "I knew what had been going on," Stewart said. "For some reason I was just drawn to it. I was just fortunate the authorities allowed me to be of some help. Coffee, food, anything I could possibly do, I did."

"HUNDREDS DEAD IN HUGE QUAKE" read the headline in the Wednesday, October 18, edition of the *San Francisco Chronicle*, produced despite a power blackout at its Fifth and Mission building. It hardly seemed like overstatement given the damage caused by the largest Bay Area earthquake since 1906. Working on historical models of rush hour traffic flow, authorities estimated that at least a couple of hundred people had been killed on the Cypress Structure. By noon on Wednesday, they had given up hope of finding any more survivors. It had become a recovery effort. It took months to make a full accounting of the death and destruction caused by the Loma Prieta earthquake. According to the U.S. Geological Society, 63 people lost their lives as a result of the temblor, 3,757 were injured, and there was $6 billion in property damage.

It was a strange time for those in the business of baseball. Clearly the game was a low priority in the wake of the disaster. Yet there was a World Series to consider. Representatives from the A's, Giants, and Major League Baseball and San Francisco civic officials met to discuss what, if any, role baseball might play in the coming days or weeks. At a candlelight meeting at the blacked-out St. Francis Hotel, Commissioner Vincent struck the perfect tone. "I don't think cancellation of the World Series is appropriate," he told the national media. "Right now we're hopeful to play next week. We have to remember we are guests here. Our modest little game is not a top priority. We will not play while this community is in a state of recovery, while the hunt for victims goes on."

Giants owner Bob Lurie said he had steadfastly opposed moving the World Series elsewhere. La Russa supported Vincent's position. A preliminary inspection of Candlestick Park by structural engineers from the San Francisco Department of Public Works and 10 structural engineers from a private company that had done repair work on the stadium in the early 1980s revealed no significant damage. Stadium manager John Lind said a full inspection would take three to five days.

◆ ◆ ◆ ◆

The A's and Giants got back to work on Thursday with both teams engaging in intrasquad games with varying degrees of enthusiasm. All of the A's convened at the Coliseum except Rickey Henderson, a no-show who didn't respond to a message left on the answering machine at his Hillsborough home.

Practicing in the wake of such a major natural disaster proved to be a surreal experience. "When we realized how bad this was," Mark McGwire told reporters at the A's practice, "baseball didn't mean a damn thing, then." Carney Lansford, a Bay Area native, said that when the World Series resumed at Candlestick Park, "I do not want my wife there and I do not want my friends there." La Russa cited baseball's history of being "part of the healing" process after tragedies and war. Stewart lamented that "this has turned into the Earthquake World Series." Parker was fatalistic. "You're born to die, man," he said. "We're just trying to do a job."

At Candlestick Park, reliever Steve Bedrosian reported for practice wearing a construction hat. Whatever levity that inspired was fleeting. Center fielder Brett

Butler said he could take or leave baseball under the circumstances. Would've-been Game 3 starter Robinson had trouble shaking images of victims being pulled out of the Cypress Structure rubble. Ten days after achieving his crowning moment in baseball with his single off Mitch Williams, Clark said, "I haven't thought a second about baseball for the last few days."

Similar conversations were taking place all over the Bay Area—in workplaces, in bars, around the kitchen table, on talk radio, in newspapers. Some expressed sentiment that the World Series should be canceled. Vincent continued to defer to local authorities while holding out hope for resumption in a relatively timely manner. The Bay Bridge was declared closed for two months as the Bay Area Rapid Transit (BART) system announced it would expand its service to 24 hours on Monday. The Marina District still smoldered. SFPD commander Isaiah Nelson told Vincent that an adequate police presence probably would be ready for a Tuesday game. By Thursday, estimates of casualties on the collapsed Cypress Structure were revised sharply downward. Based on examination of the rubble, there had been lighter-than-normal traffic when the earthquake hit. An Oakland police sergeant wondered if perhaps the World Series had something to do with that.

Rickey Henderson made it to Friday's practice, pleading ignorance of the Thursday workout. La Russa let it slide, considering the circumstances. La Russa also made a couple of announcements. He would come back with Games 1 and 2 starters, Stewart and Mike Moore, in Games 3 and 4. Welch would get the Game 5 assignment—if the Series went that far. And La Russa also pushed back against those who wished the World Series to be canceled. His points were valid. The San Francisco 49ers had rescheduled their Sunday, October 22 home game to Stanford Stadium. But they were still playing, and no one was calling that insensitive or disrespectful. Stanford University had a home game scheduled for Saturday. "You guys are working," La Russa said to reporters. "Other people are going back to work. I have a lot of problems with those people who say we should call off the World Series."

Nearly 24 years later, he felt the same way. "I remember I had a [team] meeting," he said. "My answer was: should we cancel it out of respect? Okay, let's consider that. I said, 'They're playing college football, they're playing pro football, stage plays, all the other entertainment. We're the only ones [being asked to cancel].' I said, 'Everything's resuming in life, and at some point, we're going to resume our life.'"

The Giants held a second day of workouts as well. Craig announced Robinson as his Game 3 starter and pegged Scott Garrelts to start Game 4. The team sent a contingent, including owner Lurie, Rosen, and third baseman Matt Williams, to the Moscone Convention Center to visit people displaced by the earthquake. They distributed baseballs, posters, and caps to people who had lost much of what they owned. "It's not all the Giants organization can do, nor is it all we will do," Lurie told reporters at the event. "But it is a start."

As concerns grew over the upcoming Monday commute, in which working people would start to get back into their normal lives and typical work schedules, and even as it was announced that Washington state would be sending three ferries to the Bay Area to provide alternate sources of transportation, clouds were appearing on the horizon. Rain clouds. Wet weather was forecast for the weekend and into early the next week. It was exactly what two teams faced with an extended break in the middle of a World Series didn't need to hear. "How in the world are we ever going to get ready at this rate?" Clark said.

◆ ◆ ◆ ◆

For more than three days, searchers, growing increasingly pessimistic about finding any more survivors of the freeway's collapse, combed through the rubble of the Cypress Structure. The stench of death hung over the West Oakland neighborhood. The task grew ever grimmer. Still the work went on because no one officially wanted to give up hope.

On Saturday, October 21, 89 hours after the earthquake, a rescuer peered down through a small hole cut in the rubble and saw movement in a crushed Chevy Sprint. Buck Helm, a 57-year-old, 240-pound longshoreman, was inside the car. And he was alive. Getting him out took time. Construction workers had to support the crumbled freeway before even attempting the rescue. And as the rescue party—composed of first responders and engineers—made its way through the cement tangle, it had to stop every few feet to install more supports. Finally Helm was removed from his car, placed on a backboard, slowly lowered to the ground, and taken by ambulance to Oakland's Highland Hospital.

A dehydrated Helm had broken ribs, a skull fracture, and kidney failure. He was listed in critical but stable condition. His rescue energized the crews working at the Cypress Structure. Oakland mayor Lionel Wilson came to the site to watch. News of Helm's rescue rocketed around the Bay Area. The misery and destruction caused by the earthquake had made people feel powerless and small. Now here was a guy who had fought back. Helm gave a boost to the regional psyche and he was a character to boot. He worked in Oakland and returned to his home in Weaverville, a four-mile drive north, on weekends. When the quake hit, he was headed to Emeryville to play poker. A friend driving five to 10 seconds ahead of him just made it out of the danger zone. Helm just missed. Helm's son, Greg, told reporters that his father survived because "he's an ornery old fart."

Also on Saturday at the Coliseum and at Candlestick Park, there were signs of clubhouse fever. La Russa's pitching plans—Stewart in Game 3 and Moore in Game 4—had 19-game-winner Storm Davis feeling unappreciated. On Friday he said he understood La Russa's decision. He wasn't as diplomatic on Saturday. "What they're saying to me," Davis, a free-agent-to-be at season's end, told writers, "is, 'We have enough pitchers.' If that's the case, I'll go somewhere else." "If he thinks that's the way things work around here," La Russa responded coolly, "he can go ahead and file."

Rain limited the A's to an hour on the field. Craig gave his pitchers the day off. Some players hit in the indoor batting cage. "The week off, the earthquake, the rain now, it's just tougher to get guys fired up," said Craig to reporters, adding that the team hoped to find a local college with a gym big enough to accommodate something resembling a full-team baseball workout.

On Sunday, October 22, San Francisco mayor Art Agnos and Vincent agreed to push back Game 3 until Friday night. Vincent denied the immediate speculation that ABC had pushed for the Friday game for ratings purposes. "I'm telling you," Giants catcher Terry Kennedy joked to reporters about the seemingly endless delay, "we'll be coming in from a workout, and there will be turkey and dressing in the dining room."

The rain continued, and both teams canceled their workouts. There was a rumor the A's were considering heading to their Phoenix spring training headquarters, so they could continue to practice. Rosen had a two-word response to that report: "Bon voyage."

It was an NFL Sunday, and the CBS pregame show enraged La Russa. "The [broadcaster] was talking about a question of whether the World Series is going to continue," La Russa told reporters, "and he's standing right in front of Stanford Stadium where the 49ers are going to play. For the life of me, I can't see how you can say it's not right [for baseball] to play and then come along and say it's all right for these other forms of entertainment. If anything, we should be thankful. Do you know how many people we took off the streets [on Tuesday]?"

Craig reversed field, naming Garrelts his Game 3 starter with Robinson pitching Game 4. On the fifth day of the delay, it seemed like a drill or some kind of fantasy baseball exercise. The A's and most of the Giants took Monday off, but more logistical problems arose. The Rolling Stones were scheduled to appear at the Oakland Coliseum on November 4 and 5. Their contact called for the stadium to be vacant for five days prior to the concerts. A seven-game World Series would end in Oakland on November 1. Some agreement would have to be brokered just in case.

At Highland Hospital, Helm nodded his head to tell doctors he had no pain. His condition was upgraded to very serious. Doctors said if he continued to improve over the next 24 to 48 hours, he would be "out of the woods."

Tuesday was a day of decision. Limited by wet weather to two hours of work at the Coliseum, the A's decided to travel to Phoenix for two workouts. They would leave Wednesday morning and practice at Phoenix Municipal Stadium, their spring training home, that afternoon. They would have a team dinner Wednesday night, practice again Thursday, and then fly home for Friday's resumption of the World Series.

In the summer of 2013, La Russa explained the reasoning behind the decision. "I'm a reader," he said, "and Pat Riley's book *Showtime*, I read that. He talked about the Lakers. Right at the beginning of the postseason, he'd take the team somewhere outside of town, and they would take two or three days together. They'd work out, no distractions, and they would make a commitment. I went, 'Wow, that's really good.' And all of a sudden, they say we're going to play on Friday, and the forecast was for rain [Wednesday]. Right away I called [GM] Sandy [Alderson] because I was thinking about Pat Riley. And he called [owner] Walter [Haas], and Walter said [okay]. So I brought the team in and I said, 'Pack your bags. Tomorrow we're going to fly.' A couple guys grumbled a little bit. I said, 'Hey, fellas, we're on a mission.' I was taught the philosophy of no regrets. You cross every T that you can."

At Candlestick, Craig said there would be no more intrasquad games until Thursday. "This is what they wanted to do," he told writers, referring to his players. One of those players, Kevin Mitchell, was asked about the A's decision to skip town. "That's up to them," he said. "I'd rather sleep in my own bed. If it pours down rain the next couple days, maybe they'll look smart for doing this." On the concert front, rock promoter Bill Graham expressed fears the Rolling Stones dates at the Coliseum could be in jeopardy with 120,000 tickets already sold and the band scheduled to travel to Texas immediately after their November 5 date in Oakland. Alderson expressed hope to reporters that the Coliseum board would "think we're a priority. Maybe," he added, "we could be the opening act."

As if to restate the nature of the ultimate landlord/tenant relationship, the San Andreas Fault produced a 4.5-magnitude aftershock at 6:27 PM, one week and 83 minutes after the earthquake that stopped the World Series in its tracks. In a related development, Agnos received assurance of Candlestick Park's structural integrity.

A lot had happened in a week's time. The nature of the World Series had changed. It had come to mean something other than what it had signified during Games 1 and 2. Then it represented a clash of partisan interests for all the right reasons. Were you an A's fan or a Giants fan? Were you American League or National League? Oakland or San Francisco? Canseco or Clark?

The earthquake inspired Bay Area residents to set their differences aside and celebrate their similarities. As with Dravecky's comeback game, a baseball-related event segued into a testimony of the human spirit. No matter their partisan affiliation or provincial allegiances, Bay Area residents suddenly were on the same side. La Russa, who since coming to the A's in 1987 had felt the A's were a second citizen to the Giants, sensed a new normal. "For all the rivalry we hear about," he told writers, "we're probably a lot closer to the Giants spiritually than we've ever been. We've both gone through the same thing."

La Russa had pushed for the trip to Phoenix so the team could get good work in and hopefully reconnect. He didn't anticipate what might have been the biggest benefit of their Arizona excursion. "As we're flying in," La Russa said, "the pilot comes on and says, 'If you get a chance, on the right side of the plane, you should see the cars waiting to get to your workout.' And everybody was just, 'Wow.' What we found out was, when the word got out, for two days parents took their kids out of school in the afternoon. To see a team in the World Series? This was unique. So here are guys who have been burdened with guilt and all this kind of stuff, and we come out and we get there. The bus pulls up, and we dress and we get out there like at 3:00, and people start cheering."

Sixty reporters and 10 camera crews were at the workout. The 6,000 fans who showed up donated $9,200 to the Red Cross Relief Fund for earthquake victims.

As if that wasn't enough positive news, the Rolling Stones and the Coliseum board reached a compromise that would allow Game 7 of the World Series (if necessary) and both Stones concerts to go off as scheduled. The concerts would be pushed back a day, and the team and the Coliseum board would share overtime construction costs.

After their workout in Phoenix, the A's had a team dinner at an Italian restaurant where players were encouraged to speak from the heart, tell jokes, and say whatever was in their heart. It was a team-building experience right out of Pat Riley's book and it led to another spirited practice in front of another cheering, fawning crowd on Thursday. "It was a relief," La Russa said, looking back. "It wasn't that we forgot [about the earthquake]. Our ownership would not let us forget. I don't think it made that big a difference, but it was a hell of an experience for these guys for one night, two workouts. We flew home and the next day we played and we hit home runs. They hit some home runs, too. But our guys didn't look like they'd missed a trick, did they?"

Meanwhile, the Giants practiced on Thursday inside empty Candlestick Park, quiet except for the construction work being done to shore up the stadium for Game 3 of the World Series. In hindsight it's easy to suggest that the A's trip to Phoenix gave them a significant competitive advantage. But in real time, the 10-day delay was uncharted territory. There was no handbook on how to handle such a situation. The Giants decided to stay put and get in whatever work they could. "I'm satisfied with the way we've prepared," Williams said to reporters. "I think the way we've gone about it suits our club's personality."

But hindsight paints a vivid picture about the A's unprecedented venture to Phoenix. "That was really helpful," Eckersley said. "It was the right time to do it. For obvious reasons it was a little bit of a depressing time. I don't remember the fans or any of that stuff. It's all a blur. [But] I've never seen more focus ever. Remember, this was a team that screwed up the year before."

"The people did come out and watch, which was cool," Stewart said. "I don't know that it gave us an edge. I think [the Giants] worked out, too. I think that the earthquake was still in the back of our minds. We were concerned, worried that we were doing the right thing. When they said we were going to play, it was just a matter of getting back to business."

Twenty-four years later, Clark didn't mince words. "In retrospect it might have been an advantage for them," he said. "But then looking back on it, I felt the sense of need here in the city. We stayed here. We did not go to Phoenix or Scottsdale. We did quite a bit of stuff away from the ballpark as far as community. That definitely needed to be done. Like I said before, it's just a game. This ain't about life and death. I definitely felt a need to be in the community. What do you do? How do you react? All that stuff's going through your mind. The one thing you think about is: *I've got to be a citizen. I'm a citizen of San Francisco. I didn't lose anybody. I'm fortunate enough to run out on a baseball field and play a game. There's a lot of people coping with a lot of worse stuff.*"

Chapter 12

World Series Games 3 and 4

With the Bay Bridge out of commission, the A's had no choice. They had to bus to Candlestick Park via the San Mateo Bridge for Game 3 of the World Series. Friday afternoon traffic in the Bay Area is typically a nightmare. The A's could have flown to Denver in the time it took them to drive from Oakland to San Francisco. Oakland's Game 3 starter, Dave Stewart, slept most of the way.

The World Series was about to resume. But the winning and losing of Game 3 seemed almost secondary to the fact it was being played at all. The Series had begun in a climate of partisan rooting interests defined by T-shirts, bumper stickers, and civic wagers. The earthquake had united people from both sides of the crippled Bay Bridge and from all corners of the socioeconomic spectrum. Communities that had suffered no appreciable damage felt a kinship with communities that would take years to rebuild.

So it was a different atmosphere before Game 3 than it had been on October 17. There was a long moment of silence for those who lost their lives in the disaster—a total that now had become clear would number in the dozens instead of the hundreds. A dozen earthquake heroes, including the man who discovered the barely alive Buck

Helm on the Cypress Structure, threw out the ceremonial first pitches. The cast of the play *Beach Blanket Babylon*, clad in its campy attire belted out "San Francisco," the anthemic title song from the 1936 movie that celebrated the rebirth of the city after the 1906 earthquake. And 62,038 fans, who had been handed the lyrics as they entered the stadium, sang along.

Candlestick Park thrummed with communal good will and shared experience as Scott Garrelts opened the game by getting Rickey Henderson to ground out to shortstop and then allowed a first-pitch single to Carney Lansford. That brought up Jose Canseco. In his first official career World Series at-bat in 1988, Canseco had mashed a grand slam to center field in Dodger Stadium. He had gone hitless in 23 Fall Classic at-bats since. On this stage at least, he was a sleeping giant.

Garrelts missed with his first pitch. His second went whizzing over Canseco's head, sending the A's right fielder ducking out of the way. "I wanted to say, 'Thank you,'" Oakland catcher Terry Steinbach told reporters after the game. "You don't want to wake him up." Canseco took a menacing step toward the mound. Tempers quickly cooled. Two pitches later Canseco singled to left field with Lansford taking second. Garrelts retired Mark McGwire on a ground ball that moved the runners to second and third. But Dave Henderson doubled off the top of the fence in right-center field, missing a home run by a couple feet at most. Lansford and Canseco scored for a 2–0 Oakland lead.

Matt Williams got one run back with a solo home run off Stewart in the bottom of the second inning. It remained 2–1 after three innings. It was a mild, still night, hardly unusual for early fall in San Francisco. After the gales of August and September, the city experiences some of its best weather in late summer and early fall. It's temperate and calm. When those conditions applied to Candlestick Park, the yard played like a bandbox.

Dave Henderson, leading off the fourth, launched a home run to right-center field. One out later Tony Phillips homered to right. Giants manager Roger Craig was taking no chances. Garrelts had been hit on the elbow by a McGwire line drive in the third. By that point he had given up two long balls in the span of three pitches. The Giants couldn't afford to lose the game. Craig asked Garrelts for the ball and handed it to reliever Kelly Downs.

Downs escaped further trouble, and San Francisco catcher Terry Kennedy cut the lead to 4–3 with a two-run single in the bottom of the inning. The A's, however, were relentless. Canseco ripped a three-run home run to left-center in the top of the fifth, and Dave Henderson followed one out later with another solo shot. In three plate appearances, Hendu had put one ball off the top of the fence and two balls over it. It was Lansford's turn in the sixth. His homer made it 9–3. It was Oakland's fifth home run of the game, tying the World Series record set by the 1928 Yankees.

Lansford added a two-run single in a four-run rally compiled against Atlee Hammaker in the eighth, which gave Oakland a 13–3 lead. All that was left was the accounting. The final score was 13–7. Having allowed three runs in seven innings, Stewart earned the win. It made him the first pitcher ever to win two games in the league championship series and two more in the World Series in the same year. He liked the sound of that. "I've got something to stick my chest out about," he told writers.

While the A's were unanimous in their belief that their trip to Arizona had been of great benefit, Craig was firm in his belief that he had done all he could to get his team ready to play under difficult circumstances. "Their going to Arizona didn't win the game for them tonight," Craig told the media. "I know this in my heart. I have my team as mentally prepared and as physically prepared as they could be. Maybe they were a bit rusty. They looked a little sharper than we were. They're a better club than we are right now." Asked what changes he might implement for Game 4, Craig said, "I'm going to play my outfield a little deeper."

Game 4 of the 1989 World Series was beginning to feel a lot like August 1988 for the Giants. Their starting pitchers were falling all around them. Rick Reuschel, the All-Star Game starter, was out after having been hit in the right shoulder by a batting practice line drive. Relegated to the bullpen late in the season after spending time on the disabled list, Hammaker and Downs had been cuffed around in the World Series. Mike LaCoss, who began the season as the Giants' closer, hadn't started a game in four weeks and had a 6.75 ERA in two postseason outings. Dave Dravecky and Mike Krukow, who accounted for two of the Giants' three wins in the 1987 National League Championship Series against the St. Louis Cardinals, had thrown their final major league pitch. "You're forced to take guys and put them in an unfamiliar situation," Will Clark said almost 24 years later. "You're taking a reliever and making him a starter or vice versa. And you're trying to do it in the middle of the season. Or in this case, trying to do it in the World Series. It's like, 'Oh, come on.'" Also reflecting back, A's manager Tony La Russa said, "If they'd had their pitching, it would have been a better Series. They didn't."

The Giants' choice for a Game 4 starter was the Caveman. Don Robinson hadn't started a game since September 25 and had pitched just eight and one-third innings in 49 days. He had suffered pain in both knees and his left hamstring during the final month of the regular season. He had been flown to Pittsburgh to be examined by doctors who knew him from his days with the Pirates. He couldn't pitch without a calf-to-thigh brace on his right leg that was clearly visible through his uniform pants.

He was a metaphor for the Giants, a fine talent operating at less than his best. Likewise, Rickey Henderson embodied the A's at that moment in time, a brilliant athlete at the absolute top of his game. He swatted Robinson's third pitch of Game 4 over the left-field fence for a 1–0 Oakland lead. Robinson got out of the first inning with no further damage. Mike Moore, Oakland's Game 4 starter, gave up a bunt single to Brett Butler in the bottom of the inning. Butler never made it past first.

Dave Henderson doubled to lead off the second, and Robinson was back in the soup again. He retired Steinbach and Phillips. Then Craig ordered him to intentionally walk Walt Weiss. That brought up Moore, who because of the designated hitter, had batted just once, unsuccessfully, in 451 regular-season games. In fact American League pitchers were hitless in 70 World Series at-bats dating back to 1979. Robinson threw two high fastballs, and Moore swung through both. "You doubt that Robinson has a scouting report on Moore, don't you?" chuckled ABC broadcaster Al Michaels. "Has trouble with the thrown ball," analyst Jim Palmer cracked as Robinson delivered an 0–2 fastball.

But there was something Robinson, catcher Kennedy, Palmer, 62,032 Candlestick Park fans, and millions of TV viewers didn't know at that critical juncture. It was yet another ancillary benefit of the A's quick trip to Phoenix. While the position players practiced on the main field at Municipal Stadium, the A's pitchers had taken batting practice on the secluded back field. "We played some (intrasquad) games on the back field, splitting up the pitchers," pitching coach Dave Duncan told reporters once Game 4 was in the books. "[Moore] must have hit four, five balls over the fence. He consistently hit the ball hard. He's got a good swing."

Robinson didn't get his 0–2 pitch as high as he wanted, and Moore swung and laced a line drive to center field. Seemingly unable to believe what he was seeing, Butler froze in his tracks. He turned and retreated toward the fence, but it was too late. The ball sailed over his outstretched glove. Two runs scored, and Moore wound up at second base. The A's led 3–0.

Moore wasn't finished embarrassing the Giants. Rickey Henderson, the next hitter, grounded a sharp single to left field. Kevin Mitchell was on it quickly, scooping it up and preparing to throw to the plate. If Moore had little experience hitting at the big league level, he had no experience running the bases. Yet third-base coach Rene Lachemann brazenly waved him to the plate on what could have been a close play even for an experienced runner. It was as if he was taunting Mitchell and the Giants. Mitchell's throw was late, and Moore scored standing up for a 4–0 lead. Craig made the slow walk to the mound to relieve Robinson and summon LaCoss.

LaCoss held the fort for two innings before giving up three runs in the fifth. A run in the sixth off Jeff Brantley made it 8–0 A's. It was over before Giants fans had anything to yell about. Or was it? Mitchell's two-run homer off Moore in the sixth had the feel of a consolation prize. Greg Litton's two-run homer off reliever Gene Nelson in the seventh was a novelty. But the Giants weren't done.

Later in the seventh, they tacked on two runs against Rick Honeycutt to trim the lead to 8–6. Robby Thompson was on first base. Clark, the potential tying run, was digging in at the plate. The fans began to make a little noise. Honeycutt hung a breaking pitch, and Clark just missed it. He slammed his bat to the ground in frustration as Canseco corralled his high, harmless pop fly in right field. That brought up Mitchell, who had spent the season as hot as any hitter can be. La Russa called for Todd Burns for the righty-on-righty matchup.

Finally Candlestick Park was shaking for the right reasons. Mitchell worked the count to 2–2 and then blasted a pitch to deep left field. In their hearts, Giants fans saw a game-tying two-run homer. Some A's fans might have seen it the same way. Rickey Henderson raced back to the fence then and, gauging the ball's flight, drifted to his right along the warning track. Wearing a big smile, he snapped the ball out of the air with a flourish.

The A's tacked on a run in the eighth. The Giants had seen their last base runner of the season. In the summer of 2013, Dennis Eckersley, who hadn't fully recovered from his rotator cuff issue from midseason, still recalled warming up to pitch the ninth inning. "I knew I was going to pitch the ninth no matter what," he said. "I was warming up, and Matt Young was throwing next to me and he was throwing 100 mph. My shit was like broke. I'm like, *Why am I going into this game?* It's the little moments you remember in your head. But the adrenaline was firing, man."

Eckersley retired both Donell Nixon and Jose Uribe on the first pitch. The final out was a tribute to the A's defense, an often overlooked facet of Oakland's game.

The Giants' Butler slapped a grounder to the right side. McGwire made a diving attempt, but the ball was just beyond his reach. No matter. Phillips was moving left from his second-base position. He fielded the ball with a lunge. Eckersley, of course, was right where he should have been, sprinting toward first base. He caught Phillips' throw head-high as he stepped on the bag, showcasing the deft fielding and teamwork of the A's, who were suddenly world champions. "It was the ultimate for my whole life at that moment," Eckersley said. "It wasn't crucial. It wasn't a one-run game. But it's in Candlestick Park. I grew up in the Bay Area. I went to watch the Giants at Candlestick. It could have been a strikeout. What are the chances of getting the ball in your glove to finish it? It was like I was supposed to be there. That's my gift."

After stopping briefly to confirm the out call with first-base umpire Al Clark, Eckersley celebrated his gift with a wild fist pump. Phillips was on him in a flash, enveloping him in an embrace. Jubilant Athletics headed for the Eck-Phillips hugfest on a dead sprint from the dugout, bullpen, outfield, and infield. Weiss, McGwire, and Steinbach buffeted Eckersley in the first wave. The second wave rolled over them like a pounding surf. "They smoked me," a smiling Eckersley told reporters.

La Russa and his coaches brought up the rear. Phillips was the first player La Russa encountered. He stopped, spread his arms wide, and then wrapped them around his second baseman and trainer Larry Davis. The celebration was joyous but not riotous. The A's flash mob quickly broke up into a series of individual embraces while some Giants watched quietly from their dugout, and others headed down the stairs to the tunnel that led to their clubhouse.

Oakland fans cheered the final out and the initial celebration. Giants fans pushed back with a low-level chorus of boos. Oakland fans pushed back against the pushback, regaining the floor with cheers and whistles. But like the A's on-field demonstration, the noise died down quickly. The World Series had been completed and had produced a deserving winner. But there were still bigger things to think about.

◆ ◆ ◆

It already had been decided there would be no unseemly champagne celebration out of respect for victims of the earthquake. "Ownership—and we had the best ownership—said no champagne, no celebration," La Russa said in the summer of 2013. "So there were just hugs, very muted. We got in our cars and drove to the Coliseum, and they had some food and they had the trophy, and we had our own little party there with all the families. It was nice." The Bay Area was still in mourning.

Candlestick Park's flags flew at half staff for Games 3 and 4. So the postgame show went on without the customary histrionics. But it was clearly meaningful for the A's.

Stewart was voted the World Series MVP to the delight of his teammates. To the surprise of no one, he wished he could cut the trophy into 24 pieces, so that all his teammates could share it. Then in the same clubhouse, which had been shaken like a snow globe on October 17, forcing dust from the rafters and smoke from the air ducts, team owner Walter Haas accepted the World Series trophy on behalf of the A's for the organization's fourth championship in 18 years. "Our heart goes out to the people of this area who suffered in the last 10 days," he said to the players in the clubhouse and millions of ABC viewers. "The Oakland A's are the world champions of baseball. But we've got a lot of champions here and we've got to work together to rebuild this area. It's the best part of the world to live, to work, to visit, and to play baseball."

Bill Rigney, 71, had spent a lifetime in baseball, having played eight years, all with the Giants. He had managed three teams (including the Giants) for a total of 18 years. He had spent several years as a consultant with the A's. Now he had his first World Series ring. "This is wonderful," he said with tears in his eyes.

On the Giants side, there wasn't much to say. Kennedy reflected upon his second World Series experience—he was with the San Diego Padres when they were defeated in five games by Detroit in 1984—and concluded he had seen the two best teams of the 1980s. "The '84 Tigers and the A's this year are similar teams," he told reporters. "They had the same look in their eyes. They smelled it, went after it like tigers on the kill, and they weren't going to let it slip away."

Craig was asked if he would have considered retirement had the Giants won the World Series. "It would be a lie if I said 'no,'" he told reporters. The Humm Baby, who for four years had advised his players, "Don't get your dauber down," knew his team had been whipped. Late in the summer of 2013 he was satisfied he and his players had done the best they could under trying circumstances. "We played so many simulated games," he said. "Guys were getting tired of it. I told them, 'It's going to be just as bad for them.' But their starting pitching, they came back—Stewart and Moore. I didn't have two guys like that. You've got to go out and do the best you can. All our guys got their work in. They were ready physically but maybe not mentally."

Clark, in the summer of 2013, recalled the challenge of trying to regain personal and professional equilibrium after the earthquake. "Once you start the season in February, if you get an off day here and there, that's a good thing," he said. "You never have two days back-to-back, much less 10 days. Here we are in the middle of the World Series, we're down two games. And for me it was almost like back in spring training again, trying to figure out how to put a bat on the ball. The rest of it speaks for itself. The A's won Game 3 and Game 4 and looking back on it they had a phenomenal team and they proved it all year long. We came out on the short end of the stick. But I'd like to have seen what happened if we played Game 3 that day."

Taken at face value, the 1989 World Series was a dud. You could make the case, and people have, that it was the least competitive, least interesting edition in World Series history.

- For the first time since 1966, the winning team never trailed and the losing team never led.
- The 18-run differential was tied for largest in World Series play.
- The Giants' team ERA of 8.21 was the second-highest in World Series history, trailing only the 9.26 mark of the 1932 Chicago Cubs.
- The 92-point disparity in batting average (.301 for the A's vs. 209 for the Giants) was the largest in World Series history.
- It was the lowest rated (16.4) of any televised World Series.
- More than one wag dubbed it the Fault Classic. (*San Francisco Chronicle* columnist Herb Caen rechristened Candlestick Park "Wiggly Field.")

But the Bay Bridge World Series achieved something few sports events ever do: It assumed an integral, vital role in the life and times of the communities it served and the people it entertained. The "modest little game" that commissioner Fay Vincent spoke about united people. It healed. It became part of the important discussion on grieving, resilience, and getting back to a normal way of life. It is almost certain that the intense interest in the originally scheduled Game 3 saved lives because countless would-be commuters were in front of their TV sets and therefore not in harm's way.

To this day it occupies a special place in the heart of civic-minded Stewart for one reason. "That reason is that in all the years I grew up and lived in the Bay Area, it was the first time both sides had to work together," Stewart said. "It brought a good feeling in San Francisco with regards to Oakland and a good feeling in Oakland with regards to San Francisco. That was the best part of the whole thing."

Chapter 13

The Aftermath

Two days after their muted postgame celebration, the A's held an understated rally at Jack London Square in Oakland. Local newspapers estimated that 4,000 to 5,000 people attended. There was no parade down Broadway, as Charlie Finley's Swingin' A's had received in the early 1970s. In fact the public event was optional for A's players. Jose Canseco, Dave Parker, and Terry Steinbach were among the no-shows. "We took a ferry from near where the Coliseum was," Tony La Russa said, "and pulled into Jack London. There were maybe a couple thousand people. There's a couple of pictures of us there. We got back on the boat and we left, and that was it."

The fans who showed up lavished affection on A's players. Dave Stewart drew cheers when he held the World Series trophy aloft, as did Rickey Henderson when he declared it the "greatest day in my career." But the context of the time was inescapable. Broadway was sprinkled with earthquake-damaged buildings, which had been condemned. Oakland City Hall was shuttered, pending repair. Buckets were passed among the crowd to collect donations for earthquake relief efforts. Less than two miles away, demolition of the collapsed Cypress Structure continued.

It was a far cry from the choreographed civic extravaganzas you see today. La Russa's second World Series-winning team, the 2006 Cardinals, drew an estimated half-million people for the victory parade in St. Louis. But you'd be hard-pressed to find a member of the 1989 A's who felt cheated. "You see the way it's done now," Dennis Eckersley said. "But at the time, no. When you win a championship—I had been around 15 years—hey man, whatever. We won. You know something? That's cool. It was meant to be. It was what we were supposed to do." Stewart addressed the possibility of a more demonstrative celebration. "It would really have been nice," he said. "But at the same time, I got it. I understood."

◆ ◆ ◆ ◆

On Novembar 18, four weeks after he had been pulled from the rubble of the Cypress Structure and eight days after his 58th birthday, Buck Helm died. His death from respiratory failure surprised his doctors, who believed he had been making steady progress toward a full recovery. His rescue lifted spirits all over the Bay Area. He had become an unwitting symbol of fortitude. His death seemed as shocking and cruel as the earthquake itself.

There were, however, other symbols of recovery. The same day Helm died, the Bay Bridge re-opened to car traffic to much fanfare. The day after that, the San Francisco 49ers lost to the Green Bay Packers, dropping their record to 9–2. That was the last game they would lose all season. Once again Bay Area residents found a communal touchstone in sports. Led by rookie head coach George Seifert, the 49ers finished the regular season 14–2 and pulverized their three postseason opponents by an aggregate score of 126–26. An estimated 75,000 fans lined the championship parade route on San Francisco's Market Street.

In time the Cypress Structure was torn down. The silver lining to its demolition was that the West Oakland neighborhood divided by its construction was made whole again. San Francisco eventually demolished the damaged double-deck Embarcadero Freeway, restoring the open feel and scenic beauty of the city's waterfront north of the Bay Bridge.

The Federal Emergency Management Agency advised Oakland to raze its red-tagged City Hall, which had a huge crack in its signature clock tower, but residents pushed back. The building, which opened in 1914, was a point of civic pride. Not only was City Hall rebuilt—in an $85 million project that required jacking the massive edifice off its foundation—it was placed on shock-absorbing isolators to help it survive the next big quake. It reopened in 1997. Likewise, San Francisco repaired its damaged City Hall at a cost of $181 million.

It took 24 years, but the cantilevered eastern span of the Bay Bridge, a section of which had collapsed in the Loma Prieta earthquake, was replaced by a sleek $6 billion span featuring a distinctive suspension tower. The Marina District, downtown Santa Cruz, and Watsonville have been rebuilt. Projects to retrofit Bay Area transportation infrastructure continued for years after the earthquake. The surest sign of recovery: complacent Bay Area residents now have to remind one another to keep enough batteries, water, and food on hand to ride out the next, inevitable disastrous seismic event. Time will tell to what extent people have taken those reminders to heart.

◆ ◆ ◆ ◆

Bart Giamatti, commissioner of the game he loved for 51 weeks before his death on September 1, 1989, once wrote about how baseball begins in the spring, blossoms in the summer before leaving you to face the fall alone. That may be true of the games. The business of baseball never ends.

The day after Game 4, Storm Davis, irked that he was not included in La Russa's earthquake-retrofitted World Series pitching plans, told reporters he wanted assurances that he would be a part of the team's starting rotation in 1990. Apparently he didn't like what he heard. He filed for free agency on November 3 and signed a three-year, $6 million deal with the Kansas City Royals in early December. (He later returned to Oakland for a 19-appearance cup of coffee in 1993.)

Parker, 38, coming off a season in which he had 97 RBIs and finished 11th in the MVP voting, understandably believed that he had earned a two-year contract. The A's, who still lived in a world where $500,000 represented all the pencils in the world, offered him one year. Parker signed with the Milwaukee Brewers for two years and $2.9 million. Under normal circumstances, there wouldn't have been such a lucrative option for super-sub Tony Phillips, who played six positions for the A's in 1989. But their pockets lined with cash from Major League Baseball's new four-year, $1.1 billion television contract with CBS, owners were in a spending frenzy. The Detroit Tigers signed Phillips to a three-year contract worth $3.25 million. (He later returned to the A's in 1999 for his final season.)

Those losses were not inconsequential. But Rickey Henderson was the biggest offseason priority for the A's. Acquired in June in the last year of his contract, he energized the A's offense, scoring 72 runs and stealing 52 bases in little more than half a season. He was a beast in the postseason, batting .441 with 12 runs, 11 stolen bases, and three homers in nine games. General manager Sandy Alderson had taken a leap of faith in trading for Henderson, believing he might be able to talk him into re-signing for a hometown discount. New York Yankees GM Syd Thrift, who had been unable to negotiate a long-term deal with Henderson, was skeptical. "We're going to find out just how much he loves that Oakland area," Thrift told reporters.

Henderson filed for free agency on November 2. Three weeks later he re-signed with Oakland for the biggest contract in baseball history: $12 million over four years. It was soon surpassed by other megadeals. Within months Henderson complained that the deal didn't provide for a $150,000 Ferrari Testarossa and stated his intent to renegotiate the deal if he had a big 1990 season.

♦ ♦ ♦ ♦

Ten days after the final game of the World Series, the Giants found themselves on the short end on another kind of scoreboard. On election day in San Francisco on Tuesday, November 7, voters defeated an initiative for a new downtown ballpark by less than 2,000 votes out of more than 170,000 votes cast. It was the second ballpark initiative to be defeated in San Francisco in three years, and both came on the heels of a postseason appearance by the team. In Scottsdale, Arizona, voters approved $8.4 million to build a new 7,000-seat spring training ballpark for the team. "We're going to have to face this reality," San Francisco mayor Art Agnos said at a news conference. "We're going to lose the Giants."

The earthquake undoubtedly had an effect on the vote. Regardless of the financial details, it was difficult to fathom building a new ballpark when so many existing, vital structures were suddenly in need of repair. Given that months earlier the board of supervisors had voted to amend the Giants' lease to make it year-to-year, only one thing was for certain: the Giants would play the 1990 season at Candlestick Park. After that, who knew?

Six days after the failed vote, there was more discouraging news. Dave Dravecky, whose comeback from cancer surgery on his pitching arm inspired millions inside baseball and out, announced his retirement on November 13. Doctors had found a new tumor on his upper left arm, in which a bone had snapped in his second comeback start. The same bone had been re-broken in the celebration after the Giants beat the Chicago Cubs in the National League Championship Series. Dravecky had been remarkably upbeat regarding a second comeback attempt in the wake of his postsurgical injuries.

Away from the spotlight, he was struggling with simple daily tasks such as getting a good night's sleep. He had sought and received permission to leave the team after the earthquake had put the World Series on hold. "My wife went to [general manager] Al Rosen and asked if we could have permission to go back [to Ohio]," Dravecky said. "I was sleeping upright in a La-Z-Boy chair. It was taking its toll on me. I needed to be home. I was still sleeping upright in November. I think it might have gone into the holidays. I was a bear to be around. I wasn't getting my sleep. My journey—on the outside to those who watched—I've heard people say over and over how well I handled it. If they only knew. If they went home with me and saw the struggle before even coming back and how hard it was to keep going every day, how in the midst of this journey having depression without realizing it, and that after my retirement I would have to face. I was struggling as a husband and a father because of all this stuff going on. We were just trying to get through the day. It's not an easy thing to do. It's a very difficult journey. All that really helped me over time to see how important his thing called life really is."

Dravecky could walk away from baseball, but there was no escaping the cancer that recurred in his left arm. Over the 18 months between his retirement and the spring of 1991, the disease and the increasingly aggressive treatment conspired to render his left arm—once the source of great pride and wonderful memories—a source of pain, betrayal, and frustration. In the end he welcomed the June 18 surgery at the Sloan-Kettering Cancer Center in New York City, during which doctors removed his left arm and shoulder.

One of Dravecky's former teammates, Kevin Mitchell, was voted the National League's Most Valuable Player in 1989, outdistancing runner-up and teammate Will Clark and joining Willie Mays and Willie McCovey as the only West Coast Giants to win the MVP. He also was named MVP by *The Sporting News*, known then as the bible of baseball. He was to receive the award at the winter meetings in Nashville, Tennessee. A limousine was sent to the airport to pick him up at the appointed hour. Mitchell was a no-show. Manager Roger Craig finished second in the Manager of the Year voting, losing out to his good buddy, Don Zimmer.

On the field, the Giants finally gave up on right fielder Candy Maldonado, whose productive seasons in 1986–87 were followed by confoundingly subpar years in 1988–89. A few days after Dravecky's retirement, they signed Kevin Bass, who grew up in Redwood City just south of San Francisco, for $5.25 million over three years. Maldonado wound up with the Cleveland Indians on a one-year deal for $825,000, a $75,000 pay cut from his 1989 salary.

Like the A's, the Giants paid dearly for their 1989 success. In January, Mitchell signed a one-year deal for $2.083 million. It amounted to a raise of more than $1.5 million, the biggest increase in baseball history at the time. A few days after that, Clark was signed to a four-year, $15 million deal, the largest the game had ever known. "He plays like a Hall of Famer," general manager Al Rosen told reporters, "and he should be paid like one."

Despite the teams' many stars, the Bay Area's status as a robust two-team market was fleeting. While the A's endured as a tour de force in the American League for a few seasons after 1989, the Giants quickly faded, finishing in third place in 1990, fourth place in 1991, and fifth place in 1992. Their attendance dwindled accordingly, from fifth in the NL in 1989, to eighth in 1990, 10th in 1991, and 11th in 1992.

Owner Bob Lurie grew increasingly desperate to ditch Candlestick Park even if it meant ditching his hometown of San Francisco as well. In 1990 he turned to Santa Clara County in the South Bay Area, where officials put together a proposal for a 45,000-seat, $152 million stadium that would open in 1994. Lurie called it the last hope to keep the team in the Bay Area. He even agreed to rename the team the Santa Clara Giants. The plan called for voters in five cities to pay a 1 percent utility tax to help fund the venture. The proposal was defeated on November 7, 1990, by 3,491 votes out of 272,537 cast.

Lurie gave it one last shot in 1992. San Jose proposed to its voters a 48,000-seat, $265 million stadium financed in part by a 5 to 7 percent utility tax. Proponents of the stadium outspent opponents, $1 million to $13,000. Yet Measure G lost on June 2, 1992, by 9 percentage points, 54.5 to 45.5. It was the last straw for Lurie. Two months later he announced he had agreed in principle to sell the Giants for $110 million to investors who would move the team to a domed stadium in St. Petersburg, Florida.

Even before Lurie's bombshell, San Francisco mayor Frank Jordan was attempting to assemble an investor group to keep the team in San Francisco. It seemed a quixotic endeavor, but it had a friend in high places. On September 9 NL president Bill White, a player on the 1958 Giants, announced the sale was on hold and that he was open to considering a counteroffer from a San Francisco group. A local investor group headed by Peter Magowan, president and CEO of the Safeway supermarket chain, was cobbled together. Its offer didn't quite stack up to that of the St. Petersburg group; in fact it called for Lurie to take back $10 million in equity. That was good enough for NL owners, who voted down the Giants' request for relocation and approved the Magowan group as the team's new owners.

The deal had yet to be finalized when Magowan boldly signed Barry Bonds, the plum of the free-agent market, to a record six-year, $43.75 million contract. Bob Quinn took over for Rosen as general manager. Hitting coach Dusty Baker replaced Craig as manager. In 1993, with Bonds winning his third MVP award in four years, the re-energized, resurgent Giants won 103 games, battling the Atlanta Braves down the stretch before being eliminated from the division race on the season's final day. A new era had dawned for the franchise, and there was no mistaking that it had a new alpha dog in Bonds. After the 1993 season, Clark, disappointed by the contract offered by the Giants, signed a free-agent deal with the Texas Rangers.

In December of 1995, plans were announced for a privately financed waterfront ballpark in San Francisco's China Basin. San Francisco voters gave it overwhelming approval in March 1996, and the Giants moved into what was then known as PacBell Park in 2000. They returned to the World Series in 2002, losing in seven games to the Angels. In 2010 the Giants finally won their first World Series since moving to California.

◆ ◆ ◆ ◆

In the postgame locker room after their Game 4 win against the Giants in the 1989 World Series, Stewart told reporters he thought the A's could win "maybe five or six more" world championships. "But you don't know," he said. "Egos become involved. If this team stays together and doesn't get a big ego, we can do anything. The only team that can beat the Oakland A's is the Oakland A's."

In 1990 the Athletics, led by Rickey Henderson's MVP effort and a Cy Young season from Bob Welch, became the first team since the 1976–78 Yankees to play in three consecutive World Series. For the second time in three years, they swept the Red Sox in the AL Championship Series. Their reward was a legacy rematch with the Cincinnati Reds, whom the Swingin' A's had defeated in seven games in the 1972 Fall Classic. If the 1988 World Series had been an opportunity lost for the A's and the 1989 World Series had served as redemption, the 1990 World Series was a head-scratcher. A good Oakland team was swept every which way a team can lose—a 7–0 shutout in Game 1; a 5–4, 10-inning squeaker in Game 2; an 8–3 spanking in Game 3; and a 2–1 spirit-breaking loss in Game 4 in which the A's managed just two hits—both in the first inning. La Russa later said he missed an opportunity to set the proper tone before the World Series against the Reds. "I'm much more upset about 1990 than I am about '88," he said in the summer of 2013.

In June 1990 Canseco signed a five-year, $23.5 million contract, the largest in baseball history at the time. That was the deal that inspired Canseco to inform La Russa that he had become more of a performer than a ballplayer. It also inspired Henderson to complain about being underpaid. Canseco underperformed during the first three games of the 1990 World Series, going 1-for-11. He looked so lost at the plate that La Russa held him out of the starting lineup for Game 4. In turn, Canseco's wife, Esther, referred to La Russa as a "punk." The incipient dynasty seemed to be collapsing under its own weight.

A little more than two months later, on New Year's Eve, Carney Lansford had a snowmobile accident in which he seriously injured his left knee. He returned in late July of the 1991 season but had to abort his comeback after five games. It was a fitting metaphor for the '91 A's—they never got going and finished in fourth place.

Lansford returned in 1992, and the band was back together for one last tour. The A's won their fourth division title in five years. Eckersley won the Cy Young Award and MVP. Mark McGwire hit 42 home runs. But injuries limited Henderson to 117 games. And the A's finally reached their tipping point with Canseco. On deck before his first at-bat in a home game against the Baltimore Orioles on August 31, Canseco was called back to the dugout and informed he had been traded to the Texas Rangers.

The ALCS against the Toronto Blue Jays, a heated playoff nemesis from the past, turned late in Game 4. With the A's leading 6–4 and three outs from tying the series 2–2, Eckersley gave up another titanic postseason homer. This one, off the bat of Roberto Alomar, tied the score. The Blue Jays won in 11 innings, took the series in six games, and earned some payback after losing out to the A's in 1989. Stewart left Oakland as a free agent at season's end, and Henderson was traded at the deadline in 1993. Both went to Toronto where they won World Series rings with the Blue Jays. (Henderson returned to the A's in 1994–95 and in 1998. Stewart returned in 1995; he retired, tearfully, in midseason with a 3–7 record and 6.89 ERA, saying, "I've always wanted to be the solution to the problem—not the problem.")

The 1994 season was truncated by a players' strike, which cost the A's vital revenue. A more ominous development occurred around that time—beloved owner

Walter Haas was diagnosed with cancer. He sold the team in 1995 for $85 million to Steve Schott and Ken Hofmann with the stipulation it be kept in Oakland. Haas died on September 20, 1995, as his favorite team was battling for a playoff berth. "We knew he wasn't right health-wise," La Russa said. "We were tied for the wild-card. Walter dies. All these incredibly talented athletes, sometimes arrogant, egotistical—everybody lost a huge edge. We lost nine in a row at the end of the season. It was the wrong kind of tribute, but it was a hell of a tribute to loving him."

After that season La Russa left Oakland to manage the Cardinals, with whom he won two World Series in 16 years. Eckersley joined him for two years. McGwire was dealt to St. Louis in July 1997. He played four and a half seasons with the Cardinals, the most memorable of which, 1998, saw him hit 70 home runs to shatter Roger Maris' long-standing single-season record of 61. It was hailed as a Ruthian effort that helped heal the wounds of the 1994 strike season. But as one stain upon the game began to fade, another was spreading. There was growing suspicion of widespread performance-enhancing drug use in baseball. Ultimately, both Bash Brothers—McGwire and Canseco—admitted to using steroids. (The Giants' Bonds, even in the face of voluminous and damning circumstantial evidence, denied using PEDs.)

Meanwhile, back in Oakland, new owners Schott and Hofmann oversaw a teardown and rebuild of the franchise. Working on a limited budget, the A's experienced four consecutive losing seasons. Then under the creative smarts of general manager Billy Beane, they used an 87–75 record in 1999 as a springboard to four consecutive postseason appearances. They lost each first-round playoff series in the fifth and deciding game.

After 10 years of ownership, Schott and Hofmann sold the team to an investor group fronted by real estate developer Lew Wolff. Though delightfully spirited A's teams reached the postseason in 2012 and 2013, the organization's dominant narrative involved Wolff's desperate attempt to ditch the outdated O.co Coliseum, a desperation perhaps only Lurie could fully appreciate. Wolff sought to move the team to San Jose. But thus far he has been unable to make that happen. The Giants, you see, hold territorial rights to the San Jose market. Those rights were granted to them before Lurie's final stadium vote there in 1992. They were granted—free of charge—by the A's.

◆ ◆ ◆ ◆

Time moves on, and so have the boys of the summer of 1989.

Dave Stewart runs Sports Management Partners in San Diego, an agency that "provides professional and personal representation for Major League Baseball players."

Dennis Eckersley is a baseball analyst for the New England Sports Network (NESN), which broadcasts Boston Red Sox games and TBS.

Tony La Russa travels around baseball on behalf of the commissioner's office. He also continues his work with the Animal Rescue Foundation (ARF), which he founded, in Walnut Creek, California. He was elected to the Baseball Hall of Fame in December 2013.

Will Clark, who lives in Arizona, makes regular appearances in San Francisco during the baseball season as a special assistant with the Giants.

Dave Dravecky does motivational and inspirational speaking for the Endurance ministry he founded with his wife of 35 years, Jan. He is a community ambassador with the Giants and lives in Turlock, California, near his two kids and two grandkids.

Roger Craig is retired and living with his wife, Carolyn, in San Diego. The Craigs split their time between a ranch outside town and a condo in Mission Valley. The Humm Baby visits regularly with his four kids, seven grandchildren, and four great-grandchildren.

Mark McGwire is in his fifth season as a major league hitting coach, and his second with the Los Angeles Dodgers.

Jose Canseco seems to be doing more tweeting than anything else.

Terry Steinbach is in his second season as a coach for the Minnesota Twins.

Dave Henderson runs Dave Henderson Baseball Adventures, camps for amateur adult fans.

Mike Gallego is in his sixth season as third-base coach for the A's.

Walt Weiss is in his second year as a big league manager with the Colorado Rockies.

Ron Hassey is in his sixth year as a minor league manager and third with the New Orleans Zephyrs of the PCL.

Billy Beane is in his 17th year as the A's general manager (and 10th as minority owner).

Rick Honeycutt is in his ninth season as Dodgers pitching coach.

Curt Young is in the third season of his second stint as A's pitching coach.

Storm Davis is a pitching coach for the Cubs Single A team in Dayton, Ohio.

Kevin Mitchell is teaching hitting to pre-teen and teenage kids in San Diego.

Matt Williams became manager of the Washington Nationals after four seasons as a coach with the Arizona Diamondbacks.

Robby Thompson briefly filled in as the Seattle Mariners' manager in 2013 when Eric Wedge was recovering from a small stroke. He was let go as the team's bench coach following the season.

Steve Bedrosian is retired from a career in coaching and was following his son, Cam, who was pitching in the Los Angeles of Anaheim Angels system.

Brett Butler is in his first season as third-base coach of the Miami Marlins.

Craig Lefferts completed his first season as pitching coach for the Single A Vermont Lake Monsters but did not return.

Mike LaCoss is CEO and founder of ibaseballchannel.com.

Atlee Hammaker is an owner of Smith and Hammaker, an IT company in Knoxville, Tennessee.

Jose Uribe died in a single-car car accident on December 8, 2006, in the Dominican Republic. He was 47.

Candy Maldonado is an analyst for ESPN Deportes.

Hitting coach Dusty Baker was fired after the 2013 season after six years as manager of the Cincinnati Reds.

Donell Nixon is president and CEO of his brother Otis Nixon's Strikeout Foundation, and a professional baseball instructor.

Greg Litton may not have won a World Series ring with the 1989 Giants, but he earned a degree in diamond grading and apparel and is an appraiser/manager at a jewelry store in Pensacola, Florida.

Ken Oberkfell is manager of the Lincoln, Nebraska Saltdogs, an independent league team.

Tracy Jones is a talk show host on WLW radio in Cincinnati.

Chris Speier was fired along with Baker following six seasons as a coach with the Cincinnati Reds.

Bob Brenly is a broadcaster for the Diamondbacks, the team he managed to a World Series win in 2001, and TBS.

Mike Krukow is a broadcaster for the Giants.

Mike Laga is running the Mike Laga Youth Baseball Association in Northampton, Massachusetts.

Jeff Brantley is in his eighth season as broadcaster for the Cincinnati Reds.

Acknowledgments

I t has been a recurring question asked of me over the 35 years I have been a print journalist: do you think you'd ever like to write a book?

For 34½ years, the answer was: not really.

For most of the first three decades of my career, I wrote three to four sports columns per week. I considered them 800-word snapshots. Books, to me, seemed like the equivalent of the kind of massive oil paintings I had seen hanging in the halls of Congress. And that seemed like a colossal amount of work. So the first person I need to acknowledge is my wonderful wife, Ann, who, after being informed I had been pitched an offer to write a book about the 1989 baseball season, said: "You need to do this."

Not only was she right, she took extra bath and bedtime shifts with our two-year-old daughter Carolyn so I could be free to excuse myself after dinner and ride the time machine back to 1989. I couldn't have undertaken a project such as this without the support of Ann, Carolyn, and my oldest daughter, Dana.

Being a newbie at the business of writing books, I'd like to acknowledge the wise counsel of Noah Amstadter and Jeff Fedotin of Triumph Books. They answered my rookie questions with patience and sound advice.

Special thanks to Tony La Russa, Dennis Eckersley, Dave Stewart, Will Clark, Dave Dravecky, and Roger Craig for being generous with their time—both during their heydays with the A's and Giants, and in the summer of 2013, when I came calling to ask questions they had answered dozens of times. Their thoughtful reflection helped bring the summer of '89 back to life.

I also would like to thank Tom Barnidge, my former sports editor and current metro colleague at the *Contra Costa Times*, for reviewing a rough draft of the book. His feedback, at a time when I was questioning my ability to deliver a semi-readable manuscript, was much appreciated.

Sources

Publications

San Francisco Giants 1987, 1988, 1989, 1990 media guides

Oakland Athletics 1989, 1990 media guides

1988 Major League Baseball World Series media guide

Periodicals

Contra Costa Times

Los Angeles Times

The New York Times

San Jose Mercury News

San Francisco Chronicle

Websites

Baseball-Reference.com

Baseballmusings.com

News.Google.com

Newspaperarchive.com

Sportsillustrated.cnn.com/vault/

Personal Interviews

Tony La Russa

Dennis Eckersley

Dave Stewart

Will Clark

Dave Dravecky

Roger Craig